FEAR THE STRANGER

The Murders of
Susan Maxwell,
Caroline Hogg
and Sarah Harper

Former Deputy
Chief Constable
Hector Clark
with David Johnston

MAINSTREAM
PUBLISHING

EDINBURGH AND LONDON

*To the British police service and my long-suffering
family*

First published in Great Britain in 1994 by
MAINSTREAM PUBLISHING COMPANY (EDINBURGH) LTD
7 Albany Street
Edinburgh EH1 3UG

Reprinted 1994

ISBN 1 85158 646 6

A catalogue record for this book is available from the British Library

Typeset in Palatino by Litho Link Ltd, Welshpool, Powys
Printed in Great Britain by Butler & Tanner Ltd, Frome

Contents

Introduction

This is a story I tell with a sense of pride overshadowed by a deep and powerful feeling of sadness.

Some may see it as the story of a vile, serial child-killer. It is not though. It is the story of three lovely little girls whose lives were snuffed out in acts of unparalleled evil. The 1983 murder of Caroline Hogg, who was just five years old, bore striking resemblances to the killing one year before of eleven-year-old Susan Maxwell. I was asked to head a joint investigation into the two murders. By the end of the case over ten years later, in 1994, another murder and two other serious crimes involving children had been added to my task.

The inquiry was to take many dramatic twists and turns over the years. Detectives in the team I headed spoke to thousands of people across the United Kingdom and abroad as we tried to track down the man who had brought such devastation to three families. I demanded total commitment, hard work and perseverance from the team and was not disappointed.

The hunt for the murderer in what became known as the Maxwell, Hogg, Harper killings was the first of its kind. It was the first time a chief officer was appointed to oversee an investigation crossing force, and indeed national boundaries. It was the first major inquiry to have such widespread back-up help from computers.

Worryingly, after Robert Black was identified as a suspect in our linked inquiries there was no single piece of hard evidence to tie him to the crimes that had shocked the nation for so long. We were able to convict him only after a 'reverse' investigation: we believed we had our man, the evidence needed to be found to prove it. That may sound a dangerous practice, but one factor unique in this inquiry was that after Black's arrest we did not uncover one single substantive piece of evidence that pointed away from his guilt, let alone to his innocence.

This book is not a rose-tinted view of a major investigation, minus its faults. Where we, or indeed I, were wrong I am happy to hold up my hands.

My most fervent hope is that the words which follow will give a special understanding of the magnitude of the task faced by the British police service in 1983, the suffering and devastation of the parents of three delightful little girls who did not deserve to die and a true appreciation of the evil of the man at whose hand they perished.

Inevitably there is a limited amount of information I have, quite rightly, had to leave out of this account. The missing facts do not detract from the story, which should stand as a lasting reminder of a difficult job carried out against the odds.

H.G.C.
Edinburgh,
May 1994

CHAPTER ONE

The Stranger Strikes

The long wait for the jury to reach its verdict on Robert Black was, for me, totally unbearable. The hunt for this evil man had taken up the best part of ten years of my life. Now the moment of truth had arrived.

Our case was solid. In court the lawyers had not let us down during the trial, but the thought that juries sometimes do reach the wrong conclusion would not leave my mind. It was near enough eleven years after my appointment as the head of what was then a double child murder investigation and the day of judgment had finally come.

During my career as a Tyneside detective I had often sat in the Crown Court in Newcastle to watch as villains were put away at the conclusion of successful cases. Since I left the city for promotion in Scotland a new court complex had been constructed but the old Moot Hall courthouse was reopened specially for this case.

The jury walked slowly back into the court at the end of their long deliberations and all the mixed emotions of the long hunt for this taker of innocents visited me again. There was the sheer bloody sorrow for three sets of bereaved parents. There was the memory of anger and frustration as the massive inquiries hit brick wall after brick wall over the years. There was the elation of success, tempered today with the powerful apprehension of potential failure.

As we waited for Mr Justice Macpherson to come back to his court I could only wonder, 'What if the jury gets it wrong?' I knew full well that Robert Black murdered three children in the process of fulfilling his lust for pre-pubescent girls. Were the jury convinced? They should have been.

I knew a verdict of not guilty would devastate not only me but every single police officer from around the country who had worked on the various aspects of this case over the years. Thousands of detective and uniformed officers had been involved in the hunt for this man who now sat, apparently so calm, before the court. They had been on his trail since 30 July 1982 and he had eluded them for eight years.

Now there was the chance for this long and distressing case to come to its end. That would give me, and a great many more, a deal of satisfaction. More importantly it would give the families of three lovely little girls the chance to finally close a long, sorrowful chapter in their lives.

I could not help reflecting what other evil this man might be responsible for. We knew fine well he was guilty of three murders and one abduction attempt, on top of the harrowing ordeal he had already admitted subjecting a six-year-old to. The question that kept coming back was this: How many more? What number of little girls suffered at his hands? Could it be that a man so base as this had managed to control the lust that the court had heard about in such graphic and sickening detail, except on five occasions?

It remains my firm conviction that he did not. I believe Robert Black is guilty of causing a great deal more suffering and misery than we know about. He had, after all, spent years travelling the highways and byways of Britain, accountable to no one, free to do as he would in his job, with only the loosest constraints.

THE STRANGER STRIKES

I watched intently as the jury took their seats in this modern courtroom. As I looked up at the ceiling and closed my eyes for just a second my mind went back a decade, to what had been for me the start of it all, a visit to the seafront area of Scotland's capital city.

Portobello, to most Scots, conjures up images of family holidays and happy days out at the seaside. For me, I am afraid, it does nothing but send a chill through the whole of my body. It was at this seaside resort in the eastern suburbs of Edinburgh that my involvement in what was to become Britain's biggest ever child murder hunt began.

The area is now a bit shabby, a bit rundown, yet in places beginning to show signs of the attempts that are being made to revitalise it and, once more, make it a place for a family day out. I suppose it has a rugged charm like many east coast resorts. For some it has a fatal attraction.

On any summer's day when the sun does manage to break through the Presbyterian grey of the Scottish sky people still flock to the beach in droves. Often on warm evenings the seafront will be bustling as local folk and a declining number of holidaymakers walk their dogs, amuse their children or just go for a drink in one of the many bars that stretch out along the coastline. The eighth day of July in 1983 was just one of those nights. Being a Friday there were perhaps just one or two more people there than normal, a few more children allowed to stay up a bit later than usual, for a stroll on the prom. The school year was long since over in Scotland.The thought of that evening still turns me cold. It is a feeling that returns with each visit to the area.

Mingled in with the crowds at Portobello on any night like the one in July to which I am referring, are men with evil intentions. They are by no means unique to Portobello. My long police experience has taught me, sadly, that where children play, especially in the summer, will be a hunting ground for men who get their sexual thrills out of youngsters.

11

The media use the blanket word paedophile to describe such individuals. However, the perversions of man come in many forms, and so it is amongst those drawn to places like Portobello where youngsters are at play. Some may be there only to watch, others may get their thrills by engaging a little girl or little boy in seemingly innocent conversation. The really dangerous ones will have more sinister intentions.

Be in no doubt, the stranger is not a figment of an over-anxious parent's imagination. He is real, he is tangible, and, worryingly, he exists in many seaside places, swing parks or anywhere else that is a magnet for childlike fun. It was no different that July night. The parents who had so long warned of the danger posed by strangers could have no inkling that their worst fears were about to be realised. For the child the danger of the stranger was only discovered too late. As little Caroline Hogg skipped amongst the holiday crowds that evening she was being watched. For once the eye transfixed on the pretty little five-year-old was not that of her loving mother or father. It was the eye of an abductor.

The very fact that Caroline was out at that time of night, about seven o'clock, was a triumph for a persistent child over the common-sense of its parent. Annette Hogg did not let her children play on the promenade by themselves. It was only a matter of yards from the front door but she knew it could be a dangerous place.

Caroline had been insistent, and it seemed a shame to turn down her polite plea for a few minutes more fun on such a lovely night. She'd just had a super time at her friend's birthday party. The grandmother she loved had been to call. There was no harm in a few minutes more play.

As she left the house to look for her little friends someone was waiting to end her playing forever. The Hoggs' home, in Beach Lane, Portobello, lay in a street at right angles to the promenade. Looking down the street over the prom, the sea was visible from the front gate.

As the little girl walked out she was quite a striking sight that night. Her lilac and white gingham party dress was somewhat out of keeping in comparison to the casual clothes of the holidaymakers. At least she had listened to her dad and taken off her party shoes in favour of something more sensible, a pair of trainers. Caroline, who had just finished her first year at Towerbank Primary, stopped first at the swing park, just past her school.

This little corner of Portobello where they lived was a close-knit community. Even though the population is swelled by seasonal workers and people living in rented flats in the traditional Scottish tenements and subdivided larger houses, the locals knew a high percentage of the faces they passed in the streets around the front. And so it was with the Hogg family. Caroline's progress towards the promenade would later be well charted by those who knew her. As she passed by that night there was nothing to worry about, nothing to alarm the people who recognised her.

Hindsight, as ever, would put a different perspective on the events of that night. Many, when questioned later, thought they should have paid more attention to what they saw. Many thought they should have taken more notice of the scruffy man who seemed to be staring at the playing children and at Caroline in particular. Some did make a subconscious note of him as he watched the little girl with the pretty blonde hair tied back in bunches, but at the time they saw no reason to be diverted from their own business.

One of Caroline's little friends saw him, the scruffy man. He thought nothing about it either, until the police started searching for Caroline and suddenly everyone was asking about the man, the stranger. Another youngster had just finished work in the cash kiosk at Fun City. She had gone home, then back out on to the promenade near the amusement park. Caroline was sitting at the edge of the prom dangling her feet in the warm sand. This girl also remembered Caroline talking to a stranger. Scruffy, he was, needing a wash and a shave. There was, she later recalled, nothing to suggest the trouble Caroline was getting into. As she talked to the stranger she laughed. There was a smile on her bright face.

Just before eight o'clock, the teenager who worked the children's roundabout in Fun City, right on the seafront, remembers Caroline having a ride. She sat in the little toy bus. The ride was paid for by a man who was not Caroline's father. The fare in those days was 15 pence. The teenager had not seen the man before.

The amusement park was less than five hundred yards from Caroline's front door.

As this was going on at Fun City, back at the Hogg household in Beach Lane, we later learned, mum was becoming a little worried. Caroline had been told she could stay out for only a few minutes. She had been away half an hour when Annette asked one of the other children to go and have a look for her.

Stuart Hogg had been initially reluctant to leave his friends, but he did. Then other members of the family joined in. Within a short space of time the whole family, friends, neighbours and the police were all scouring the area around Caroline's home.

The few minutes before this little domestic drama was acted out were the last John and Annette Hogg were to enjoy as normal parents. A heartache that would never leave was about to settle on their lives. They were being turned into the parents of a murdered child.

Caroline Hogg simply vanished off the face of the earth that night. She was there, on the promenade with the scruffy man, then at the funfair, then gone. Within a couple of hours the local radio station was broadcasting news of her disappearance. Many ordinary members of the public went down to Portobello straightaway to help search for the little girl. Most of the Scottish newspapers had stories about her going missing, the following morning, on the Saturday. News of the search for the girl missing from her Edinburgh home was in the national newspapers on Sunday.

I became aware of Caroline's disappearance over that weekend through police circulations and press reports.

Edinburgh is covered by the Lothian and Borders force, which also has responsibility for the large area that stretches from the Firth of Forth down nearly to Berwick-upon-Tweed at the English border.

The July weekend of her disappearance I was the Assistant Chief Constable of the force immediately to the south, in England. Our patch began at the Scottish border. Northumbria Police and Lothian and Borders usually had little to do with each other. They were in different countries, operating under different legal systems. There was, of course, a fair bit of cross border crime but this was handled by the respective southerly and northerly divisions of the two forces.

I was not involved in the search for Caroline at that precise moment but I do recall thinking that her disappearance was rather similar to the mystery of what had happened to a little girl in our own patch the year before. Susan Maxwell, a farmer's daughter, had gone missing one July afternoon. It too was on a Friday. She had, it later transpired, been murdered. The Northumbria and Lothian and Borders Police forces had been co-operating closely over the, as yet, unsolved inquiries into her death. The two organisations were soon to be linked in one of the longest and most complicated murder investigations ever to be carried out in Britain. Certainly, for the many hundreds of officers involved in it over a period of years, it was one of the most distressing.

As the police called in to hunt for the missing girl began their work, my mind was mainly on other matters. I had been ACC in Northumbria for some time. My career was far from over and I was on the promotion circuit, looking for a Deputy Chief or Chief Constable's position. There was no desperation to leave Tyneside, however. I was born and brought up in Northumberland and had spent most of my working life in and around the area. Northumberland is arguably the most beautiful county in England and the way of life it affords suited me and my family well. I had promised them that if we were ever to move for a new job it would only be to an area where a similar quality of life could be enjoyed. So, many of the posts that fell vacant after my decision to seek advancement were excluded for this reason alone. Where I live has always been very important to me. You cannot spend your formative years in a small and lovely village like Felton, Northumberland, and then be happy in some grim industrial town in the Midlands.

Two Deputy Chief Constable posts had already eluded me in places where I thought we could settle, Cambridge and Dorset. The day Caroline's body was found I was preparing to go for an interview to the Warwickshire force which was looking for a new Deputy Chief Constable. On arriving at their force HQ there was an urgent message waiting. I had to telephone my own Deputy Chief Constable in Northumbria, Fred Chambers.

The call was connected straight through to his office and he delivered a message that was to set the sternest challenge of my career. He said that it had been decided to link the abduction and murder of Caroline Hogg with that of the other little girl, Susan Claire Maxwell, the farmer's daughter who had been just eleven when she was snatched off a roadside near her home village of Cornhill on Tweed, just a matter of yards south of the Scottish border. They wanted me to lead the dual investigation.

Susan's body had been found some time earlier in Staffordshire. That was the year before Caroline Hogg's murder, and to date there was not a single active lead in the hunt for her killer despite a very large inquiry. Caroline Hogg's body was found dumped, like Susan's, in a lay-by in the English Midlands. The decision to link the inquiries had been taken, Fred told me, by the Chief Constables of the four forces involved. The four were the two from the areas from which the children had been taken and two more from the separate force areas in which their bodies were found.

The size and nature of the challenge being offered was immediately apparent. Although I had not been directly involved in the Susan Maxwell murder inquiry, I was one of the most senior officers of the force that had spent a year investigating every aspect of it and drawing a blank at each turn. I was painfully aware that the hunt for Susan's killer had virtually petered out. Only a token number of officers then remained involved in the investigation and they were merely tying up loose ends. There would be all sorts of complications to come to terms with. Not least the fact that the two abductions had occurred under separate legal jurisdictions. Scots law and police practice is quite separate and distinct from the English system. This would create problems in the future.

I knew all four of the Chief Constables who had set me the task, some well, some less so. The discussions between the four had taken place at Ponteland, a small town on the western outskirts of Newcastle-upon-Tyne, and the site of the Northumbria Police headquarters. My own boss, Sir Stanley Bailey of Northumbria Police, was one of them because Susan Maxwell had been abducted in his area.

Sir Stanley Bailey was a powerful character, one of the stalwarts of the British Police service. Stanley was a man with a reputation for not suffering fools gladly and he was an experienced investigator, himself having been involved in, and subsequently run, some very major inquiries.

Charles Kelly was the Chief of Staffordshire, the force covering the area where Susan Maxwell's body was found. He was supportive of the idea to link the investigations, though it has to be said that as the months, and eventually years, went on I did not see very much of him.

The Leicestershire force was involved because it was in their area that Caroline's body was discovered. Their Chief Constable, Alan Goodson, was a great help to me in the early days of the inquiry. I found him to be an absolute gentleman. At that original meeting he was very supportive of my appointment, I later learned, and during my involvement with him he always came over as kind and understanding. I am not, of course, saying the others were not. Sadly, Alan Goodson has since died.

The fourth of these men was Sir William Sutherland, then without his knighthood, the man who would eventually become my own boss and my good friend. He's a perceptive and knowledgeable operator who gained many years' experience in English forces before returning to his native Scotland to run the Lothian and Borders Police. Bill Sutherland had been heavily involved on the night the IRA bombs went off in Guildford. One of the benefits of the friendship, both professional and social, that I built up with him, was that he would always tell me when I was wrong – and sometimes I was. Now any need for sycophancy is over, I guess that if there is a finer Chief Constable in the British Isles I have yet to meet him.

So these were the men who gave me the challenge. Fred Chambers' phone call included a genuine opportunity for me to decline, but it took no more than half a second to accept the job. It did not need a second call. From the moment words of agreement left my mouth all thoughts of making the highways and byways of Warwickshire safer faded. I threw the interview and headed north as quickly as possible.

Caroline's body had been found in a lay-by off a main road through the Midlands, near the town of Twycross, on 18 July 1983. The Chief Constables met on the 20th but my appointment was not announced until the Friday of that week, 22 July. A news conference was called at Northumbria Police HQ in Ponteland. It was obvious my appointment was going to be taken as confirmation of intense press speculation that now a double child killer was on the loose.

I suspected the press call would be well attended; in fact there was not a spare seat in the room. Interest had no doubt been heightened by the fact that Caroline's abduction had come at the end of the week in which the inquest into Susan's death had finally been held, finishing with an inconclusive verdict.

It may have been the end of the inquest but the hunt for the killer was to be by no means over. The Susan Maxwell murder hunt had been a very large inquiry that was, a year on, virtually exhausted and faltering to a standstill. With the fresh impetus of a second killing every aspect of the investigation was to be completely reviewed and extended still further.

It was clear from the outset that co-ordination was going to be the key to success. The many lines of inquiry were already very complicated and in some ways cumbersome. By the time I took over as the supervising officer appointed to head the linked investigations, one was a year old and virtually run out of steam, the other was a matter of days old, following the discovery of Caroline's body, and a large and vibrant inquiry. In addition, because foul play had been suspected from such an early stage in the missing person inquiry looking into Caroline's disappearance, the matter had been treated to all intents and purposes as a murder hunt from the outset.

I established my own headquarters in a bungalow in the grounds of the Ponteland HQ building. Inevitably, I suppose, it was dubbed Hector's House by both officers and the press, after the children's television programme.

My linkman at Lothian and Borders Police was one of the finest policemen I ever came across. Eventually I would succeed Stan Pringle as Deputy Chief Constable of that force, in 1984, on his retirement. For the time being though he was a tower of strength to me. Soft in nature but strong in purpose, he provided manpower, equipment and other resources at the drop of a hat, sometimes seemingly from thin air. We thought the same way, and his friendship was one I appreciated at that time, and since.

It fell to me to become quickly established as the leader of the inquiry and yet at the same time be careful not to step on too many toes by appearing to arrive from the outside to show them all how it was to be done.

One of my first moves was to seek an early meeting with Sir Lawrence Byford, HM Chief Inspector of Constabulary for England and Wales. It was he who had conducted a full review of the Yorkshire Ripper inquiry. There had been criticism of the fact that Peter Sutcliffe had been interviewed nine times by police in the hunt and yet remained free to go on killing. One of the recommendations of his report into the affair was that a senior officer should be appointed to oversee major inquiries which straddled force boundaries. I was the first person to be so appointed in the 'Byford role'. The purpose of my meeting was simply to see what lessons there were for me. The Ripper hunt had been massive, involving many forces and thousands of officers. It was obvious my investigation was likely to follow a similar path, and because the Byford report was never made public I had to find out what I could learn from it.

The magazine *Police Review* made great store of my talks with Sir Lawrence. They even devoted an editorial to the subject. That leader ended by addressing a stark warning directly at me. Over the years it may have haunted me but it certainly never put me off. 'There is nothing much we can do to help you. If you succeed, we'll all be for you. If you fail you are on you own.'

So, filled with determination, enthusiasm and commitment I was off to Edinburgh, where so much of my time would be spent in the coming months. My first task was to discover more fully what had happened to Susan.

CHAPTER TWO

The Parents' Anguish

Liz Maxwell had been quite certain within minutes of her daughter failing to arrive home from a tennis game. If she was missing, then she must have been snatched from the mile and a half of country road that lay between Coldstream and the family home at Cramond Hill Farm.

Liz's husband Fordyce had been out on the combine-harvester that July afternoon in 1982. He worked Cramond Hill with other members of his Borders family. The farm is just outside the little village of Cornhill on Tweed which is the last settlement in England before the Scottish border, formed there by the River Tweed, the famous salmon river.

The village is small, it lies about 15 miles west of Berwick and is dominated by two features. The Collingwood Arms Hotel, named after the family of one of Nelson's admirals whose family for generations occupied the big house, is one. The other, more modern, landmark is Rutherford's garage, the BMW dealer where farmers from all over this rich border country buy their family cars.

It was hot that afternoon, one of the hottest afternoons of the summer so far. 'Susie wanted to play tennis. It was a lovely afternoon and we were all in the garden,' said Liz years later recalling the time which was to be the start of an inner torment that would never leave her in peace. 'Susie wanted to go on her bike, but we didn't want her to go on the bike because of the traffic.' The road from Cornhill to Coldstream is the A697, the middle road between Scotland and England. Tourism is a major industry in the border country. That afternoon, as most others in the summer, there was a constant stream of traffic on the route. Tourist cars mingled with local people going about their ordinary lives.

Instead of cycling, Liz asked Susie if she would mind walking. Her daughter had never before walked to Coldstream by herself. But there could be nothing dangerous after all. They lived in a small community and if she walked there and back there could be no harm in it. All along the route, Liz supposed, she would be passing, and in turn be passed by, people she knew. Anyway, as it happened, she got a lift to the game; one of the farmworkers was heading into town. It was, though, still the intention for Susie to walk back herself.

In the event that plan altered too. Liz changed her mind and went to pick her daughter up – the natural caution and consideration of a caring mother. 'It was a very hot afternoon, I thought she'd be hot and sticky after playing tennis for an hour and too tired to walk back. So I put the wee ones into the car and drove over to Coldstream.' Liz like so many in those border villages speaks with a strong Anglo-Scots accent, basically Northumbrian with a spattering of Scots words. As she drove the car, and the little ones, the short distance from the farm to the main road and over towards Coldstream, she kept her eyes on the side of the road, expecting to see Susie at any moment.

Quite a bit of the route Liz drove that afternoon is lined with mature trees in full leaf, that give shade and shelter to the road. Nearly the last house in Cornhill is the local police station, a one-man affair, a far-flung outpost of the Northumbria Police. Coincidentally, one of the first buildings across the bridge and Scottish border in Coldstream is another police office, the southernmost station of the force from which I have now retired.

The bridge over the Tweed at this point is a stone structure one hundred yards long with five arches spanning the river. It has a parapet which stands waist high to an adult and a little cottage on the Scottish side where marriages used to take place many years ago. At several road crossings of the border there are these marriage houses where young couples eloping from England would tie the knot, taking advantage of Scotland's younger age of majority and the right, north of the border, to marry without parental consent.

Liz had not been expecting to drive all the way along the road that afternoon, right into Coldstream town, but she did, right up to the Lennel Tennis Club. There was no sign of her eleven-year-old daughter anywhere along the road, or at the club. She was nowhere to be seen as Liz drove back either. As soon as the by now worried mum reached home again she phoned the friend with whom Susie had been playing tennis.

'She said she'd left Susie at the corner of the road on the outskirts of Coldstream. I started to panic then and Fordyce said to just phone the police straightaway.'

Liz was frantic. She and her husband quickly became aware that although a number of people had seen Susie on her journey home, the sightings stopped at a spot just past the end of the bridge, on the English side. The shepherd who usually would be found in the next field was not there that afternoon to watch as the little girl walked by.

Quickly the police realised there was a chance of something very serious being wrong. It was not just a case of a little girl who had decided to stay out a bit longer than she should. Officers had spoken to people who'd been going over and back across the bridge that afternoon and discovered there was a period of just a minute or so between people seeing Susie, and other people being equally certain they had not seen her.

Liz was convinced that someone must have stopped to ask for directions and grabbed her little girl before driving off again.

Soon extra officers were being drafted into the area. Dogs were out searching the river-banks. Further downstream more people were watching the waters of that famous salmon river in case, that day, there was a body in it.

'The first night was the worst,' said Liz. 'When darkness fell and she wasn't home it was dreadful. I was just eaten up by fear and panic. It is impossible to describe. I kept thinking, "Where could she be?".'

Fordyce said they were more concerned that she was hurt. 'That's what was worrying my mind. That she was lying injured somewhere and could not raise the alarm. I certainly thought she was still alive then. The night just seemed so long. It was certainly light very early.'

Liz says with great understatement that she did not get much sleep that night, and then allows the truth to come through as she adds, 'Nor for the next number of years really.'

In the morning they had to begin the dreadful task of telling members of their family further afield of what had occurred. Liz's father could not speak at first when he heard the news. He was told Susie was missing, and straight away took that to mean that Susie was dead.

As Fordyce spent every waking hour with the search parties, Liz remained at home, talking. Talking to anyone and everyone who wanted to speak to her. There were reporters, more and more of them, as the days went by. Friends, family, acquaintances all eager to offer help, comfort, advice.

The couple are both journalists to trade. They had met through newspapers. They knew how to handle the news media, and were only too aware of the importance of keeping their daughter's disappearance on the front pages. Each time there was a story published there was a picture of Susie along with it. There was always the chance, while that picture was staring out of news pages across the country, that someone would recognise her. Susan's picture in a newspaper might make a reader realise that the little girl just moved in next door was not a distant relative or whatever. If Susie had been abducted and was still alive and living somewhere, the perpetrator would have concocted some story to explain her presence. Liz, like the police ourselves, worked on the theory that it only takes one person to make the connection to solve a crime. Publicity could have jogged the memory of someone who'd just had a fleeting glimpse of her in a passing car, or at a petrol station, or seen a little girl being bundled into a house or shed. The possibilities were endless, and the chances real enough to keep Liz answering all those questions from the reporters.

The people out searching ensured not a single part of the area was left unturned. Fordyce was working with the police and volunteers ploughing their way through thickets, searching quarries, drains, and ditches. 'At least it kept me doing something,' he says. 'It kept my mind occupied and stopped me sitting round thinking too much.'

There was, inevitably, more pain inflicted on the couple by necessary police routine. The parents were extremely well known in the community but the officers investigating their daughter's disappearance could leave nothing to chance. Fordyce was actually Susie's stepfather. For many reasons, and sometimes seemingly for none, stepfathers have been known to be responsible for the unnatural death of their step-daughters. And so it was, inevitably, that Fordyce was questioned closely, and at length, about his movements that day. His relationship with Susie was discussed too.

Fordyce had been expecting it, and he was ready to cope with the interview when it came. However, the process was something of a shock for Liz who, with all the many things weighing down on her mind at that moment, had not even entertained, for just one second, the slightest chance that the detectives and uniformed police looking for her missing daughter could think that her husband might have had something to do with her removal, apparently from the face of the earth.

The interview was perfectly routine, but thorough, and it did not take long for the team to realise they were going to have to look elsewhere for their suspect. It was equally clear to Susie's parents that they were somehow going to have to find the inner strength to keep going, not least for the sake of their other children, Tom, then aged three, and Jacqueline, who was two years older.

I discovered later, after my involvement in the case became total, that Liz and Fordyce Maxwell had impressed everyone that came across them with their dignity and composure. They managed their grief, despair, and anxiety with a degree of resolve few of us could ever hope to achieve in similar circumstances. They discovered the main stumbling block that there was appeared when dealing with their other two children, and beginning to try to explain to them, at such tender ages, what was going on.

'I don't think I was ever brave enough to tell them what had happened', Liz said. 'We had a big family and I am not sure who, but one of them told the wee ones as best as they could.

'I tried to divert the children in other ways. They went to play with their cousins and things like that. I don't think we saw a lot of them over that fortnight that Susie was missing. They were so little and so dependent. They had a sister who was here, and then gone the next minute. How can you explain that when you are so confused and frightened yourself? We found it very difficult to put thoughts into words.'

Even now, all these years later, you can hear the pain return to these parents for whom grieving is still, in all likelihood, their most common emotion.

They have left Cramond Hill now, and live in a Georgian house in Berwick-upon-Tweed, at the mouth of the river that flows past the scene of Susie's abduction. Fordyce and Liz have both gone back to full-time journalism. She on the local paper, the *Berwick Advertiser*; he with *The Scotsman*, based in Edinburgh. For years after Susie's disappearance Fordyce wrote a regular farmers' diary in *The Glasgow Herald*. Its humour built up a large following both within and outside the agricultural community. He has a talent for telling stories. A talent shared with many of his fellow border folk over the ages. Now he's agricultural editor of *The Scotsman*, a Scotland-wide daily paper.

Susie's disappearance had a major impact on her little sister Jackie, even though she was only five when it happened. She still remembers Susie going off to play tennis and not returning. She also remembers people started giving her presents, and it wasn't even her birthday. People were sending messages to her mum, and they didn't usually.

'When it was her birthday, a little time later, there were photographers there to see her cut the cake. The next day the picture was in the paper, usually with Susie's picture close by,' said Liz. 'It's hackneyed and it's probably a cheap tactic on behalf of newspapers but we were prepared to do anything. At least it helped me feel as though we were doing something else towards getting her back. I thought if I can get her picture in every paper in the country, if it's on television every night then the more the better. I talked myself silly saying the same thing over and over again. As long as journalists kept coming I kept talking.'

Fordyce said they were prepared to do absolutely anything to get the publicity. 'It was also something to divert you from this inner hell. Sitting at home was agony. Each car that came could be bringing good news, or news that everyone had been fearing.'

A fortnight after the abduction Liz had been asked to appear on the *Jimmy Young Show*. The Radio Two programme pulled in millions of listeners throughout the country and was exactly the sort of opportunity she wanted. It was about an hour's drive to reach the BBC's nearest remote studio. An off-shoot of BBC Radio Newcastle, the studio was actually based in Alnwick Castle. Liz had no idea, as she drove through some of Britain's most lovely scenery to the broadcast, that down in the English Midlands police had made a grim discovery. The badly decomposed body of a little girl had been found in a lay-by in Staffordshire. It was Friday the 13th of August.

On the radio Liz described Susie and gave a moving account of how devastated she and the rest of the family were by the disappearance. Maintaining her composure throughout, she asked anyone who knew the slightest scrap of information about Susie's abduction, or her present whereabouts, to contact the police.

Some time after she arrived back at Cramond Hill there was a visitor. It was not good news. Detective Chief Inspector Fred Stephenson, who had been in charge of the missing person inquiry, was there with other officers.

'They came in and said, "Sit down." I thought this is it. He said, "I've had the police at Uttoxeter on the phone and they have found a little girl." He didn't say, "She's dead." He said, "This little girl is not alive." I'll always always remember this, he said, "This little girl is not alive". I just remember the feeling of coldness start in my feet and work its way up through my whole body. I just went totally numb. I didn't cry and didn't shout. I didn't feel anything. I felt nothing. It was just the most terrible moment I've ever had.

'They came back later that afternoon and told me they could confirm it was Susie. They had confirmed it from dental records. It was one of the first things they had asked – who her dentist was. I thought then "What on earth do they want to know that for?" She was so badly decomposed they could not identify her and so they had to use these kinds of methods.

'The first thing I said was "Can I see her?" but they just said things like, "It's been very warm." I think I really knew what they meant and that they were just trying to shield me from the worst of it, but I thought if I had just been able to see her one more time it would have helped.

'It probably would not have done though. That has struck me a lot, the fact that she was lying outside vulnerable to birds and insects and mice. It was bad enough for her to be dead, but to think of her lying there in a strange place and us not knowing where she was. Her thinking that we must have forsaken her. Her last thoughts, I would have thought, must have been, "Why are my mummy and daddy not coming to get me? Why are they not coming to rescue me?"

'That's what's always haunted me.'

Fordyce, like many in his position, prefers to find answers for the inevitable questions. Speaking before the trial of Robert Black he said: 'I prefer to think that it was all over very quickly, that she blacked out and didn't really know what was happening. Whether that's true or not I just don't know, but it helps me get through the rest of my life.'

Fourteen long days went by after the discovery of her body, and then Susie's funeral took place in Cornhill's little village church. Liz wanted it to be a celebration of her life as much as a farewell. The congregation sang Susie's favourite hymn, *All Things Bright and Beautiful*.

Liz said: 'I was about the most calm person there, but it was automatic pilot. It was all just a false front. It was almost as though it was someone acting me, not just me.'

After the service a friend of the couple from *The Glasgow Herald* took Fordyce to one side and said it was the first day that he had been ashamed of being a journalist. The newsman was referring to the photographers who just minutes before had been scrabbling round the graveside trying to get a 'good shot' of the heartbroken couple.

Neither Liz nor Fordyce had even noticed them. Liz says, quite the reverse, she did not mind the press being at the funeral. 'Let people realise that this is what it comes to. You walk behind your child's coffin – it's something that no one ever wants to do – and then watch this coffin going into the ground.'

The first Susie's mum and dad had seen of their little girl's coffin had been in the church on the night before the funeral, on the day the body was brought up from Staffordshire. It hit them how small it was.

During the days that followed, something strange happened to the couple. They noticed that some of their friends and neighbours would come to the house and not mention what had happened. It drove them mad. Liz says she began to wonder if they did not know about Susie's death. Perhaps it was all in her mind. Also there was the vast number of letters from people in similar circumstances. Not just the parents of murdered children, but people who had lost young ones in many ways. Some people went on to write regularly, on anniversaries, or at Christmas. There were hundreds and hundreds of letters.

It caught on. Little Jacqueline started writing to her parents too. She would hand them little notes all sealed up in an envelope saying something like, 'Dear Daddy, I've had a good day at school.' She was quiet about it though. She's been quiet about Susie ever since. It took several years for Jacqueline to even say Susie's name and then never voluntarily.

Her parents put this down to the resilience of children. Fordyce says children are able to accept things a lot more easily than their parents. 'For quite some time we did not want them to just accept what had happened. I wanted to make sure they remembered her and kept her memory alive. We would go over things and look at photographs.

'One day we were talking with Tom about what he would be like when he was older, what he'd be like at middle school. He said, "Will I ever be eleven?" It was a heart-stopper for a boy to think it was natural for a child to die at eleven.'

Susan had died at the age of eleven though. One year later, not many miles further north another little girl, Caroline Hogg, was to be taken in similar circumstances at less than half Susan's age. I was winging my way to Scotland.

CHAPTER THREE

A Double Murder Hunt

Having spent part of the weekend of 22 and 23 July 1983, after my appointment as the head of the joint inquiry, reading up on the Susan Maxwell case which had been largely handled by my own Northumbria Police force and Staffordshire Police, I made for Edinburgh. The Caroline Hogg inquiry was then based in Leith Police Station, right in the docks area of Edinburgh. It is a somewhat dour and drab building from the outside, but inside this former town hall boasts a wealth of beautiful Victorian municipal furnishing and decoration, and, more importantly for me, at the time of my first visit, a lively and vibrant inquiry.

The welcoming party early that Sunday morning was led by the man who was to become my effective number two in the investigation, the then head of Lothian and Borders CID, Brian Cunningham. He was the senior officer investigating Caroline's murder and was a man with whom it was easy to strike up a good rapport. Brian Cunningham had been head of CID for some years and had quite a reputation as a wily operator. It was clear that the way he had set up first the large missing person inquiry, and then the Edinburgh end of what became a murder hunt, provided the basis of a solid investigation. The first thing people notice about Brian is his cheerful disposition. Immediately friendly, he is a tallish and softly spoken man. I was to come to realise he was a 'star' of the early part of the investigation. Of the old school, he was suspicious of modern styles and techniques but nevertheless totally effective in what he did. He welcomed my participation in the inquiry from the outset and his professional and social support were appreciated.

Another key member of the team was a fellow Geordie, one I had brought up from Northumbria. Detective Chief Inspector Les Orange was one of the Newcastle detectives I most admired. We had worked together on several tough cases in the past. He was a real sleuth in every sense of the word, a man whose ideas were immensely sensible, his thought logical, and his care of me outstanding. Les and I often had long, wide-ranging discussions of the case, sometimes failing to agree. However, what emerged was a powerful team of two English detectives coming to Edinburgh to head up the investigation into an essentially Scottish crime with English dimensions.

Although I am a countryman by birth and inclination, I have always been of the opinion that the best detectives came out of the cities, at least in a practical sense. Les was of that ilk. We housed ourselves at Heidi Toolin's Royal British Hotel on Edinburgh's famous Princes Street, fed ourselves at the Leith Assembly Rooms run by Molly Neil, and watered ourselves wherever, and whenever, we could.

Just as I had four Chief Constables to work with, so my investigation had four main centres. For the Susan Maxwell case we had Northumberland and Staffordshire, where her body was found. The Caroline Hogg case was split between Edinburgh and Leicestershire, where her body had been discovered.

In those few first days, the most striking feature of the investigations for me was the large number of fine officers who were involved in the hunt. They were driven on by a sense of revulsion at the savagery of the subject of their investigation. The by-product of that determination so often found in police officers is a service to society. The whole of Britain was shocked at the prospect of a killer on the loose who had claimed at least two little girls' lives. The team trying to hunt him down took strength and encouragement from that shock and it served to increase their resolve to reach a successful conclusion to the case.

In Edinburgh we had officers like John Henry, Stuart Henderson, who went on to become involved in the hunt for the perpetrators of the Lockerbie disaster, Charlie Nunn, David Garbutt, our computer expert, now Deputy Chief Constable of the Grampian force, Tom Wood, another shrewd operator, now Assistant Chief Constable of Lothian and Borders, and many others. In Staffordshire, Detective Superintendent Derek Boden was heading the hunt, effectively the lead force in the Susan Maxwell murder inquiry, and Detective Inspector Peter Herward assisted. Detective Chief Superintendent David Baker, at the Leicester end, and Detective Chief Inspector Fred Stephenson in Northumbria were other key team members. They were all good detectives with a driving ambition to clear up these dastardly crimes. Indeed that was the aim of all the service, such was the feeling nationally of revulsion and fear.

So I had through the four strands of this inquiry excellent, keen and experienced officers, each convinced that hard work on the case would bring with it the result we all wanted. But I needed to be certain that a sense of common purpose filtered through the whole team. We all had to be pulling in the same direction, all singing the same tune. To help achieve this goal I drafted a statement of intention and a set of ground rules, and circulated them to all the officers in the various teams. These must remain confidential to the police service and, for that reason, I shall not reveal their contents here. Suffice to say they were written to ensure that all actions and inquiries taken by team members from the bottom right up to the top were done in an effective and efficient way. It was essential that the same high standard of work was achieved by all, and it was equally crucial that the standard was maintained no matter how long the investigation went on.

I wanted to meet Caroline's parents as quickly as possible, both to give me a feel for the case and, more importantly, them a feel for me. It is vital in circumstances like these for the relatives to have an opportunity quickly to establish faith in the police in general, and the officers in charge of the inquiry in particular. A time like this is difficult enough for any family. It is hard to imagine how anyone could begin coping with the tragic loss of a lovely daughter in such circumstances. The minds of the relatives will have time for nothing else as they go over and over their role in the events which led up to the disaster, and in turn examine the roles of everyone else. For this reason, in my view, it is essential for senior officers to quickly establish in the relatives a feeling of confidence, if for no other reason than to give them one less thing to worry about.

There was, of course, already a policewoman detailed to work closely with the family and act as a liaison point between them and the inquiry. PC Karen Walker had done a good job. She later revealed in some of the radio and TV programmes made about the case over the years how she had become completely involved. Karen said to one interviewer, I recall, that she went into the assignment determined to maintain a professional and non-involved approach. She later admitted to finding that goal impossible to achieve. Movingly, she said she even found herself believing that Caroline was still alive in the days immediately before her body was found, when it was painfully obvious to other police professionals on the case that all the evidence pointed to her being dead. This officer's work was nonetheless vitally important. I was grateful for her involvement and I know she did a fine job.

I wanted Mr and Mrs Hogg to know that my appointment was an indication of the significance and importance the police service generally was placing on these awful circumstances. Even now, after it is all over, I remember quite clearly going to Caroline's home at Beach Lane, Portobello. The lane is part of a maze of side streets in the seafront area of the suburb. The backs of the houses on the Hoggs' side look out on to the backs of the next street. The front looks out across the playground of the local school to more houses about 400 yards away.

The house in which they lived at this time is quite unusual. It is half of two Victorian semi-detached, flat-roofed homes situated a couple of hundred yards from the beach. There is a tiny front garden bounded with a stone wall topped with high, spiked iron railings. The whole area round about is dominated by the school. It is one of the most unusual schools I have ever seen, and a forbidding looking one at that.

Towerbank Primary is a massive stone building, three storeys high. It sits right in the middle of this area of housing made up of a mixture of old and new homes, and, on a rough day, you can hear the roar of the waves from Portobello beach. The tower that gives its name to the school, and many other landmarks in the area, is a rather peculiar building as well. I would guess at it being well over one hundred feet high and now semi-derelict. Despite the fact I must have walked past it hundreds of times, I never had time to find out exactly what it is, or was. Maybe a Victorian seaside attraction, maybe some genuine historic relic.

Right next to the tower at the bottom of Beach Lane was the Tower Amusement Arcade, now called something else, the sort of place terribly attractive to any young child. Caroline had been warned away from the arcade by her parents. She knew full well that it was out of bounds.

John Hogg, a self-employed plumber, ran his business from the house. As Brian Cunningham and I walked up to the front door I noticed the date above it, 1893, the year the home was built. We were quietly greeted and ushered into the comfortable front room. Out of the bay window you could see the school yard where Caroline and her friends often played.

As we sat there, I slowly explained who I was, and what task had been given to me by the four Chief Constables of the forces involved. I explained the terms of reference of my appointment. The piece of paper I had been given not long before required just two things of me:

1. To supervise and direct all aspects of the investigations into the deaths of Caroline Hogg and Susan Claire Maxwell; and
2. To explore the extent to which computers and modern technology may be of assistance, and implement as appropriate.

As Brian Cunningham sat nearby, I assured the grieving couple that a lot had already been done to try and find the man who had brought them such pain, and that no effort would be spared in the future to bring him to justice, no matter how long it might take. However, I was careful not to give any assurances over whether or not the man would eventually be found.

In over 70 murders either investigated or overseen by me I have only ever once given such a promise. That was in the case of another multiple child killing.

The first time I met Mrs Eileen Turnbull, the mother of Eileen Lynn Gibson, who was killed with her two children at Alnwick, in Northumberland, in 1979, I made a pledge to arrest the murderer. That was a very different set of circumstances though. The pledge was honoured.

Here I was dealing with something completely different. If the same man was responsible for both Susan and Caroline's death then he had already eluded police in a massive year-long inquiry that had spared no effort to try and track him down. Indeed this fact had to be one of the foremost thoughts in my mind. If there had been matters overlooked in Susan's case, or things that had been done wrongly, or avenues left unexplored, then it was up to me to make sure that such matters were put right, if they could be and, more importantly, ensure that the same mistakes were not allowed to happen again. The fact that two children had in all probability died at the hands of this man made the job all the more urgent. Until he was caught there was, ever present, the frightening possibility that he could strike again, to snatch another little innocent from the street.

Part of the problem with the Yorkshire Ripper case had been

that the murders were coming so thick and fast the team became snowed under with work. It was impossible for them to get to the bottom of any particular major line of inquiry before a more pressing need became apparent with a new killing. In my investigation also, and to an extent more distressingly, there was always the chance that we may be looking for two killers: perhaps the murders were not by the same person. One killing could have been a copy-cat of the first.

This aspect demonstrates very well the difficulties of detective work. Linking inquiries can be useful; it can also be disastrous, if eventually you discover the cases in hand were not linked. We could never afford to eliminate a suspect entirely just because he was totally alibied for one of the killings. There was never going to be a point at which we could say, with certainty, that a suspect was not our killer because he was firmly alibied for one of the murders but not the other.

All these thoughts were running through my mind as we sat in that neat front room trying to bring comfort and reassurance to a couple who had just lost something so precious, and had seen their lives destroyed in the losing. The best I was able to offer was a powerful promise, and one that was borne out; that the police service generally, all the forces involved at that moment and any others which may be drawn in during the days to come, would make extreme, indeed supreme, efforts to trace this man, this stranger.

Despite Mrs Hogg's trauma and her weepy state, I think she may have taken some comfort from those assurances. I am certain that both John and Annette Hogg were, even at that early stage, more than aware of the vast operation that was underway.

Brian and I were both struck by what a decent and, I suppose, ordinary couple we were dealing with. Two older girls from John Hogg's first marriage stayed with them in the house, along with Caroline's elder brother Stuart, who was twelve. Annette Hogg, understandably, looked all of her 31 years that afternoon. John, eight years her senior, was more calm, but was obviously equally distraught inside.

The relatively long time between their daughter's disappearance and the discovery of her body had taken its toll. Like any parents they had hoped and prayed for her to be returned to them safe and alive. Indeed as part of a deliberate ploy to help keep the publicity surrounding her disappearance going, it had been revealed at one of the regular news conferences how the missing girl's mum and dad thought she may have been taken by a woman desperate for a child of her own, and was being well cared for.

Maintaining the publicity is an important part of the job for the police. Just as Liz Maxwell had realised a year before, you are as well to put up with most of the demands of the media because that way the case stays in the newspapers. Crime, at the end of the day, is solved largely by members of the public. If, as in this case, a mother's anguish viewed on television and reported in the newspapers pricks the conscience of a person shielding a killer, then justice is done more quickly, and perhaps another life is spared: that of the next potential victim.

I became involved only after Caroline's body was found. It was clear to me though that mum and dad, like the police, had been only too aware of the reports of the scruffy stranger stalking their daughter that night, from an early stage. No one could fail but to give those accounts the sinister interpretation they deserved.

It may seem strange for a man who has as many years service in the police, and is a veteran of so many murder inquiries, but I still find it difficult talking to the relatives of victims of crimes, like this one, which are so senseless. It is a difficulty made so much worse when the victim is a child. To have a youngster full of fun and innocence taken from you in such circumstances is the fate parents probably fear more than any other. When it does happen the result is, of course, quite devastating. It is hard to see exactly from where people in this dreadful position find the strength to continue with their lives. They do, though, and those of us brought in to help can only admire their courage and try and ensure we offer what we can to ease their pain. For a police officer that can only mean one way: to do a thorough and effective job.

At the same time, I confess to having a tear in my eye on this occasion, as in so many others. No murder is justifiable. Some come near to being understandable, but the taking of a child's life will always be the most outrageous crime in any policeman's book. Anyone who says they are not affected in the way I was is either quite insensitive, or simply telling lies.

In some ways this is wrong. In any murder case you should have the same strength and the same resolve and determination to succeed. Inevitably, though, the fact that the victim is a child, an innocent young girl, must have some effect on your commitment.

The determination I felt walking silently away from that house was one I sought to engender quickly into the whole team based at Leith Police Station, a couple of miles away, first with the senior officers in lengthy discussions and then with the entire squad attending briefings at Edinburgh and Leicestershire where Caroline's body was found. Later, too, on visits to Staffordshire.

The discovery of Caroline's body had brought with it few clues. She was found, by a tourist stopping to stretch his legs, lying in a lay-by near a busy main road – very similar to the circumstances in which Susan's body was found the year before. This time it was the A444, a favoured route for commercial traffic running between Nottingham and Coventry.

The geography of the lay-by was very similar to the one where Susan's body had been found. It was separated from the road by a narrow strip of grass, it had quite a lot of undergrowth, trees to the rear, and the odd house nearby. A classic place to dump something. Far enough away from the road and houses to allow your actions to pass unnoticed. Close enough not to stick out like a sore thumb, to appear to passers-by as someone looking for a quiet place to get up to no good.

Caroline's parents had given us very detailed accounts of the few hours leading up to her disappearance. It had been a perfectly normal day for a perfectly normal family.

She and her brother Stuart were the children of Mrs Hogg's first marriage. They had been adopted by John, but no one who met them would ever imagine they were not his natural children. Outside, little Caroline could be shy, like so many other children, but not at home. She was often seen whizzing about on her bike. That Friday it was broken. She liked nothing better than to go out and play with her 'wee pals' living within a few yards of the Beach Lane home. Sometimes they would play in the pedestrian area of the new houses behind their house. Other times the school playground would be the favoured venue for their endless games.

The one rule her parents had laid down over and over again was to detail the areas that were out of bounds when she was out with her friends. She was strictly forbidden to go to the beach, the park, the promenade or the fun-fair, without an adult.

However, as these things happen, on this Friday, in the late afternoon, Caroline had overstepped the mark. She had been 20 minutes late for tea. The rest of the family had eaten at about five o'clock, without her, when their calls to her to come home had gone unanswered. But she did return, not long afterwards, to a normal family scolding. Her tea was cold, but she had made a token effort at eating it.

Then she wanted to go out again.

She wanted to go for a walk. There was no one available to go out to have fun with her, so instead a compromise was reached, and the little girl went along to the High Street with her mum and grandmother to take 'Nana' to the bus. On the way back mother and daughter stopped to buy a sweet to share and Caroline skipped home, chomping merrily.

By now it was almost seven o'clock and the little girl's request for just a few more minutes outside was met with a firm 'No.' The firmness faded, and another compromise was reached. 'Take off the party shoes and put something sensible on and you can be out for five minutes,' her parents had said. So, still wearing her lilac party dress, Caroline went for one last play in the evening sunshine.

Not long after, John and Annette decided to go out themselves, and so Mum went to fetch Caroline in for bed. She was, worryingly, nowhere to be seen. With increasing desperation first Mrs Hogg, then other members of the family, started to search the area around the house.

Then, the by now anguished mother found a little boy who said he'd just seen Caroline with a man on the promenade. But they could find no sign of her, or the man, there either. Frantic, Mrs Hogg dashed round everyone she could think of in the area, then raised the alarm by phoning the nearby local police station.

John Hogg told the policewoman that had been despatched to look into the disappearance that he could not believe Caroline would have gone into Fun City by herself because she had been told so often to stay away from it.

Already it had been clear to the first officers involved in her disappearance that this was not an ordinary case of a child wandering off to return later, perhaps a bit frightened but unharmed.

From the outset, Caroline's parents were sure that if it was their daughter that had been seen in Fun City with the man, then she had been enticed there, with all the sinister implications of that simple phrase.

Searches went on late into the night, well after the summer sun had sunk over the tenements that stood between Portobello and Edinburgh. By the next morning the police inquiry was spreading further and further afield. We had alerted the media and appealed for help from the public, either through increased awareness in their everyday lives, or by turning up to help search the massive area round Portobello seafront, and inland, up towards Edinburgh. By 10 a.m. on Sunday an army of volunteers was on the beach and promenade eager to play their part: 600 civilians helped over 100 police comb the area for any sign of the youngster.

All the time we were uncovering more sightings and reports of this man seen with Caroline. He wore glasses. He was scruffy. He was definitely with Caroline. He paid 15 pence for her to ride on a kiddies roundabout. She had sat in the bus on the little carousel. More worryingly, Caroline, according to the witnesses, was still with the stranger when he left Fun City by its western gate, the one that leads to the car park. They were hand in hand.

One of Stuart Hogg's friends told how he'd seen Caroline walk off towards the promenade. Just a few minutes later her Mum had been out looking for her. This youngster told us how Stuart had ignored his Mum's first request to help look for his sister. Seconds later, on its firm repetition, he was off.

Another youngster had seen a scruffy man leaning on a fence and smoking a cigarette. He looked weird. This girl told her Mum about him. This witness was only young but the abduction of Susan Maxwell the previous summer had stayed in her mind, and made her pay attention to what she saw.

Officers had spoken to more and more children who were out that night about the scruffy man so many of them had seen. Some thought he was drunk. Others saw him staring at the children as they played. One of the youngsters estimated the stranger was watching one particular area for over half an hour.

Then we had the vital evidence of an eight-year-old boy. He saw Caroline with the man. He was certain the stranger was scruffy. This little boy had walked right past Caroline and the man as they strolled together. Caroline had not replied to his greeting. The eight-year-old told officers later that he thought it was odd that Caroline had not spoken to him. She lived next door to his granny and he knew her quite well. He saw she was holding the stranger's hand, but she looked frightened. He clearly remembered Caroline was afraid. Equally he was certain the man had glasses and a bit of a beard. His eyes were funny. His glasses were like bottle tops, he said, but of course meant bottoms.

By the time I had arrived at Leith Police Station that Sunday morning all this evidence was to hand. There was one powerful conclusion to be drawn from it all: and that was that the scruffy man truly was the stranger children had to beware of, and he had taken Caroline away.

Before Caroline's body had been found police appeals for help in the search for the missing child produced a response that was quite fantastic. On the Sunday nine days after she vanished two thousand people responded to a request for help in conducting searches of areas not covered by earlier ones, or re-checking other likely places. Co-ordinated by more than 140 policemen, the volunteers fanned out right over the city of Edinburgh and up and down the coast of the Firth of Forth. The rugged areas of Holyrood Park and Arthur's Seat, the dented hill that dominates the Scottish capital, were combed in hours with the help of civilian volunteers in an operation which, if carried out solely by the police, could have taken days. Even the security staff at the Palace of Holyroodhouse, the Queen's official Scottish residence in the centre of Edinburgh, were asked to check the Royal policies for any sign of the missing child.

The next day the newspapers reported a complete blank. One of the organisers, Superintendent Ron Stalker, appeared in print saying: 'I am afraid at this stage I have to report we have turned up nothing at all.'

At this time we were keeping one good clue up our sleeves. Brian Cunningham and his team had, amongst other things, an artist's impression of the stranger, but had decided not to release the picture to the press at that moment in case the move proved counter-productive. The image had been compiled using the recollections of just two people, who had seen him for only a few seconds. They could not be sure exactly how accurate their recollection was, and premature release may have worked against the inquiry. In the event, this artist's impression was invaluable to the investigation and, as it turned out, stunningly accurate.

On 18 July 1983 Detective Chief Superintendent David Baker of Leicestershire Police stood in a lay-by near Twycross and made a terse announcement to a small group of press men. A child's body had been found and his officers were liaising with police looking for what he described as a five-year-old girl missing from her home in Edinburgh.

There was no doubt whose body it was. Caroline was identified in a number of ways. The baubles that had held back her lovely blonde hair were there, and so was a locket she wore around her neck. Apart from these she was naked.

The four Chief Constables had acted quickly after this sad find, and I had arrived in Edinburgh. But what sort of man had they selected to carry out this vital role?

CHAPTER FOUR

The Man in Charge

The majority of my police career has been spent serving the force which covers the county of my birth, Northumberland. I was born and brought up in Felton, a village in the middle of this county, which used to be bisected by the A1, the Great North Road. In fact that road was one of the main features of the village. On Sunday evenings in the summer people would gather in droves to watch the endless nose to tail traffic as people headed back into the urban conurbations of Newcastle and surrounding towns after a day out in the beautiful north of Northumberland.

Now the village is bypassed, thankfully. It is a little haven of peace nestling on the banks of the River Coquet which flows from the Cheviot Hills down into the North Sea at Amble. I well recall attending, as a police officer, the opening of the village bypass by the then little known junior transport minister, Kenneth Clarke QC MP. He more recently went on to commission the Sheehy inquiry into the police which made several controversial and unwanted proposals to change the structure and organisation of the service.

My first home in the village was the butcher's shop. Father was a master butcher and our house and shop were at the bottom of the hill near the river, in the middle of Felton. We moved homes eventually because of a slight disaster. A runaway lorry careered backwards down the hill one day crashing through the front of the shop. No one was hurt but the Clark family moved further up the street to a larger shop, on the level, out of the downhill danger zone. The house that went with the shop was also bigger than my first home; my two brothers, sister and I had more room to spread about.

Life in those days in Felton was a curious mixture of rural tranquillity and organised activity for young and old alike. There was a village policeman but no one troubled him much. Then youngsters did not take the risks with the police they do now.

School was the local village one. The headmaster, Mr Sanderson, wielded a long whippy cane, Miss Young, the teacher, used a shorter more stocky number. From experience I can say both were equally effective; neither did me any harm and I believe their use today would not go amiss in stemming the rise of juvenile crime.

After the village school, I went to college in Newcastle. Friday night was a rush home to help my father with the weekend meat orders. On Friday nights I delivered meat to half the village, the rest was done first thing the following morning. Cycle trips to outlying farms in total darkness were quite hazardous.

Recreation centred round the river. It held a mystic fascination for us, drawing youngsters from the village and surrounding areas to its banks to fish, or into its waters to swim in the then seemingly long, hot summers. The Coquet is a good trout and salmon river but, at times when bites were few and far between, I confess to landing undersize fish along with the rest of the village.

Children then were untroubled from the sort of experiences I was to go on to investigate in later life. Our other great entertainment was taking to the roads and fields around the village and going off for hours. The walks were as picturesque as their names suggested. The Blades, Bell's Land and the Duke's Banks were just three of them.

There was danger of course, but it was a threat posed by natural obstacles like trees with weak limbs or fast-flowing rivers, not the threats posed by other humans. There was a warming predictability about village life in those days. Most faces were known, indeed most names were known. Our habits would be fairly regular and would bring us into contact with the same people on a regular basis. Some may think it's claustrophobic to live life in a place where encounters could be so easily predicted, but for youngsters like us it was reassuring and comforting. Juvenile crime for me and my friends in those days in rural Northumberland never got beyond raiding the odd orchard and nearly getting caught once, and playing 'knocky nine doors' down the main street. Pretty anti-social, sure, but laughably innocent in comparison to activities today for some youngsters.

I would have to admit to not being far away the day another lorry ran back down the hill, on the south side of the river valley known as The Peth, in Felton, after missing a gear. It turned over at the bottom sending its load of oranges flying. There wasn't a house in the village short of marmalade for months.

Football was, and still is, a passion. I played first for the village junior team, then the big team. I played with Sunderland AFC for two seasons but being a committed Newcastle supporter that was an achievement I did not shout about then, or now. I even made the village cricket team in the summer months but there were many others more talented than I in that game.

Saturday nights were spent usually at the pictures in either Alnwick to the north or Morpeth to the south. There was no cinema in Felton, although at the local army camp at Felton Park there were occasional NAAFI film shows.

Pals for youngsters in small communities are most important. Friends are established not just through general activities and sport but through just passing the time of day. The two I remember best were Bruce Armstrong and Jim Routledge. Bruce still lives nearby. Jim joined the RAF and became a commissioned officer. Many years later we were to stand alongside each other at RAF Turnhouse, near Edinburgh, where he was stationed and we would parade, meeting and greeting members of the Royal Family arriving in Scotland. Jim travelled the world with the RAF but has now gravitated back to Felton where he lives in retirement.

Village life, for those who have not enjoyed it, may seem rather sheltered and hardly an ideal preparation for a career in a pretty tough world. The converse is true. In villages life is much more real and nearer the bone. In a small place like Felton one can gain a worldly wisdom and confidence that would be more difficult to achieve in the town. So, I think, it was for me.

My first job was working for the estate that owned a great deal of the land round the village of Felton. I was employed as an office junior at the estate office in Alnwick Castle, the magnificent home of the Dukes of Northumberland. It was good work and enjoyable but neither challenging nor exciting. And so it was that I was given over to a feeling of relief rather than trepidation when, in 1952, National Service called. I joined, not through choice, the Royal Air Force and began my service career with training in statistics, which stood me in good stead for later life. I was asked to express a preference between working home or abroad, and on plumping for the latter was posted to Dalcross, now Inverness Airport. This was my second foray into Scotland, the first being a short family holiday in Edinburgh, staying at a boarding house at the top of Leith Walk, the long straight street that joins the centre of the city to its port area of Leith.

I was later posted to a station in Bedfordshire, where my interest in football was allowed to flourish. I played for the RAF side there, but was later signed, as an amateur, for Luton Town. I found it quite embarrassing to be dropped off at the camp guardhouse after the game on Saturdays.

The team manager then was a former Scottish inter-nationalist by the name of Dally Duncan. He was extremely well known, having played in the 1946 Derby County side that had won that FA Cup. I was with Luton in 1954 and 1955, and was somewhat surprised to be offered a professional signing by Dally when I came out of the RAF. Tempting though it was, I was realistic enough to admit to myself that I did not have the ability to make it professionally in football. Also, like many from the northern counties, I had a lurking desire to return to the North-East.

Once back the Duke's estates held no attraction for me. I had just finished an exciting time in the services; I did not want to go back to a good enough but predictable and unexciting job. So instead I joined the police, my local force, the Northumberland County Constabulary. In June 1955, after initial training, I was sent to Whitley Bay for the usual probationary period.

My first Chief Constable was Alan Scroggie, a Scot from Edinburgh, who later became one of Her Majesty's Inspectors of Constabulary. Usually, a probationer would not have much to do with a Chief Constable but I remember him as a powerful, awesome man. He now lives in retirement in the picturesque East Neuk of Fife, a string of lovely fishing villages along the north shore of the Firth of Forth. In later life I got to know him in a much better way, when he would call at my Edinburgh office, leaving his wife guarding the car unaware of the nature of the refreshment we would enjoy over a chat about, often as not, the north-east of England.

By 1957 my probation period was behind me and I was married and embarked on course as a career detective. Two detective sergeants had a major influence on my development in the CID in those days. It was then that good habits were learned and bad practices avoided. The first major influence on my professional life was Alan Bailey, whom I would later succeed as head of Northumbria CID. The second was Denis Procter, later a chief superintendent and now, coincidentally, living in retirement in Felton. Both had fine qualities, not particularly as detectives, strange though it may seem, but as practical policemen, good organisers and excellent senior officers. I learned a lot from them.

But it is not just the senior officers that you learn the trade from. There were many men who did not advance through the ranks but still made a major contribution to my development. Charles Lockwood for one. From Charlie and others like him you learn a lot and receive help and guidance for which I was grateful.

By 1965 I was a founder member of the regional crime squad in the north-east. Television portrayed us in the series *Softly, Softly*. I was a detective sergeant by now and, through the crime squad, mixing with officers from other forces and learning from their different ways.

In 1969 amalgamation of our rural force with Newcastle and Tynemouth brought further opportunities. I have always argued, much to the chagrin of colleagues in the former county force, that the towns produce the better detectives. So I jumped at the chance to work in the tough west end of Newcastle with a harder breed of criminal and with more serious crime to investigate. It was a short period but an important part of my development.

Promotion, in 1970, to the rank of chief inspector brought with it bad news. I was returned to uniformed duties in Morpeth and the neighbouring town of Ashington, described by many as the largest pit village in Europe, now sadly without a coal mine at all. I enjoyed my time there but prosecuting village parking and petty crime was not to my taste and I was only too happy to go back into CID work in Tynemouth and Whitley Bay after really just a year away.

There was a further amalgamation. The force joined up with parts of Durham Constabulary to form Northumbria Police, taking in the metropolitan areas to the south of the Tyne and some of the rural areas of County Durham. The rank of detective superintendent was bestowed on me in 1973 and then three years later I was made, first, deputy head of CID, and then head on Alan Bailey's retirement. It was a dream beyond my wildest expectations. It was a time of sharply increasing serious crime with the north-east seeing the emergence of criminal gangs involved in gambling and the beginnings of drug trafficking. I needed support and got it from every quarter. Conscious of the risk of ignoring some by omission, I specifically refer to Fred Moffatt, Jim Anderson, John Lawton, Cecil Hall, Peter Docherty, Eric Sanderson, Ken Jewitt, Bunny Osborne, Tom Garside, Joe Bulch and Bobby Hodgson, all Northumbria colleagues.

During my time as a senior officer murder was on the increase at an alarming rate and its detection was a priority. I can say with due modesty that I investigated or supervised in over 70 murders. Sections of the media argue that they all resulted in arrests and in the true sense they are right. In 1975, however, I was involved in the investigation of the murder of Old Polly McKay in the daytime stabbing outside her home in the shadow of St James' Park, the football ground of Newcastle United. The investigation was led by Brian Johnson, now the long-time Chief Constable of Lancashire Constabulary. We failed on that occasion, but failure produces an odd quality, that of enhancing or further extending one's professional education and capabilities.

In any event the CID career, which I first craved and then achieved, was to end in 1981 when I was appointed as an Assistant Chief Constable in Northumbria. A promotion to this rank without leaving home was fairly unusual but welcome. I was assigned to deal with uniform operations and traffic. Later crime was to be my responsibility, which was more to my liking.

When Susan Maxwell was abducted in 1982 I was not really involved in the investigation, although I do recall the Chief Constable, Stanley Bailey, asking me to 'look things over', presumably to check to see if anything had been missed. The only suggestion I could make was for Northumbria and the other force involved, Lothian and Borders, to search every lay-by within 100 yards of the A697 road for 50 miles north and south of the point of Susan's abduction. The exercise bore no fruit but Susan's body was subsequently found in a lay-by, albeit hundreds of miles away. My suggestion was not clever in any way, merely the product of logical thought.

So this is the man that the Chief Constables got to head their joint investigation into the murder of two little girls that had shocked the whole country. They were arguably getting a person of proven ability with vast detective experience. More importantly, they were getting someone absolutely determined and committed to succeed.

As a consequence I admit that at times I expected too much of people working for me on the investigations but make no apology for it. My instinct told me we were in for no easy task and from the outset I wanted everyone on the case to put into it the resolve my instinct was telling me would be necessary. It was obvious no one man was going to manage this job on his own. A team was needed. I was the man the Chief Constables were looking for to lead and inspire that team.

CHAPTER FIVE

Leads and Dead-ends

From the Leicestershire end of the investigation, we had the few clues that could be discovered from Caroline's body. By 22 July 1983, when I took over, not all of the information we would eventually receive from the scientists and doctors was to hand. More tests had still to be done. A lot of information had been gleaned though. It told us that Caroline had not suffered any injuries to her skin or flesh which in itself was most unusual in child murders. It told us she had not been strangled, a common method of killing in cases like this.

None of the back-up services were able to give us two of the more important pointers we needed. Those were: exactly when Caroline died and the method by which she had been killed. The time of death was vitally important because it could give indications as to what might have happened between the time of her abduction and the discovery of her body. The method of killing may have yielded clues as to the type of person we were looking for.

Entomologists were called in to study the cycle of the insects that had laid eggs and hatched in her little body as it lay in the open air during those warm summer days. They estimated as best they could, that it had been in the lay-by for between four and six days. That meant her killer had disposed of the body between four and six days after abducting her. Between 12 and 16 July.

It has to be remembered that an inquiry like this can quickly take on massive proportions. When you have a missing person, especially a child, people want to help and the public provides a great deal of information, a lot of which has to be followed up before its usefulness can be evaluated. Then, once a body is found the sort of information volunteered by people changes, but its volume does not decrease. The number of jobs that have to be done multiply exponentially. There are also the inquiries we are generating ourselves. Tracing and interviewing as many people on and around the promenade as possible and eliminating them. Trying to build up a picture of the scruffy man from witnesses, not helped in this instance by the extreme youth of some of those who saw him that night.

Then there are hunches. After Caroline's body was found, for instance, Leicestershire officers were stationed, on a weekly basis, beside the A444, one and a half miles from the village of Twycross, near the lay-by where she had been dumped. Amongst other things, they noted the registration number of every single vehicle that passed by over two periods of three days. It was a long shot, but they just wanted to make sure that if the killer used the road on a regular basis, and his vehicle number appeared elsewhere in the inquiry, we would match the two up and start asking questions.

There were lots of people who had been on the front of Portobello during the crucial minutes who elected to 'eliminate' themselves. They decided, without reference to anyone, not to come forward in response to widespread appeals from myself and other senior officers, having concluded that they had nothing of importance to add. They were certain they had not seen anything. But the very fact that they knew they had been in certain places at certain times, perhaps watching a specific occurrence, meant that they might have been able to make a contribution to our attempts to build up a complete picture of what was happening on the promenade during the time Caroline moved from her house to the last sighting of her at the amusement park. If they were certain they saw nothing, that negative report might be of importance to us because of the context it allowed other sightings subsequently to be viewed in.

We eventually ended up with 27 people who saw Caroline on or around the promenade that night and recognised her because they knew her, or had such good recall of what they saw that they were later able to identify her after studying her picture. Half of these people also saw the scruffy man.

The house to house inquiries round about were very intensive. People think you just knock at the door, ask if anybody has seen anything, get a negative response and go on your way to the next house. We had officers checking all the occupants against the voters roll, asking people to describe their movements. And then checking it all with the neighbours. On the electoral register it may say Mr and Mrs Bloggs at No 12. They confirm they live there alone. Then the neighbour says, quite innocently in response to questioning, 'Oh yes, Mr and Mrs Bloggs live there with their son Jamie.' Jamie is seen and has questions to answer. So it goes on. You double-check, and that way get to people who are trying to hide someone, or something.

We had, all the time, possible suspects being phoned in by the public, candidates being put forward by officers themselves, and we sought out people with convictions for similar offences in the area. In this case we looked at people with convictions for murder, attempted murder, rape and assault with intent to ravish, who fitted roughly the descriptions of the man we were being given. Most put his age in his thirties so there was no point in looking at people outside that age range, although a margin of error has to be catered for.

We went to every single force in the country, every criminal intelligence office, to draw up this list. The sad thing is that there was not then, and still is not now, one central point that you can go to and be confident that you get everyone you are looking for. I say be sure. You can get most, but there are no guarantees you will be told all. People fitting the profile in the force that covers Edinburgh, that is Lothian and Borders, and the neighbouring forces – Fife to the north, Central Region to the north-west and the eastern divisions of the massive Strathclyde region to the west – were traced, interviewed and eliminated. The same in Northumbria, Cumbria and the other north of England police forces. A similar operation was being carried out in Leicestershire, Staffordshire and the nine forces surrounding those areas.

We spoke to hundreds of the country's less savoury characters, and as a by-product cleared up quite a lot of more minor crime. It's often a feature of an operation like this that a potential suspect confesses to a minor offence to give himself an alibi for something more serious. You knock on the door of a man with convictions for sex offences against children, because of where he lives, near the scene of the crime under investigation. He may well have been half expecting it. Occasionally, he may be prepared to be honest and admit quite straightforwardly to another offence committed at the time we were interested in, when all we were trying to do was eliminate him from the list of possible suspects for our crimes.

Sometimes people could not be eliminated by questioning and checks like these. So as a last resort we put them on to an identification parade. This technique was used as sparingly as possible. There is a danger if you hold too many ID parades the only thing that will be achieved is to get your witnesses, the people you may have to rely on if the case ever gets to court, practised in the art of not picking out culprits. The passage of time does nothing for identification either.

We were eventually able to identify at least six men who were on the seafront that night clearly for immoral purposes. They were there to watch the little girls. Some, I am sure, would never have dreamed of doing anything more than just watching. Some would have got all the thrill they wanted by simply engaging a child in conversation; all the half dozen had convictions for this sort of offence. I suppose any of them had the potential to commit a more serious offence given the chance.

It is a sad fact of life that these people hang around places such as Portobello, and it's by no means confined to there. They are the sort of people you could find at nearly any place where children play. A lot of them do go just to watch, but it is a fact that there are more indecent assaults in places like this than anywhere else, underlining this potential danger in even the most attractive of beauty spots.

One such man was identified sitting in the swing park that Caroline had walked past. He was known to police in Edinburgh and had convictions for offences against children. He appeared to be behaving in an odd way from the descriptions we got. His head was in his hands. We needed to speak to him urgently. He was tracked down and brought in for questioning. To help establish myself and also set standards of the way in which I expected these matters to be carried out in the future, I conducted the interview with the suspect personally. Brian Cunningham and I gave him a very firm questioning, quite a hard time indeed.

The man lived by himself in lodgings and we stripped his room completely. Eventually we concluded that he was not involved in Caroline's disappearance, and he was released without any charges being made. Just a few weeks later he killed himself. I sent officers to his home in case we had come to the wrong conclusion and the suicide was as a result of guilt. However, that was not to be the case and although no notes were left by the man, it was clear his death at his own hand was brought about by matters completely unconnected to the inquiry.

The press has taken my appointment as confirmation of their speculation that one person was responsible for both murders. Front page headlines proclaimed, 'Susan's killer may have struck again', 'Monster on the loose', 'Find him or he'll kill again'.

Although always confident in my own mind that we were looking for just one killer, I was determined not to exclude the chance that there were two. At news conferences, for instance, I was always careful to keep alive that possibility. Quoted in *The Scotsman*, I said at one such briefing for reporters: 'It appears we are looking for one man, but different people may be involved.' I also, perhaps foolishly, added: 'I have been appointed as a result of research carried out and lessons learned after the Yorkshire Ripper inquiry.'

The press jumped at that. Several papers quoted me as saying that this investigation would not make the mistakes seen in the Peter Sutcliffe case. That was unfair and out of context. The problems with the Ripper case were all down to the system used to record details of the evidence, the only system that was available at the time. A huge database had been kept on manual files and cards and as the inquiry became ever larger, the mechanics of the investigation, the recording system, was creaking under the strain. It was this case, showing the need for better ways of handling such large volumes of information, that gave the impetus for the search to develop computer systems to help.

I had a substantial involvement in the hunt for the Yorkshire Ripper and realise exactly the immense pressures that it created. Unless one knows the background to the case one should not be critical and certainly I am not, and was not. That inquiry killed a good friend of mine and seriously affected the personal lives of many others.

Back to the investigation I had in hand and in many ways the public were the best weapon we had. There was such a good description of the number one suspect that I thought I would be able to pick him out myself from a whole room full of people, so well did I feel I knew him. We wanted someone out there to do the same thing.

Certainly people tried. An appeal for holidaymakers to send us snaps and rolls of film taken at Portobello was met with enthusiasm. For a few days we were probably receiving more holiday pictures and undeveloped film than Boots the Chemist. And it was an operation that bore fruit. Rolls of film came from as far away as Australia and Japan. All of it was developed and studied carefully. A few frames gave us good leads on the movements of people round the area. None gave us a picture of Caroline out and about that night with, or without, her abductor.

However, in one photograph there was a clear shot of a scruffy man who, caught in the snap second of a shutter's movement, seemed to be staring intently out across the beach towards the sea. We had the photograph blown up as much as possible and saw that in many ways he resembled the man who had been described to us so many times now. Just sticking up above the wall was the end of a bicycle handlebar, and the top of a saddle. The man was obviously with the bike. He also wore dark glasses.

That picture was circulated within the force to see if any officers could identify him, but none did. As a safeguard I had detectives go round every cycle shop in the city to see if any of their staff members could recognise him. Again no one could. Some days later the incident room got an excited call from an Edinburgh city centre cycle shop. A man had come in for spare parts for his machine and the assistant behind the counter recognised him from that picture, which he been shown by the officers days before. With this lead we traced the man, and it turned out he was a sex offender who had served seven years in jail for raping a young girl, just a mile from the point of Caroline's disappearance.

This episode demonstrated to us how easily mistakes could be made. He should have featured in the inquiry because of his conviction, and had not. He should also have been recognised by the officer who had dealt with his case some years before, when that enlarged holiday snap was circulated in the force. There was a weakness in the system and a weakness on the part of the officer who failed to recognise the man. It served to remind everyone that a whole inquiry can be let down, or even lost altogether, by just one short cut, one omission. As it was, the suspect was eventually totally cleared and eliminated, but it was a situation that should not have arisen. I was not very happy that it had. The police officer concerned was 'spoken to'.

So it seemed perfectly clear that Caroline had been abducted by the scruffy man. He had been seen almost, as it were, selecting his intended victim. He was standing by the fence round the swing park not far from Caroline's house. He was seen speaking to her, walking hand in hand with her on the promenade, and then paying her on to the Fun City roundabout. The last sighting of him was walking, with the little girl, out of the gate towards the carpark, where it was fairly safe to assume that he had some kind of transport waiting. We could be fairly certain because once Caroline and he left the fun park there were no more sightings of them at all. If he had continued on foot from Fun City in any direction there were people who would have seen him and in the hours and days after her disappearance the publicity was massive. The trail went stone cold as they left the sight of the last witness in the funfair.

We had no indications or leads on the vehicle that we presumed had been used. Intensive attempts to find out about it were made, but no person has ever been found that saw the stranger and Caroline get into a vehicle, or drive off.

One potential major breakthrough did present itself to us though. It proved to be a tough nut to crack.

There was an incident on the A697 road slightly later the same night Caroline disappeared that made the entire team excited when it was reported to us. The A697 is often known to people in the east of Scotland and England as the middle road. It is the route which lies between the main easterly road linking the two countries, the A1, and the main road running down the centre of Britain at this point, the A68. More importantly for us, it forms the main road that runs right through the middle of Coldstream town and over the bridge from where Susan Maxwell had been abducted the year before.

Police were contacted by a Michael Flynn, an Edinburgh man. He had been driving north up the A697 with his wife, returning to Scotland after a holiday in the south. It was 9.25 p.m. and the couple were about nine miles north of the Borders village of Greenlaw. They were almost forced off the road as they met, nearly head on, a blue Ford Cortina car heading south.

Mr Flynn skidded to a halt, as did the driver of the other car.

Mr Flynn, a former police civilian employee in Edinburgh, had a good look at the driver. His description of him loosely fitted the description we were being given of the stranger seen with Caroline. More important than that was the fact there was a little girl, a frightened little girl, in the car. She was standing up between the two front seats. She had blonde hair swept back at the sides, tied in bunches, like Caroline's had been, and big, black eyes.

Obviously the fear on the little girl's face may have been put there simply by the car in which she was travelling grinding to a halt in such a near miss. Equally there may have been fear there long before the close encounter. There were words exchanged between Mr Flynn and the mystery driver, but he made hardly any response.

The incident happened at a spot only some 20 miles north of Coldstream and assumed great importance in the inquiry. There were only two ways in which we were going to get to speak to the driver of the car. Make a successful public appeal for him to come forward, or the hard way. Go out and find him.

Mr Flynn's description of the car was enough to pinpoint it as one of a model produced by Ford during a period of two and a quarter years. The car company during that period had offered purchasers many shades of blue. We were faced with the prospect of trying to track down the man through his car which, we hoped, would be found within the registration details of over 120,000 blue Ford Cortinas of this model held by the DVLC in Swansea. Our hope, on the August day that I first made public the lead, was that the driver would come forward. The appeal won national newspaper, radio and television coverage. He did not contact us.

In the hours after that news conference I experienced the most painful and distressing part of my role in the hunt. Brian Cunningham and I attended Caroline's funeral. She was laid to rest in Piershill Cemetery not far from the family home, in an area of Edinburgh that would be very significant as the investigation entered its later stages.

Mr and Mrs Hogg had withdrawn completely into themselves, understandably, by this time. They had made themselves available to the press on a small number of occasions after being persuaded by ourselves that their presence at a news conference would help generate the sort of publicity that may just help us find Caroline. Then after her body was discovered they had been unwilling to go in front of the cameras again. I knew the funeral of their daughter would be of great press interest, and I was equally aware that such interest would only cause further distress to a family that was already going through enough.

On my instructions, all knowledge of the burial was kept entirely secret and the service remained totally private to the family. Just in case, each entrance to the cemetery was discreetly watched over by police officers to keep the occasion secure, personal and private.

During the emotion-filled graveside service only a few of the little girl's closest relatives were present. Her little white coffin was adorned with a simple bunch of pink roses. On them a card which read: 'We will love you always, our darling Caroline. Mum and Dad.'

The next day, the daunting task of trying to track down that Cortina driver continued. Although I had only just made public the hunt for the man it had been under way for some little time. Again though, as the senior officer, I had to take steps to try and shortcut this part of our hunt as far as possible, purely because of the potential size of it. Brian Cunningham and myself had to come up with a plan to make this line of inquiry as simple, fast but most importantly, effective as we could.

The first thing we had to bear in mind was that if the driver had not been connected with Caroline's disappearance he could hardly have failed to see the publicity surrounding our search for him, and he should have come forward. I had always been at pains to stress that the man was being sought as a witness, quite genuinely, to make it as easy as possible for him to contact us.

If he was to be found we had to have a structured approach to the task. It was decided to concentrate on the registered keepers of blue Ford Cortinas living in the areas where we were already running detailed checks on sex offenders. In the force areas in and around Edinburgh, the border counties and the English Midlands. Officers spent weeks tracing the keepers, interviewing them at length as to their movements and checking the alibis they gave for that night. In all nearly 22,000 keepers of blue Ford Cortinas were seen and spoken to.

In addition to the registered keepers of the cars in those areas, we ran a double-check with the database we had built up of sex offenders. No matter where they lived, men with convictions that put them into our potential profile of the killer, and who owned a blue Ford Cortina, were visited and again questioned in great detail. The answers we got from them were checked, and double-checked.

Prior to this case, all police murder inquiries were managed on an entirely manual recording system. It was exactly the same way major inquiries had been managed for years and years. In some ways effective, but more often than not open to human error. The misplacing or loss of a single index card in a box file could negate the entire investigation. One key fact overlooked, one name that got stuck behind a filing cabinet could be the difference between success and failure. In the Caroline Hogg inquiry Lothian and Borders Police already had a dedicated mainframe computer which had the capacity to take all our data. They were ahead of the game. This was in the days before a specific police system was devised for major inquiries. A software programme was hurriedly written for us, and as a result of it mistakes were less likely to occur. Accurate checks on information were now possible between the forces involved.

The Susan Maxwell inquiry, on the old manual files and cards, stood on its own. Checks had to be made on both systems. The whole joint investigation record was to be put on a more formal and satisfactory basis when another murder was included in the series. More of this later.

In the middle of August, we carried out a reconstruction of Caroline's last known movements. I must say I am not a great believer in these events, but they do serve some purpose and every line of inquiry has to be exhausted. There is the chance of throwing up a hitherto unknown witness, unlikely in this case, and it proved to be so. They do, of course, help keep the publicity going.

The effect of press coverage can be vital. All the time during an inquiry such as this publicity is essential. It brings forward new witnesses and new leads with them. It can also have the effect of playing on the conscience of a person who may either be shielding the killer or be suppressing real fears that they know the identity of him or, more likely, are related to him.

On 12 August, Caroline's part in the reconstruction was taken by the daughter of one of our own officers. PC Allan Beck and his wife Jenny were only too willing to allow little Marion to assist. She looked not unlike Caroline, a fact that was instrumental in the family's decision to take part. Mrs Beck told newsmen that night: 'When the wee girl went missing and I saw the pictures of her I thought, "That could be my wee girl." I just hope that this helps and someone, somewhere saw something.'

As I had feared, that reconstruction turned up hardly anything we did not already know about the events of the night Caroline vanished. But now, five weeks after the disappearance, and 21 days after the start of my own involvement, I was heartened by the vast mountain of information we did have. Most importantly, we had a very good idea of what our culprit looked like. Sustained attempts to track down a glimpse of him in the corner of a holiday snap had failed. Equally, hours of video film handed over by sightseers had failed to capture him, even for a split second.

We had gone to the length of tracking down, first through our own detective work, and then Interpol, a woman from Preganziol near Treviso in Northern Italy, who had been described by several witnesses as a sun-tanned woman with a video-camera. She had been one of a party of Italian tourists staying at a hotel in the county of Angus and the owner of the establishment recalled them talking about filming near the sands at Portobello and contacted the incident room to tell us. But despite all that effort, no luck. She had held on to the tape shot during the evening of the abduction, but there was nothing on it for us. And nothing either from the tapes sent from Australia, Japan and other countries.

Other leads were fruitless too. Officers flew to Germany to interview one gentleman, Herr Fritz Witte, a teacher from Witten in what used to be West Germany. He had gained something approaching notoriety in the press, who had got hold of his name. He was portrayed as a suspect when in fact he was really only a potential witness who may have seen something that night because we thought he might have been in key locations during the vital minutes. This lead too turned into a wild-goose chase despite the willingness of Herr Witte to do all he could for us.

As the inquiry grew it became apparent that unless a sudden and, I have to confess, unexpected breakthrough came, then we were in for a long hard slog. The by-product of this slog was a mountain of information that grew and grew.

CHAPTER SIX

Running Out of Steam

The double murder hunt was at times in danger of becoming overwhelmed by the volume of information that was building up.

The picture we were seeing in the inquiry was one that I had been faced with before, during my time as head of CID in Northumbria. Then it was the Yorkshire Ripper hunt. There was a strong connection to the Sunderland area of the north-east because of the taunting messages that were sent to the Ripper Squad. The man sending them spoke with a pronounced Wearside accent. These purported to be from the Ripper himself; the tapes, and some letters sent to the police, bore a Sunderland postmark. For quite some time the various items were regarded as genuine and a considerable effort was put in to try and track this man down through this avenue. It was subsequently shown to be the work of an extremely sick individual who ended up costing the inquiry thousands of wasted hours and substantial sums of money. The identity of the hoaxer was never conclusively established.

Now, that whole inquiry is often referred to as a flawed investigation; the adjective 'bungled' is regularly trotted out in connection with it. This criticism had nothing to do with the Sunderland end of the inquiry or indeed West Yorkshire Police themselves. It was more the product of a recording system that was far from perfect. The reality then was quite different from the public's and media perception now. It was a very good investigation, in the main, led by excellent detectives from an efficient police force. It was, however, one that was let down by the way in which information was collated, stored and checked. Computerisation of any sort was a long way off at the start of that episode and was therefore not available to the squad. If it had been, then the inquiry may well have taken a different, faster route.

In my child murders investigation one of the main priorities was to ensure that our information was handled in the best way possible. Indeed, my duty, in the terms of the brief given to me by the four Chief Constables, was to look at how modern technology might make our task more efficient.

The entire Susan Maxwell inquiry had been recorded only on a manual system. These were made up of record cards and files of paper, with all the inconvenience and, of course, dangers involved. One piece of paper missing, one card out of place and the case could be lost, even with the best detectives in charge. The reality of this system was, in the worst instance, that a child killer could be allowed to remain free for long enough to strike again, simply because a single card was filed in the wrong place, not put back properly after being examined, fell down at the back of the filing cabinet, or was not replaced at all. It would be several years before the development of the computer system that was eventually designed to handle big investigations. Its acronym HOLMES is now quite well known; it stands for Home Office Large Major Enquiry System.

The linked inquiries into Caroline Hogg and Susan Maxwell's murders were spread across four force areas. There were four separate strands to the hunt. Two abductions in the northern parts of Britain and two murder hunts based in separate forces in the Midlands.

It is police convention that the force in whose area a body is found takes the lead in the murder inquiry, despite the fact that often, as in our case, the majority of the clues were to be found in the area of the abductions. It may seem an odd system, but it's based on the principle that applies to all cross-territorial crime: that the force with the most serious offence in its patch leads in a joint inquiry. In most cases this works well enough, but in a murder it may not.

Our cases dealt with crimes that had started off as missing person inquiries. By the time the two girls' bodies were found both cases were, to all intents and purposes, full-scale murder hunts already. For the emphasis of control then to be switched to another force starting out cold would not have been sensible. Certainly in the Caroline Hogg inquiry, we had a huge volume of evidence available at the Portobello end of it and very little uncovered in Leicestershire. So on this occasion we departed from convention and the main inquiry was based at, and led from, Edinburgh.

The indications pointing towards the clue that would lead us to our killer could be contained in separate parts of the mountain of evidence gathered already in those hunts. We had to compare and search for common ground. To do so thoroughly, on a manual basis, was virtually impossible.

I arranged a meeting at Edinburgh police headquarters with the Lothian and Borders force Chief Constable Sir William Sutherland and people from the Scottish Office, Home Office and others who may have been able to assist. I will take help from anyone.

Lothian and Borders had recently taken delivery of a new computer system with a large mainframe for their force-wide system. They were one of the pioneers of police computerisation, and still are for that matter. My desire was to get sufficient space on that system to put all of the Caroline Hogg inquiry into it and then have the whole Susan Maxwell inquiry back record converted, that is to say the manual files in-put on to the same computer to provide one complete database for both murders.

To me this seemed vital to the success of the inquiry in the long term, but it was not to be. The move was vetoed by Sir William, for reasons that I accepted then, and now, were perfectly correct. Of course the decision was disappointing. Bill was worried that the system he had just taken delivery of was new and relatively untried. He was also concerned that, because of the massive amount of information already gathered in the two murder hunts, and the equally vast volume likely to follow, the mainframe may not have the capacity to cope with these two inquiries and continue to do the job for which it had just been purchased.

In the event, we did have sufficient capacity to handle the Caroline Hogg inquiry, using a programme devised and written by Lothian and Borders Police's own experts over a single weekend. It was interesting to note that, much later, when the HOLMES system was developed, it bore striking similarities to the programme that we developed and used.

What we ended up with was a computer system to manage, record and log the Hogg inquiry, and a manual system based in Staffordshire for the Maxwell inquiry. It worked, but it creaked from time to time. It meant that when anyone in Edinburgh carried out an inquiry in the Hogg case, particularly in respect of potential suspects, as well as checking the computer database they also had to telephone Staffordshire to see if the name had cropped up in that investigation. A backlog of checks built up from time to time, as you would expect, but although our methods were inconvenient and time-consuming, we were always able to be aware of any links between the two investigations.

From the outset I stressed how vital it was to carry out this procedure thoroughly, if we were to avoid the sort of mistakes made elsewhere. If someone was mentioned in both inquiries we had to have confidence that fact would be thrown up quickly, so appropriate action could be taken.

One of the surprising aspects of the Maxwell case that had been known for many months was just how many human links there were between Coldstream and Uttoxeter, where Susan's body was found. For example, we discovered that quite a few people crossed the Tweed bridge on the day of her disappearance and ended up in the Midlands of England, and Staffordshire in particular. A local doctor, for instance, had driven over the bridge and arrived in Uttoxeter later that very day. However, he never really featured in the inquiry because he began his journey from Coldstream sometime before Susie set out for that fateful game of tennis. He could not, though, be eliminated without being seen and questioned.

There was another task I had to carry out as quickly as possible. The Hogg inquiry was very much active and developing when I took charge. The Maxwell investigation was virtually exhausted. A few officers were still assigned to the case and there were matters to be followed up on a fairly irregular basis but it would exaggerate their importance to describe these inquiries as leads. They were, in the main, routine checks to tidy up odds and ends and to make sure each possibility had been thoroughly examined. Things were to change substantially after Caroline's body was found. A whole new emphasis and urgency was put back into the Coldstream/Uttoxeter case.

I had to familiarise myself completely with what had been turned up, with all the many facets of that earlier investigation, and, where necessary, draw conclusions on possible links. This meant trips down to Staffordshire and Leicestershire and, again, a visit to a pair of grieving parents. The farm cottage occupied by the Maxwells at Cramond Hill, within sight of the Scottish border, would become a familiar stopping-off place over the next few years.

Liz and Fordyce Maxwell were exactly as I expected them to be. The Northumbrian character is one well known to me. They were warm, friendly and welcoming – and devastated. Even after a year there was little sign of a lessening of this couple's grief, and the knowledge that the person who had killed their daughter had, in all likelihood, struck again did nothing to ease their troubled minds.

I was to become a regular visitor at this house, calling in to bring them up to date with developments, or all too frequently for my liking, the lack of them. When I called tea was always offered, not in china cups in the front room, but in a mug in the kitchen. It was an arrangement that suited me fine.

The need to know the parents in this case was important to me. There was an equally vital need to become 'up to speed' with the detail of the inquiry and the personalities involved in it, both the investigators and the investigated. My aim had to be to become as knowledgeable with the detail of the Maxwell inquiry as officers who had spent months working on it exclusively. Many hours were spent reading reports and statements and talking at length to detectives who had featured at many levels.

The abduction of Susan was so like what had happened to Caroline in many ways. It was a similarity obvious to all, not just police officers. She had been taken by a stranger. Snatched from her home environs to be used by her abductor for whatever purpose, and then discarded like a broken toy.

Every parent who goes through what Liz and Fordyce Maxwell had spends a great deal of time thinking about the events that led up to the disaster. Over and over again one little phrase crops up: 'What if?' What if it had rained, what if I had gone to get her, what if she'd played five minutes longer? 'What if' is inevitable, but totally fruitless. The simple fact is that no one involved in the events leading up to Susan's abduction did anything to make it more likely. It was an event that was not foreseeable.

Today as holidaymakers go to Coldstream, many unaware of the terrible thing that happened there one summer afternoon, they will think nothing of allowing their youngsters the freedom children need to enjoy themselves. Nor I suppose should they, beyond the basic commonsense rules. Just in the way Susan's family could have no forewarning of what was about to befall them. Things like that do not happen to people in the country. It's a problem for townsfolk.

Susan had intended cycling to Coldstream for her tennis

game, but because of the traffic on that busy tourist route, which led from her home to the town, her mum had persuaded her to walk. As it happened one of the farmworkers was leaving Cramond Hill at the same time as the eleven-year-old and offered her a lift, an offer which was readily accepted. This made Susan a little early for the rendezvous with her intended tennis partner, who was just twelve. The farmworker dropped Susie off in Coldstream, near the Lennel Tennis Club, where the game was due to take place.

She had left the farm wearing a yellow terry towelling tee-shirt and shorts. The tee-shirt had a quaint palm tree motif on it. White ankle socks and white tennis shoes completed the outfit. She carried her racket, a ball and a flask of orange juice. It was a lovely, warm afternoon.

As there was time to fill, Susie wandered into the local filling station, the Tweed Garage. Her family used it a lot, she was known there. In fact the lady on duty that afternoon, Mrs Home, even knew Susan was going to play tennis. Liz Maxwell and her daughter had been in earlier in the day and the match that afternoon was among the topics of conversation.

People spoke to me of Susan as a polite and kind girl. Her kindness was demonstrated here at the garage. Mrs Home wanted an errand run to the Post Office nearby, and Susan was only too happy to oblige. She came back with the stamps that had been asked for. Mrs Home had told her to buy something for going and the youngster was sucking an ice lolly as she returned.

I never knew Susie, of course, but I feel as though I did.

Almost prophetically, Mrs Home asked Susan how she was going to get home after the game and was told by the little girl that she planned to walk. Clear as a bell, the garage clerk remembers telling Susan not to accept a lift from a stranger. In addition one of the garage salesmen said he'd be going over towards Cornhill about the time the tennis game was due to be over. He said he'd stop and give her a lift if he drove by and saw her.

I learned the game passed off uneventfully and the young friends set off for their respective homes. The route taken by

Susan's opponent that afternoon took her part of the way towards Cornhill, and the pair walked together as far as the police station on the corner, near the end of the town. There they parted and the other girl recalled last seeing Susan looking as though she was about to cross the High Street. Her friend walked off home. She later estimated for us that it was about ten past four. She recalled looking at a clock in the High Street.

As this small scene was being played out someone was watching over the pair.

An office worker in the solicitors' firm across the road from the police station happened to be looking out of her window. She saw Susan walk past, noticed what a very pretty little girl she was, but thought nothing of it until later that night, when the searchers were out looking for the missing tennis player.

It was clear that lots of people had noticed Susan as she walked towards her home that afternoon. She'd smiled at some of them, acknowledged others, but no one had seen anything suspicious. Despite all these friends, neighbours and acquaintances being about there was another man who spotted Susan on her way home. A stranger was stalking Susan with evil intentions. He was biding his time, waiting for an opportunity to pounce.

A very complete picture of her movements had been established. Officers discovered a flour tanker had been parked in a lay-by on the English side of the bridge. His tachograph, the so called 'spy in the cab', allowed accurate timings of many of the sightings of Susan to be established. There came a point in these timings and observations, past the bridge, that there was no more sightings. About the last person to see Susan was a man from Yorkshire who'd stopped to stretch his legs for a couple of minutes on the English side. The flour tanker driver moved away after his snack and is adamant he did not pass a girl anywhere along the short road into Coldstream.

Neither did another important witness. Mrs Rutherford from the BMW garage knew Susie well and if she had passed her that afternoon she would have remembered. Mrs Rutherford was certain she was in fact not there at a time she ought to have been.

RUNNING OUT OF STEAM

The waiting stranger had struck, and Susan was gone. She had been snatched, obviously between this last positive sighting, and the equally crucial evidence of the people who were certain they had seen nothing.

From shortly after the abduction, we were aware of the one piece of evidence that appeared to point positively to Susan having been snatched. About two weeks after Susan vanished detectives had been contacted by a young psychiatric nurse who lived in the south of Northumberland, and who had passed through Coldstream on the day in question. Mark Ball told police that he saw a girl struggling beside a car almost 400 yards south of the bridge. He put the time quite precisely at 4.25 p.m. He said that he had not come forward earlier because he had been preparing for important medical examinations and had not heard about the abduction until then.

There had been intensive coverage of Susan's disappearance, but Mr Ball said he'd been virtually locked away and had certainly not seen a newspaper or heard a news bulletin during that time. This explanation took some believing. How could anyone have failed to hear or see news of Susan's disappearance?

His story was that he and his sister were travelling south on the A697, returning to their home in Blyth after a holiday in Scotland. Just past the bridge, Mr Ball had told officers, he saw a young girl struggling with a man sitting in the front passenger seat of a maroon Triumph 2000 or 2500 car. What's more, he said he saw that the little girl had a tennis racket in her hand and she was scraping it on the nearside door of the car. She was obviously in some sort of distress. There was someone else in the car, in the driver's seat. The witness told detectives he had said to his sister: 'Did you see that?', but his sister had no recollection of seeing the incident, nor did she recall her brother making the remark, or any other comment for that matter.

This had been regarded as a vital lead. To be honest, the only real lead in the whole inquiry. The senior officers in the case at the time decided to interview the owners of every maroon Triumph

2000-type car ever made. There were about 19,000 of them. I had no quarrel with this decision.

It had been a mammoth undertaking, but one that was pursued with vigour as far as it could be. There were problems, of course. Mr Ball had indicated that the car may have been quite old, so there was always the danger it had been resprayed from the colour under which it was registered, and so would not turn up in the checks. A year later, when I took over, that line of inquiry was completed, as far as it could be. There were in the region of 200 of these cars that could not be traced for one reason or another.

The view that there was a maroon Triumph involved in Susan Maxwell's abduction was still the prevailing one when I took over. For the simple reason that Mr Ball was so central to the Susan Maxwell inquiry I decided to make a re-evaluation of his evidence. There were four possibilities:

Firstly, that Mr Ball was, for whatever reason, mistaken. What he thought he saw he did not in fact see at all.

Secondly, that he was right and Susan was abducted by the two people in that maroon car.

Thirdly, that she managed to get away from them and was then abducted by someone else.

Fourthly, he was lying.

Mr Ball was re-interviewed, at length, in detail, and at times, I suppose, quite harshly. He was the vital witness, we had doubts, and we had to clear those doubts up, if we could. The nurse remained adamant about what he had seen that afternoon and stuck to his story.

Various matters led me to the conclusion that I should not give the importance to Mr Ball's story that it had commanded so far in the inquiry. One of these reasons was that I simply could not understand how anyone could exist for 13 days at Blyth in Northumberland, not all that far from Coldstream, and fail to notice any publicity about the case at all. It seemed next to impossible. So, after consultations with other senior officers, I decided to write Mr Ball's evidence out of the script. He was by no means discredited, but sufficient doubt had crept into my mind to suggest that his account did not deserve the prominence it once had been given. It did, of course, end the only lead there was in the whole distressing case. But if that lead was wrong, then the move away from it meant that some progress had been made.

The information unearthed during the maroon Triumph inquiry would always remain in the system; it wasn't discarded because of my decision, its importance was merely downgraded, rather sharply.

Profile suspects in the area of Coldstream and Uttoxeter had all been traced and eliminated long before my involvement. So there was really very little to go on. We reviewed the evidence; there were other sightings of vehicles that were imprecise, or too vague to allow development of the clue. There were several cars in and around the immediate area, and a van parked somewhere around, but initially no one was able to tie down details of it, apart from it being white and probably a Ford Transit. It had been seen on both sides of the bridge.

There were thousands upon thousands of vans like that made over a great number of years; what chance of finding that one? In detective work there is never any point starting a line of inquiry unless there is a good chance of finishing it. To merely start attempting to trace all white vans, or even Transit vans that have been registered over 20 years of production would have been utterly futile.

One new lead did eventually turn up, in the autumn of 1985. It was one that the press quickly latched on to and was widely reported. We had been aware of a man going round the farms of north Northumberland selling Nu Swift fire extinguishers. He had, in fact, sold some extinguishers in the Cornhill area not long before Susan was snatched.

There was nothing, on the face of it, particularly suspicious about the man who I shall call only Mr X. The thing that brought him to our attention initially was when he was involved in a matrimonial dispute and was spoken to by police in respect of a court order preventing him contacting his family, that he had allegedly broken. We were told that Mr X had mentioned Susan Maxwell quite often. Detectives in my investigation were contacted quickly by the local officers dealing with the domestic dispute.

We discovered the man had been travelling the northern counties selling extinguishers. He was a relatively frequent visitor to the north Northumberland area. We had become equally aware that he seemed to have stopped going back to that part of the county after Susan's disappearance. A deeper look at his background revealed he had produced some quite disturbing writing which had frequent mentions of Susan Maxwell either specifically or by implication.

He was interviewed in the normal way, for the purposes of elimination, but there were certain matters that did not add up. This, of course, required further investigation. As we delved into his background, mainly by studying his well-documented sales records, we discovered that not only had he been to Cramond Hill, but he had actually sold a fire extinguisher to Susan's father Fordyce, just a matter of two or three weeks before her abduction.

Mr X, who was in his mid-thirties, had been convicted of indecency involving his own children. As a result of this his wife had divorced him.

To begin with, our inquiries into his background were very promising and the morale of the squad took off. There was a sighting of a car, like his, in Coldstream on the day Susan was snatched. There was potential identification from two girls who had been approached as they walked near Coldstream bridge some days before the abduction by a man who could have been Mr X.

There were moments when I thought we had our man, as far as Susan was concerned, though Mr X had the best of alibis for the time of Caroline Hogg's murder. He was, on that day, quite clearly in Morpeth, 97 miles away from Portobello.

In the event, Staffordshire detectives, who were leading the Maxwell investigation, built up only a weak case against him. From sales invoices, we could put him in the Hexham area on the day of Susan's disappearance, but there was not a firm link in evidential terms to connect him with Cornhill. The case against him was totally circumstantial. He had claimed to be firstly at Morpeth in Northumberland, and we conclusively showed he was at Hexham. Then later on the day Susan was snatched, Mr X claimed to have been walking on Seaton Sluice beach, in Northumberland, not far from his home, and to have met a woman he knew. The woman was traced and told us, adamantly, that she had not been on the sands at that particular place for 20 years. It was, of course, only part of the job to show he was not where he said he was. We had to show that he was where we thought he might have been.

There were a lot of powerful circumstances surrounding his movements, but as the investigation into Mr X wore on it became more likely that he was not involved in Susan's murder at all. A file on the case was eventually sent to the Director of Public Prosecutions, but he decided, quite rightly, that there was insufficient evidence to proceed against Mr X on any charges.

He had been interviewed by officers from the squad at Crammlington Police Office in Northumberland with his solicitor and a doctor present, and released into the care of the psychiatric hospital once more, where I believe he still is.

My suspicions over him cooled really as soon as we discovered he could not have been responsible for Caroline's death. Throughout I was careful not to put all our eggs into one basket, but at the same time, from the outset of my full involvement in the case I believed one person, one man, was responsible for both killings. As I have said, I found the prospect of two people capable of such inhumanity to be on the loose rather more chilling than one man being able to take the life of a child on two separate occasions.

The potential danger of this belief was to get the two inquiries intertwined to too great an extent. They had to be treated as separate investigations at all times and yet still looked at jointly. If, in reality, they were not linked, and we placed too much emphasis on treating them as the work of the same person, a killer might escape justice just because he had a firm alibi for the murder he could not possibly have committed.

By the time Mr X was eliminated from the inquiry both the murder hunts were running very short of steam. We decided that if new clues were not going to be turned up we would try looking in greater depth at the ones we had already gathered and re-examining their importance. To this end the services of one of Edinburgh's police surgeons, Dr Nichol Grey, was enlisted to hypnotise one of the potentially key witnesses to see if he could be regressed and reveal more information from some far corner of his mind.

This witness was Mr Flynn, the man who'd seen a frightened little girl in a Cortina on the night Caroline was taken. The hypnosis was not carried out to test his evidence, or to check its *bona fides*, but to see if it could be improved or enhanced. There have been cases of people remembering extra details while under hypnosis, although it is fair to say I can't actually recall an instance of something substantial turning up. We were desperate, and there was the hope Mr Flynn might just remember something else to give us a better chance, even, perhaps, part of the car's registration number. It was not to be though, and under hypnosis his memory was no better than normal.

Other leads came and went. Information on child abductions and attempts that failed elsewhere in the country flowed in. Chief Constables across the UK alerted me to incidents in their force areas that might have had a bearing on what we were doing. I looked quite closely at several such incidents, like the murder of the little girl in Norfolk, Leoni Keating, where there was an element of transporting the body, but that was cleared up and the culprit there was not even a potential suspect for either of our cases.

Then there were the . . . I suppose nuts is almost the best term. The often eccentric people who for one reason or another contact officers involved with prominent cases. Like the woman calling herself Alice who wrote twice from Dundee. She claimed that a scruffy man called Buck had incriminated himself to her. We tried to trace her and then appealed through the media for her to come forward, but she never did. More time wasted by people playing pointless and dangerous games.

By this point, the joint hunt I was overseeing was reaching the stage that no detective ever wants to arrive at. There was very little else we could do. As this time nears the officers on the squad, which is being rundown anyway, become frustrated, sad, desperate, and a whole basket of emotions emerge; because failure is round the corner and plain for all to see. Still they, and myself, were secure in the knowledge that we had conducted a good inquiry, we had done everything possible, and a few things bordering on the impossible, to try and get our man.

Throughout these years I met up with senior officers from the four forces involved on a regular basis. In the first days of the joint investigation it was every day, then every week or month, with declining frequency as the pace of the hunt slowed down. One of the last such sessions of the joint investigation was held at a hotel in the Borders. This one was different from earlier 'summits'. This time we were not reviewing progress and working out ways of developing the inquiry. We gathered at the Peebles Hydro Hotel to have a brainstorming session to see if there was anything missed out, any lead overlooked, or line of inquiry missed. Over three days at the Hydro scores of ideas were thrown around but none passed muster. Driving away from the hotel after the fruitless conclusion of the talks, I suspected all those attending would have had a heavy heart that night.

I suppose as the head of the inquiry I had to carry the can. I was, though, certain no one could point the finger and say we had made a mess of things. On the contrary we had tried our best as a team. Our lack of success was due to the luck of the quarry rather than the failure of the hunters.

No matter what people may think, and I know it is a hackneyed expression, you do live and breathe an inquiry like this. It is a major part of your life. For years I'd let off steam discussing the case with my wife Anne, but I spared her many parts of it. Still, I felt little relief that, for the moment at least, this chapter of my life was closing.

One of the worst parts of this process is having to explain to the parents involved our lack of progress. I did not detect from either family any hint that they were not satisfied with our efforts in the case. In fact, quite the opposite was true and if we were getting nowhere the families could be sure that it was not for want of trying.

Just as a measure of the thoroughness of the inquiry let me give one example of the many hunches that were followed. We had decided early on to examine the parking tickets issued in the Edinburgh area on the day of Caroline's disappearance. There were over 500 in all. Of these, 175 were put on vehicles registered to people from Leicestershire, or the south of England. Eight were issued to blue Ford Cortinas. These were thoroughly checked out, but again, to no avail.

We had closely examined 600 people whose names were put forward as a result of the artist's impression of that scruffy man on the Portobello promenade, that stranger. Some of those had come from the public, some from police officers' recollections, and some from officers leafing through books of photographs of men with convictions for similar offences. Again nothing positive.

In May of 1984, I took over the post of Deputy Chief Constable of Lothian and Borders. This left me still in effective control of the joint inquiries, but they were inquiries that were virtually finished, exhausted. The main Susan Maxwell incident room in Staffordshire, once a noisy office crammed full of people with telephones ringing and officers dashing in and out, now lay silent and locked. Once a week, a detective would open the door and check correspondence and other minor matters, and then leave it firmly closed once more. The Caroline Hogg incident room, which had been at Leith Police Station since the night of her disappearance, had been shut up and the computer terminal linking the hunt to the other forces transferred several miles to police headquarters in Fettes Avenue, Edinburgh.

In a report I prepared into the joint inquiries, I described them as extremely successful. This was an accurate assessment for internal police consumption; it was not a statement I could have made in public, because for the public the only success in police work is the apprehension of the criminal.

As I became aware, from time to time, of other incidents involving children I would sometimes travel to meet officers in charge of inquiries in other parts of the country, if there was a potential link. However, no such firm connection emerged and, whilst the murder of these two little girls was never very far from my mind, I had a new job in a new force, in a new country, Scotland, to get to grips with.

Then, late in March 1986, I was informed of the disappearance of another little girl. Sarah Jayne Harper had vanished while running an errand for her mother in the town of Morley, which is virtually a suburb of Leeds, in West Yorkshire. Sarah had left her little back-to-back terrace home on a stinking wet night to buy a loaf of bread from the corner shop in the next street, a matter of 200 yards or so from her front door. The ten-year-old was dubbed 'the missing Salvation Army girl' by the press, because she was a member of the local Citadel. Her membership of this church obviously had nothing to do with her disappearance.

After her bedraggled body was recovered from the icy waters of the River Trent near Nottingham officers from there, West Yorkshire, and myself, had to try and reach a conclusion on whether she had become the third victim of the man I was hunting. That in itself was to prove no easy task.

CHAPTER SEVEN

Has He Struck Again?

News of Sarah Harper's abduction and murder left me with mixed emotions. If she had become the third victim of the man my team and I had spent so long hunting then there was a renewed prospect of capture. A fresh crime would, hopefully, yield fresh clues to be followed up. He had been lucky twice; if he had struck again could his luck continue?

At the same time I was horrified to think that anyone could be so callous as to murder a third child. Worst of all, it seemed painfully obvious that, if it was the same man we sought, there would be little to stop him striking again, and again if he eluded us once more. This simple fact made the responsibility of leading the inquiry immense. The importance of the task was never lost on me.

There had to be a thorough appraisal of this little girl's abduction and murder to see if sufficient evidence was there to allow a conclusion on linkage. It's never easy to be certain if an offence is linked to any other if the perpetrator or perpetrators are at large still, unless there are obvious and compelling reasons.

These decisions are easy to take if you are sitting in the position of a press commentator, who gets a better story by linking the crimes and suffers no real forfeit if it turns out not be the case. There was plenty of advice from that quarter on offer to me and other senior officers as we examined in great detail all that we knew of Sarah's killing. For us, though, there needed to be a very high degree of probability before a final decision on including Sarah Harper's murder as one of a series of three could be reached.

My first inclination on the Harper case was that it was not connected to my existing inquiries. There was a substantial number of differences, even before Sarah's body was found. After that grim discovery was made, the points of similarity in the case were outweighed by the points of difference. Yes, her body had been found, again, in the English Midlands; yes, this did make it a north to south abduction; yes, she was a pretty, young girl. However, Morley in March, on a cold and wet night, has nothing to compare it to the two previous abduction scenes at the height of the summer. The victim was barely recognisable as a little girl that night as she walked the damp streets to the shop. Her anorak was pulled tight against the rain, her hood covered most of her face.

Susan and Caroline had both been brightly and attractively dressed. The man we were looking for in that case had obviously been drawn towards them. There seemed to be, in both previous cases, and most certainly at Portobello, a degree of stalking of the victim involved. We knew that the stranger was following Caroline for quite some time, staring at her, obviously entranced by her innocent features. Sarah Harper had been taken at night, in a poorly lit area and dressed for the northern winter, not an idyllic late summer afternoon or early evening.

Our man could well have been passing through Portobello and Coldstream on the days in question. Both places are on, or adjacent to, main routes through their respective areas. Because of the extensive inquiries the police had made in both those places, it was probable that had been exactly what he was doing; passing by, but stopping off for a while, perhaps with the idea of simply putting his feet up or stretching his legs. Perhaps the stranger had stopped with the clear intention of seeking out a little girl to snatch. It was equally likely that he may have been travelling by way of his employment, or may even have been a holidaymaker who regularly went north in the summer.

It seemed clear to me that in all probability he would not be passing through Morley. It was just not the sort of town that you just passed through. If you were in Morley it was because you wanted to be in Morley, you had something to do there, or someone to see.

Then, after Sarah's body was found, it was apparent that she had been dumped into the river alive. The pathologists told us she was definitely alive, but in all likelihood unconscious. The two previous girls were almost certainly dead when their bodies were disposed of. The doctors could not be certain but the indications pointed to that conclusion.

Neither Susan's nor Caroline's bodies exhibited any evidence of being assaulted or injured in their final hours. Sarah, on the other hand, had been the victim of considerable violence. She also had clearly been seriously sexually assaulted, which had not been a feature of the first two murders.

For all these reasons, and others, I and senior colleagues involved, felt that a second child killer was on the loose. It could only be a considered opinion, of course, not a final judgment beyond alteration. I was equally aware that there also had to be at least a chance that there had been a change in our man's modus operandi. It was not safe to rule out a link in this case altogether.

One other factor, which in the final analysis had no bearing on the case, was that Sarah had gone missing on a couple of previous occasions. Nothing to it. Just childish incidents, quickly resolved, the sort that occur in so many households.

The team and I were left in a difficult position. All my inclinations – hunches if you like – were that Sarah Harper had fallen victim to another killer. There was, however, a lingering doubt. That doubt was strong enough to require us to keep an open mind on the possibilities.

To ensure that, if there was a connection in this latest murder, evidence was not lost or overlooked, the officers in West Yorkshire running that inquiry, Detective Chief Superintendent

Tom Newton, Detective Superintendent John Stainthorpe and I, concluded that it would be in everyone's interests to establish computer links with the Hogg inquiry and enable telephone checks to be made with the Maxwell database in Staffordshire. This would ensure that the West Yorkshire detectives had access to all our evidence and information. By conducting things in this way we had the best of both worlds. We were not prematurely linking them with the risks that might be involved in that course of action. Equally, we were sharing our information with the new murder squad, allowing them to access the huge amounts of data that we had uncovered which may have been useful in their own endeavours.

By this time, 1986, HOLMES had been established as the normal way of computerising major crime inquiries. The new Home Office-developed computer system had already proved its value in a number of major criminal inquiries. West Yorkshire had acquired their own system and operated it in the Harper case from day one.

One intriguing common feature of the three cases was investigated and in the end proved to have nothing to do with events, but it often caused me to wonder. This was that none of the three girls was living with their natural fathers. I mention this only in passing as a matter of general interest. It is a fact that a fair proportion of children who are murdered, or are missing presumed dead, did not live with their natural fathers when they disappeared. Most have enjoyed a perfectly normal family life. The absence of the natural father had no bearing at all on any of the three cases in my serial murders, however. More generally, on the face of it, there is no reason for such youngsters to be any more vulnerable to this type of crime than any others. It is, nevertheless, quite a coincidence.

The officers in West Yorkshire dealing with the original missing persons inquiry that Wednesday night were fairly sure from an early stage that something sinister had befallen the little girl, and no time had been lost in organising a substantial search for her.

HAS HE STRUCK AGAIN?

Sarah was seen walking along the wet streets from her home in Brunswick Place towards the corner shop. Morley is a place right out of television's *Coronation Street*. The shop Sarah went to that night could have been Alf Roberts', but it is, in fact, run by a Mrs Champaneri. The little general store was in Peel Street, the road next to the street where Sarah lived.

It was never clear if she'd walked out of her home, the very first in Brunswick Place, and turned right, walking down the front of the house and then along the gable end and up the back, round three sides of a square, or whether she may have gone out of her front door and turned left, walking a few yards up the street before cutting down a short passageway into Peel Street. She was seen walking in Peel Street itself, after the cut, heading up towards the shop.

Mrs Champaneri clearly remembered serving her. She bought a loaf of white bread and two bags of crisps. She was seen by witnesses walking on her route back towards home, and then she had just vanished. No one saw her go, no one saw anything particularly suspicious. Officers had descriptions of several people who were in the area and it took time to trace some of them. One person, who had been in the shop where Sarah bought the bread, was described but was never spoken to; not for want of trying. He was at first something of a potential witness, but repeated appeals through the press for him to come forward went unanswered. As time went on, and there was still no response, his perceived role began to change from that of a witness to that of a suspect. An artist's impression of the mystery man was commissioned, compiled and circulated to the press and other police forces. He appeared to be slightly balding, he was quite thick set, and was wearing prominent, steel-framed glasses.

Still there was no sign of the stranger in the shop that night.

There was another apparent sighting of a man. This time he was seen by a different witness, in Peel Street. There would not be many strangers walking about on the streets of Morley on a wet Wednesday night in March. Perhaps it was the same man.

Then there was another man, seen this time in a van parked right outside Sarah's house.

As so often happens, Sarah's body had been found by the ubiquitous 'man walking his dog'. It was in the River Trent, at a place called Wilford to the west of Nottingham. The man with the dog had seen a body floating down the river and had made a number of attempts to pull it out. Eventually, with the help of a stick, he'd managed to drag it to the side of the waterway, just to the rear of a social club.

The pathologist who examined Sarah's body concluded that she had been seriously sexually assaulted. There were signs also of her being the victim of violence. The body had been quite well preserved in the water and the indications were that she had been in the river for about three weeks. The cause of death was registered as asphyxia due to drowning. The scientists and pathologists concluded that the little girl had probably been alive when she was dumped into the river, but it was likely that she was unconscious at the time.

The lengths to which police officers and scientists go to establish evidence in a serious case are not always appreciated by the public. For instance, in this investigation even the temperature of the River Trent at the point where her body was recovered was taken at the time the body was found. It proved to be a vital clue. Sarah's body was found to be at a different temperature than that of the water at the point of her extraction. This meant that it was likely her body had been further upstream for some time.

Officers spoke to various people employed by British Waterways, who were responsible for the upkeep of the river and canal systems in the area. Through them they were able to conclude that the body had been probably been dumped in either the Trent, higher up, or the River Soar, a tributary of the Trent. The Soar was three degrees centigrade colder than the Trent, which is warmed, on the section where Sarah's body was found, by a power station outfall at Wilford.

Officers had been told that at several points on this waterway there were obstacles, at which floating objects the size of a child's body may well have been caught up for considerable lengths of time. This was consistent with what the pathologist had told officers. He said Sarah's body seemed to have been held stationary in fast-flowing water. Then, in the recent rains which had affected the area, it had probably become dislodged and floated away downstream fairly quickly, until the point where it was found by the man and his dog.

From their experience of other bodies in the river over the years, Waterways staff were also able to tell us the sort of injuries which would have been sustained during passage over and through various obstacles like weirs and parts of the river system where debris and rubbish collect. These were consistent with some of the injuries on her body.

The conclusion of all this was that Sarah's body had been put in the River Soar at a spot close to the Junction 24 of the M1 motorway, a matter that would have some significance further into the investigation.

I visited the scenes both of her abduction and where her body was found at Wilford and spoke extensively to the officers on the case. That river had for me the same chilling feeling I had experienced at other key locations in this inquiry.

In the weeks that followed, names of suspects and witnesses coming into the Harper case were all checked against our own database in Edinburgh containing details of the Caroline Hogg inquiry. The West Yorkshire incident room at Holbeck in Leeds was live to a terminal in Edinburgh to allow for the instantaneous sharing, and cross-checking, of information. Telephone calls were made to compare information against that which was held in the Maxwell database in Staffordshire.

So although we were not treating Sarah's killing as part of the series we were investigating, it was nevertheless a linked inquiry, and I was confident that if, or when, similarities appeared, they would become quickly apparent to the experienced investigators working on the case.

About eight months into the Sarah Harper investigation Her Majesty's Inspector of Constabulary in England and Wales, John

Brownlow, intervened. As part of his routine annual inspection of West Yorkshire Police, Mr Brownlow looked at the Harper case and he strongly suggested to West Yorkshire's then Chief Constable, Sir Colin Sampson, that he should seriously consider forming one computer database for all three child murder hunts. This was not intended to be a criticism of the way matters had been dealt with up to this point. All the Chief Constables involved agreed.

Although I was not directly involved at this juncture, it was a principle I wholeheartedly approved of. It had the effect of achieving what I had been asking for in Edinburgh, almost four years earlier: that is to say one single computerised database for all the child murder investigations. Later there was a meeting of the forces involved and I was asked to take the Harper investigation into my inquiry as well.

This left me in the unenviable position of being responsible now to six Chief Constables. The two new players were the Chiefs of West Yorkshire and Nottinghamshire, Sir Colin Sampson and Charles McLachlan.

I found Sir Colin to be a kind and uncomplicated man whose force went on to make the largest contribution to the joint inquiry, with the exception of my own. He had experience and knowledge to benefit me and I welcomed the occasional briefings we had together. Sir Colin left West Yorkshire to become an Inspector of Constabulary in England, Wales and Northern Ireland before moving on to the job from which he has now retired, the Chief Inspector of Constabulary for Scotland.

Charles McLachlan, on the other hand, was not really a visible force in the investigation. He seemed content to leave it to another senior officer to handle the then seemingly impossible task of trying to solve the murders. In truth, this last criticism could have been aimed at others too. Perhaps they were just content with the way the investigation was being run and happy to leave me to get on with it. I certainly preferred it that way and would have resisted any attempt at interference from them anyway. Charles McLachlan, who also went on to be an Inspector of Constabulary, is now, sadly, deceased.

HAS HE STRUCK AGAIN?

As I say, this invitation to include the third killing could not be interpreted as a criticism of our decision not to take the Sarah Harper inquiry under my wing from the outset. We could not have been certain one way or the other. The factors that linked her killing to the other two were almost matched by those which separated them. We had employed an insurance policy that way, as I have said, to link the computer and information systems, and there had been substantial, on-going co-operation between the forces involved. That, of course, became even closer after the decision to join formally the inquiries of the six forces. I am totally confident our initial decision to regard Sarah Harper's killing as the work of someone unconnected to the first two deaths did not hamper the overall investigation in any way. In the end I was to be proved partially wrong in my original decision, or should I say our decision. The man who never made a mistake never made anything.

Now that my remit ran fully to three child murders we needed to decide, first of all, where to establish the new database. In the end we plumped for the Tyrls Police Station in the centre of Bradford. Virtually the whole of the top floor of the building was given over to us. There we constructed, from nothing, a huge computer facility with a substantial number of terminals. The inquiry was becoming truly 'hi-tec'. The West Yorkshire HOLMES facility was used.

More than 40 part-time typing staff were taken on from various agencies to back record all the information that had been gathered. Specialist police officers were involved in this undertaking. This new facility allowed us to make even more detailed and exhaustive comparisons of the three investigations.

West Yorkshire Police were well served with experts in this field. Chief Superintendent Keith Bradshaw and Detective Chief Superintendent Ian Robinson were at the forefront of computerisation. Ian had worked with the team developing HOLMES and I was extremely lucky, and grateful, to have him seconded full time to head the setting up and running of the child murders computer facility.

The new system in Bradford allowed every single piece of information in the inquiries to be compared instantly, continuously and, more importantly, accurately. There could be no mistakes. If a name went into the system, and it had already appeared in it, no matter for what reason, the operator's attention was drawn to that fact immediately on the screen. Similarly with vehicles, places and all other checkable elements of the investigation. All the information in the system was instantly retrievable. Officers carrying out any inquiry were in possession of all the material we had which related to their particular task.

So here we were, dealing with three child murders, the details of which had abhorred the whole nation, not just people in the areas where the tragedies had taken place. Our task was extremely difficult.

Again, like the Susan Maxwell inquiry, with the Harper investigation I found myself being brought in to head an inquiry that had almost petered out. There were no potential suspects. Sadly we were not getting sufficient information from the public and, after some time, no real progress was being made. It seemed to be an inquiry bordering on the impossible.

My involvement did bring a fresh impetus to matters, if only because with me came the frightening realisation, official confirmation if you like, that we had on our hands a hunt to find a ruthless serial killer of children.

To help further in the task, personnel from the six forces involved were brought into the Bradford incident room to work for the duration. This facility was called the Child Murder Bureau. It became the nerve centre of the operation which was growing from an already very large investigation into about the biggest inquiry ever seen in Britain. As such, it began to branch out from the normal techniques of detection into some new and different methods.

We had a research team looking at many different matters, consisting of officers from Edinburgh like Chief Inspectors Alec Brown and Jimmy Temple, and Detective Inspector Rex Thompson from Nottingham, Chief Inspector John Sharp from

West Yorkshire, and Inspector Bert Shevas from Leicester. There were others. These various officers worked in teams of three so that individuals were not lost to their own forces for too long a period. They trawled the database to try and identify people who could be loosely regarded as suspects. Any subsequent inquiries into these people were initiated, assessed and evaluated by these experienced detectives. We were determined to write no one out of the script, until we could be totally sure they were completely eliminated.

There really was a detailed attempt, backed by the Chief Constables, to come up with new leads and new lines of inquiry. It had been a long, hard task already; in all honesty we were getting nowhere. Desperation is not the word I would use to describe my feelings at this time, because there was a measured determination to leave no stone unturned. We needed to look up every alleyway and follow every hunch. This monster had already claimed two, probably three, innocent lives. One question was never far from our minds, and indeed the minds of others. Could we find him before a fourth child died?

The biggest fear had to be that there would be another murder, or a fifth or sixth. I did not want to end up in the same position as West Yorkshire detectives had with the Peter Sutcliffe case, with 13 murders coming on top of each other in quick succession, an almost impossible situation to deal with even utilising computers, and totally impossible without them.

Offender and criminal profiling techniques are useful to detectives, but I have never been completely impressed by the technique of psychological profiling. Having said that, it was obvious to all there was always a danger that the more our man got away with the greater the temptation there would be for him to strike again. Our inability to catch the killer may well have led him to develop a sense of security or invincibility.

We had to consider every avenue open to us in properly structuring the work. Offender profiling was one such avenue. In my view it really comes into its own as a tool after you have caught your man. Then you can use profiles of the offences and offender to back-track and link him to earlier crimes because of the way in which he is known to have worked, and indeed thought.

Quite separate from our task, but as part of the Child Murder Bureau, a research operation was set up to examine all recent unsolved cases of children disappearing and/or being murdered. This inquiry was overseen by the Assistant Chief Constable of Derbyshire, Don Dovaston, and it was given the working title 'CATCHEM'. That stood for Centralised Analytical Team Collating Homicides Expertise and Management. The CATCHEM team started work in the autumn of 1986. Don Dovaston held a news conference in late September to try to counter mounting media speculation over what this review was all about.

Don was a good and experienced investigator, and so as not to confuse my own inquiry, he was tasked with creating a computerised database concerning certain cases of murder committed in the United Kingdom over a period of 30 years. My team at Bradford were to be linked to that database. Confidentiality rules preclude me from discussing this system further, but I am pleased that this complete, accurate and helpful information is available to any future investigator who finds himself in the unenviable position I was in.

Let there be no confusion here. Don's work at Derby contained details of past cases; mine, at Bradford, simply housed the information collected during the investigations into the murders of my three little girls.

The CATCHEM team also came up with recommendations for establishing a fast response action plan if our man was suspected of having struck again. It would, of course, only have worked so long as details were reported to the police at an early stage. They suggested devising an operation to try and intercept the abductor on his route from north to south as soon as possible after a child was reported missing. Like all planning it may have had its faults; it is always impossible to take full account of the unpredictable, but if he struck again, and if he followed his previous pattern, a child's life may have been saved.

I was left to get on with my own investigations and our own research. This included looking at about 20 other unsolved incidents over the years. Some had attracted widespread publicity and speculation, others less so. We looked as far back as the late 1960s when April Fabb disappeared in Norfolk, and included cases like Genette Tate, the 13-year-old who vanished without trace on a newspaper round near the picturesque village of Aylesbeare in the East Devon countryside. None, on the face of it, appeared to be strikingly similar to what I had on my hands, but there is always scope for learning lessons or uncovering new information.

The review section of this team, in the main, gave all three of my investigations a clean bill of health. There were lengthy reports for the consumption of the chief officers of the forces concerned, but there was no major criticism of what had been done, and I may say considerable approval of the way in which our teams had carried out their work.

Whilst the inquiries could never be over until a culprit was caught, we had reached three very different points in the investigations so far.

In the case of Susan Maxwell there was a very loose list of possible 'suspects', using the word in its broadest sense. The Caroline Hogg case was entirely different, and very perplexing. I cannot recall ever having come across a murder, obviously carried out at random, where there were so many sightings of the killer. We had a large number of people talking about this scruffy, smelly man with spots, but, all these years later, we still had no idea at all where he was, let alone who he was. From the night, in 1983, that he vanished from the west gate of Fun City in Portobello he seemed to have disappeared off the face of the earth. It was perplexing, if not mystifying, that no one had fingered him. He must have lived a charmed existence to be the subject of such a good artist's impression, one endorsed by all the principal witnesses, and to have evaded arrest for so many years. It must have been, I thought at the time, that someone had a good idea who he was and had decided to either blot that suspicion out of their mind, or deliberately ignore it. People shield killers.

Could anyone be callous enough to go out of their way to shield a serial child killer?

In the Sarah Harper case, there was again the potential culprit – the mystery man in the shop and on the street, and later in a van outside Sarah's house – but no one had seen him do anything remotely suspicious and there was nothing at all to connect him directly to Sarah. But who was he?

We ended up with almost 20 people whom we had been interested in at some point but who had been largely, but not completely, eliminated from the hunt. Their alibis were not totally cast iron, so it was decided to have another good look at them, just in case.

It is interesting here to recall the sort of people who had earned themselves this position in the hunt, some without trying, and some because of what could only be described as their rather strange behaviour. These individuals ranged widely, from a professional person who had been in both Coldstream and Uttoxeter on the day of the disappearance of Susan Maxwell, to a man with convictions for child sex offences who had been discovered to be hanging around Coldstream and who could come up with no good excuse for being there.

In the case of the professional, he was unable to supply us with a solid alibi because he had been travelling and had enjoyed an uneventful journey. Whilst there was nothing to rule him out, there was certainly nothing to suggest positively that he could have been the culprit.

Then there was another man, a bachelor, living with his mother. He was a suspect in a routine case in which children playing in a street, many miles from Coldstream, in a suburb of Newcastle, complained about being approached by a stranger. This man was traced and admitted speaking to the pair, but had denied any evil intent. He had then come into our sphere when his car was routinely logged into the force computer because of the allegations by the two girls in Newcastle. It then transpired that the man had been spoken to by officers in Coldstream, just before Susan's disappearance. They had considered he was acting suspiciously. He had been parked in a field gate one evening, not far from the town, four or five days before Susan was snatched.

This was enough for us to begin looking at him a little more closely. He was a possible child molester. He was acting suspiciously in Newcastle, just days after being discovered in suspicious circumstances in Coldstream. Inquiries had then revealed he was on holiday from his work at the time Susan was snatched. An alibi for the night of 30 June was shaky, and there was a potential link with yet another approach to children near Coldstream that had also been reported to us about the same time. He was not conclusively alibied for the time of Caroline Hogg's abduction either. We could, again, neither positively rule him out nor in.

Another case was the rather strange one of the Yorkshire pitman who aroused suspicion by walking into a flower shop not long after Susan's abduction and sending a wreath to her family home in Cornhill. The assistant at the florist's shop alerted police because she thought it strange that the customer should be sending flowers when he did not know the address of the dead girl's family and had actually sought her help in discovering it.

He was found to be a divorced man, then living back at home with his parents. He had been off work with an injury during the time of the Coldstream incident. He was also a train spotter who travelled all over the country in pursuit of his hobby. Police searched his house and found photographs of the lay-by where Susan's body was discovered, as well as numerous newspaper cuttings of stories written about her murder.

He was obsessively tidy, and in his house we found all manner of papers neatly filed away. Even the receipt for the flowers sent to Mr and Mrs Maxwell was found amongst a mass of other documents uncovered when we searched, many months later. There was a train ticket to Uttoxeter for 14 August 1982. However, a check with this man's doctor revealed he had an appointment at the local surgery in Yorkshire at the time Susan was being snatched; medical records showed he had kept that appointment, an entry in his file showed he had been treated by the doctor on that day.

In their painstaking search of the house officers found a South Yorkshire bus ticket issued the year after. It was one which showed the time and date that it had been issued. It was timed for the actual afternoon of Susan's abduction. He could safely be eliminated. Just another indication of the sort of things that were being turned up.

Another man was questioned closely and investigated in great depth just because part of his pay-slip was found in the lay-by close to where Susan's body was lying. Again his alibi was not certain, but there was nothing else to put him into the frame.

The whole of the country seemed to be talking about the murders and, even when our investigation was running down, some incident involving a child somewhere in the country would spark off a whole new range of speculation in the press.

In the September of 1987 the then Prime Minister, Margaret Thatcher, paid a call at Edinburgh police headquarters with her husband, Denis. During the visit she seized on an opportunity to quiz me on the progress our hunt was making. I was amazed at the level of detail she knew about the cases and how well informed she was of the progress we were making. I suppose it was a mixture of being interested and well briefed, but I found our little chat somewhat reassuring.

The PM's visit was not the only indication of support I was receiving. The press, not always my favourite people, were extremely helpful. When publicity was required they usually came up trumps. My own Lothian and Borders Joint Police Board, and indeed the police authorities from the other forces involved in the investigations, had been patient and supportive in providing manpower, resources and finance to cover the whole wide-ranging activities of the police in these cases. No effort was being spared. The whole country seemed to have an interest. Certainly no parent could wish for anything but a successful conclusion to our labours.

The upshot of all this examination was that whilst it was indicated that some things could have been done differently, or even in some cases better, the conclusion was strong and positive.

These three abductions and murders had been subjected to thorough, rigorous and professional investigation. We could be satisfied of that. But the fact that we still were no nearer to catching our man left no room for complacency or relief.

The files never closed, but as time went on they tended to be opened less frequently. Detectives, in my experience, regard murder as the most heinous of crimes. The police service generally does not stint in the effort put into attempting to solve crimes of murder. More so when the victim is a child. Even so, on occasion, there are times when murders do go unsolved. Random child murder is the most likely category of killing to go undetected. In the vast majority of adult murders the victim is known to the killer, which always makes detection less difficult. It is human nature that most people who know a child would not normally want to hurt it, so the most likely people to abduct and kill a child tend to be strangers. This always makes detection much more difficult.

Years later I found myself reflecting on these theories after being contacted by a reporter from the then recently launched newspaper *Scotland on Sunday*. He was compiling an article for the paper's colour supplement, dealing with Scotland's unsolved murders, and he wanted it to focus on the killings of Susan Maxwell and Caroline Hogg.

The article was due for publication on Sunday, 15 July 1990, but, because it was to appear in the newspaper's colour supplement, it had to be written quite a long time in advance. On the Saturday, the day before publication, I called in at my headquarters office. Lying on the desk was an advance copy of the magazine, containing the article which had been entitled 'The Files They Can't Close'. The piece was dominated by a picture of myself spread across two pages pictured at the desk where I was now sitting reading it.

The article began: ' . . . the killing of a child provokes a response (in the police) that mirrors society's revulsion and injects an air of cold determination into the inquiry'. I had no quibble with that. The conclusion of the article was even more strikingly relevant, in the light of what was to transpire later that very day. As the reporter talked of Hogg and Maxwell he quoted me as follows: 'The kind of person that is likely to be involved in such a crime is not the kind that mixes easily with others. They are loners and itinerants, often unmarried, single persons, who are still living at home with their elderly parents or staying in a solitary bedsit.'

Then, to quote the article: 'The "kind of person" Clark is referring to might be a sex offender, pervert or paedophile. It might be assumed that such people are well documented in police records, and would be top of their list when the crime was committed.

'They are, but habitual sex offenders very often do not have serious convictions. Instead, the records show breach of the peace or petty theft. However, if you dig into the cases involved you may well find the breach of the peace involved indecent exposure or lewd behaviour, and that the petty theft involved children's clothing or lingerie.' The article concluded by quoting me directly: 'If we don't find out who committed these murders then it certainly won't be through want of trying. I can say that with hand on heart. We will go on trying for as long as it takes. My determination has not diminished.'

Whilst this last part was completely honest, the reality of the position we were in was that, over a period of seven years, three children had been abducted and murdered and despite a massive inquiry involving hundreds of people and millions of pounds we were absolutely clueless as to who was responsible.

I had been quoted elsewhere as saying that my hope was that the man would strike again, but this time would not be so lucky as he had been in the past, and that he would be caught before serious harm came to his next poor victim. As I was reading this colour supplement, eleswhere in my force area the stranger was about to strike again. Within four hours of my looking over the magazine, there was a child snatched from the street of a little village in the Borders, an hour's drive south of Edinburgh.

Within 48 hours I was standing in a police station cell looking at Robert Black.

CHAPTER EIGHT

Is this the Stranger?

I left my Edinburgh home quite early on the morning of that July Monday to head the 25 or so miles to Selkirk, in the Borders Region of Scotland. It is in the most rural part of the area covered by the force from which I retired as Deputy Chief Constable. The spectacular scenery is dotted with half a dozen towns and many villages where farming and rugby union are the main interests in life. As you head out of Edinburgh, that most cosmopolitan of Scottish cities, for the border country, one can almost feel the pace of life slowing down. It's an area where not much happens, and what little that does occur is soon known about across the whole community.

When I reached the single-storey police office in the quiet market town, Detective Superintendent Andrew Watt was already waiting for me. He had not been fully involved in the child murder inquiries up to this time but Andrew had a much bigger role waiting for him. Each weekend one of the detective superintendents based at Edinburgh police headquarters is on duty to deal with major criminal incidents that may arise. The weekend just past Andrew Watt had been told about a child abduction in one of the little border villages, covered by the force's 'G' Division. It had been a very serious incident, but fortunately for everyone involved there had been a quick arrest.

My rather muted greetings from the station sergeant underlined the serious nature of the mission that had brought us, so early on a Monday morning, to his front desk. It was fairly unusual for the top brass to look in at Selkirk. To arrive unannounced, and shortly after eight on a Monday morning, was something of a surprise.

Without any formalities the sergeant took us two visitors through the back of the office to the cells. We stood quietly in the corridor as the door was unlocked. The sergeant stood back to allow Andrew and I in.

Two things struck me immediately. The first was that the man we had come to see could only be described as scruffy, and, secondly, he smelled. It was a smell and a feeling that immediately carried me back to Portobello and the start of the journey in 1983 that had today, seven years later, led to this cell. It was a cell more used to housing Saturday night drunks than criminals of the notoriety I suspected Mr Black was about to achieve.

Apart from the smell of him, Black was, by anyone's view, scruffy. His hair was unkempt and greasy, his beard bushy and tangled. His clothes were tattered. He could easily have been a tramp taken off the streets and put into the cells.

The first words I spoke to Robert Black were, I think, my usual greeting: 'How are you doing?'

He sat motionless on the bed at the far side of the cell from the door, and merely mumbled an inaudible reply without raising his head. I inquired if he was comfortable and if he had had a cup of tea. Nothing in his responses gave any hint of a reason to stay and so Andrew and I left him to his thoughts and went to wait for the routine first court appearance Black was due to make later that morning. He had been charged with what is commonly referred to as abduction but in Scots law is called plagium, or child theft.

IS THIS THE STRANGER?

I had already been given many details of how he had been detained on Saturday afternoon in a Borders village, a few miles away, not long after he had snatched a local couple's daughter off the street, totally at random.

Because Black's little victim that day was aged under 16 the law protects her by making it an offence for anyone to publicly reveal her identity. In accordance with this rule I shall give no clues to her name or address. Suffice to say her home village of Stow is a classic one street sort of place, and is bisected by one of the main routes between Edinburgh and England. There is hardly anything for the traveller to see, indeed many must pass through this place without noticing anything special at all, save for, perhaps, the parish church which, with its high spire and ornate stonework, is quite an unusual building in this country of austere religion. There's a transport café at the top end of the village and Victorian villas along both sides of the main road. To the east heavily wooded hills shoot up. As you drive through the village it is possible to imagine hardly a soul is about. But as Black was to learn, in a small community like this there is often a pair of eyes watching you, even if you don't see them.

The little girl, aged just six, had been subjected to a horrific ordeal. She was saved from certain death by the quick thinking of a neighbour who had seen her legs disappear as she walked along the blind side of a van which had been parked just over the road from where he was tending his garden. The man, a retired grocer called David Herkes, had noted the registration number of the van, alerted the girl's mother, who in turn called the police.

There are not many police cars out and about at any one time in 'G' Division, but this day there were several close to the scene of the abduction, and they raced to the village. The men who arrived in their panda cars and traffic vehicles had been quick to ascertain what had happened. Information was being relayed by radio back to the control room as quickly as possible, to alert every officer for miles around to be on the look out for the van. Its driver would not have been aware, at this time, that he had been spotted going about his dastardly deed.

Officers were standing in the road in the middle of the village considering their next moves when the van, driven by Robert Black, came back into sight. It was instantly recognised from David Herkes' full description, and flagged down. Black was restrained and the van searched. The little girl was found in a sleeping bag in the rear. She had been bound and sticking plaster was taped over her mouth. Black had removed her shoes and socks. A bag with a draw-string was over her head, and it had been tightened around her neck. She had been indecently assaulted.

With the officers who stopped the van was the girl's father. When the abductor was found his thoughts were only for his daughter, and he immediately went to rescue her from the bundle in the rear of the van. Showing remarkable restraint the anguished dad only spoke a few words to Black. He said: 'That's my daughter, you bastard.'

Thirty-six hours later Andrew Watt and I were waiting for the man to make his first appearance in the local court charged in connection with the abduction.

As of ten o'clock that Monday morning, as we waited for the court hearing, which as usual for a first remand in Scotland would be held behind closed doors, virtually nothing was known about the man who had just been caught in the act. However, I was certain that unless, literally, my nose was very much mistaken, he was a man who would end up facing even more serious charges. Call it a gut feeling if you wish. With my experience and service one gets feelings about situations, and one is entitled to do so, in my contention, even if on occasion one is wrong.

I had been certain, as I have already said, that when I met Caroline's abductor I would know who he was from the smell, his looks and the circumstances of our meeting if nothing else. I was as near certain as possible in the court precinct that morning that I was looking at the man who seven years earlier had walked out of Fun City on Portobello promenade, hand in hand with a little girl whose life he was subsequently to snuff out.

Black was remanded in custody for a week.

The circumstances of the offence in the Borders required only the minimum of investigation. It was simply a question of taking statements and filling in the forms. Officers had discovered that after David Herkes had raised the alarm a relative of his had driven into the village and said he'd seen a blue Transit van parked in a lay-by a couple of miles up the road. The police personnel called to the scene had been radioing this information to other cars racing to the scene to join the hunt when the van was spotted heading back into the village.

The girl's dad had found his daughter in a sleeping bag in the back of the van and as he was gently lifting her out his wife had arrived on the scene. The little girl was terrified, and had very nearly suffocated. In addition to tying her hands behind her back, and sticking tape over her mouth, Black had put the bag over her head and tied it at the neck. It was actually a cushion cover with a draw-string. Was this merely to keep her quiet, or did he have a more sinister motive?

We discovered that immediately after he took her, Black had pushed the little girl under the dashboard of the van and driven out of the village to the lay-by where he had been seen. There he stopped to indecently assault her, tie her up, remove her shoes and put her in a bag. It was assumed by investigators that Black had tied up his victim and put her in the bag because he had a delivery or call to make later that afternoon. We discovered he did in fact have a drop to make; in a nearby Borders town, Galashiels.

As he was being driven to Selkirk Police Station, Black freely told the officers in the car that he had suffered a sudden rush of blood to the head, but conceded that he had always liked little girls. In the car he went on to say that he had 'only touched her a little' and had wanted to keep her until he went somewhere like Blackpool and could spend more time with her.

These words spoken by Black as he was being driven to Selkirk, and the existence of a planned stop by him minutes after the abduction, were virtually the confirmation I needed for my suspicions. Any man who could abduct a child and go on to make a delivery with a bound and gagged youngster in the back of his van was obviously experienced at his work.

Did he just happen to have a cushion cover with draw-string in his van? Had he used it before? It would take an incredibly cool character to snatch a child from the street for the very first time and be confident enough to risk being caught when making a delivery, just a matter of minutes later, with his little victim in the back of the van. Perhaps this was because he had done it before?

As we looked further into the incident, and at Black himself, my confidence that our seven-year hunt was drawing to an end began to grow.

That day in Selkirk I appointed Andrew Watt, on the spot, to take charge of investigating Black the person, his activities and his movements. I was happy that Andrew was the duty superintendent that weekend, and so had been given this task. Andrew, now retired, was a senior and respected member of the Lothian and Borders CID. He is a dour man, but not without humour, and an officer who had taken on many challenges during his career and made all efforts to ensure they were met.

Chief Inspector Roger Orr was detailed to be second in command of this stage of the operation. Roger is a trusted colleague and a good friend. He made an invaluable contribution in digging into Black's background and movements. He also saw the case through to prosecution, a demanding enough job bearing in mind the hundreds of thousands of pages of statements and other evidence that had to be managed, all whilst holding down another senior post in the force.

It transpired that Black had actually spent quite a bit of time that Saturday afternoon in the village where he snatched the girl and was later arrested. He had stopped at the transport cafe at the end of the main street, ordered lunch and then walked across the road to a newsagent's shop to buy a newspaper.

Later a 12-year-old girl told us a man had approached her in suspicious circumstances that afternoon. She said the man had stopped to ask her directions as she was walking home from a stroll out with her dog to a local park. When the large retriever dog caught up with her the man drove off. It was quite clear to us that the man was Black. His inquiry was pointless, other than the fact he was obviously looking for a victim. I believe had it not been for the dog that little girl would have been Black's victim.

After being foiled by the dog he had sat in the café looking out of the window, and may well at this point have seen his eventual target, the little six-year-old, as she walked round the village.

As that week after Black's arrest passed by officers were quickly starting to inquire into his background. We found out, from the Edinburgh bus depot where he was meant to make a delivery, that he worked full time as a driver for a firm called Poster Despatch and Storage, based in London. We had his home address, and with assistance from officers of the Metropolitan force the bedsit Black occupied at 7 West Bank, Stamford Hill, in North London, was not only searched but stripped bare and its contents carefully labelled and transported to Edinburgh, where they were laid out in the main gym hall at the Fettes Avenue Police HQ. His home contained a wide selection of child and adult pornography. His van could really only be described as a mobile abduction machine. It had rope and sticking plaster, various sex aids and other incriminating items.

We were on our way.

The more we uncovered about the van driver, who still spoke with a Scots accent despite his many years in the south, the more certain the team became that we had our man. The words in that *Scotland on Sunday* article proved to be prophetic to the point of being almost uncanny. Black lived in a bedsit. To say he exhibited signs of paedophilia was something of an understatement. He was certainly a loner. The people we were speaking to were virtually all giving us the same picture of an oddball misfit, the butt of work-place jokes, the sort of guy people didn't really want to be friendly with.

An incident room was set up at Edinburgh's newest, large police station, St Leonard's, on the south side of the city, where the next stage of the operation was to be based. We had to await Black's ultimate court appearance where he would be tried for the crime in the Borders, but I wanted no time lost in preparing the investigation into his past movements. We felt sure there had to be a way of discovering this man's movements through the 1980s up to eight years ago. Not just rough movements, like he might have been in Scotland in October 1982, or whatever. If we were to get anywhere with this hunch that Black was responsible for one or more of the child murders that had been investigated for so long, and so hard, then, because of the time scale now involved, we were going to need skill and luck.

As the preparation of the case against Black for the offences in the Borders continued the Crown Office, the prosecuting authority in Scotland, was given what's known as a 'Section 102 intimation'. That means the defence gives early notice of the intention of an accused person to plead guilty, which allows the prosecution and police to save time in preparing the case for court.

Scotland has a rule in criminal matters that restricts the period an accused person can spend in jail before trial commences to 110 days from the moment of his arrest. It can be extended for good reason but rarely is. Not infrequently serious matters before the court are lost altogether after it's discovered the 110-day rule has been broken, usually by oversight or a miscalculation of time spent on remand. Just recently a man was acquitted in the High Court in Scotland when it became clear his days in custody had been added up incorrectly and he had appeared in the dock 111 days after arrest. The judge ordered his immediate release. While that may seem, on the face of it, to be counter to the interests of justice, it is actually a good safeguard to ensure that prisoners do not languish on remand for month upon month, as can happen in England on occasion.

As I and other officers on the case reflected on what was emerging, it seemed already that there were great similarities in what happened to the Borders girl and the abduction of Caroline Hogg, from what was known of the scruffy man appearing to seek out his victim. There were also similarities emerging all the time with the Susan Maxwell and Sarah Harper cases.

In the Borders case it was clear that Black had spent quite a bit of time in the village, looking for and selecting his victim. Staff in the café talked of him watching out of the window, where there were children passing by. It seemed equally certain that had it not been for the intervention of the older girl's large golden retriever dog it might well have been her who was snatched, not the six-year-old.

Extensive inquiries were made throughout the village to see if we could trace someone who could confirm to us beyond any doubt that it was Black who had approached the 12-year-old looking for directions. We drew a complete blank. No one saw that van draw up, no one saw the girl being spoken to, no one saw the van move off again. The inescapable conclusion was that if the 12-year-old girl's dog had not bounced up when it did and she had become Black's target that day, no one would have been there to report the abduction, and we could have had a fourth murder.

The word stalking was one that we began to use when describing Black's activities, known about and suspected. He seemed to be stalking his prey in this latest attack. If it was Black at Portobello he was certainly stalking then. We had several people saying how they saw the scruffy man leaning on the fence of the play area watching the little ones have their fun. Chance and opportunity in the Borders had delivered a youngster into his hands; it may have been that Caroline had become his victim by being the first to leave the safety of other playmates and walk past the staring stranger.

The press were jumping to conclusions as we set about a more scientific approach to investigating Black's background. Due to leaks, possibly from the Metropolitan Police, newspapers, particularly the *Sun*, had printed substantial and accurate stories about the sort of materials that had been recovered from Black's house and van. The fact that he was remanded, accused of the charge on which he awaited trial and merely 'suspected' of the murders, allowed reporters to write stories about an anonymous man, in custody in Scotland, being investigated on the Maxwell, Hogg and Harper cases. Because Black was not named in these reports they did not contravene Scotland's strict contempt of court rules, designed to protect an accused person's right to a fair trial. This speculation was not helpful to us as we tried to find ways of delving into his past.

On Friday 10 August, Robert Black appeared in the dock of the High Court in Edinburgh. The court, in the imposing Parliament House building off the famous Royal Mile, is as close as Scotland gets to the equivalent of the Old Bailey. Many of the most notorious criminals in Scots history have been tried in this court and, pre-dating the building itself, the executions of many historical figures took place close by.

Black was flanked by two police officers wearing, as tradition dictates, white gloves and sitting with truncheons drawn and laid across their knees. Immediately behind the dock, which is really just the first row of bench seats that stretch to the rear of the courtroom, sat the press. The reporters' bench in this court is often fairly full, but I have never seen it as packed as it was that day. The public benches, too, had more than the usual number of onlookers and lawyers from other courts come by to idle away a spare moment. Word was getting round of just exactly what Black was suspected of.

The court stood to the mace bearer's instruction as he led Scotland's second most senior judge, Lord Ross, the Lord Justice Clerk, on to the bench.

The lawyers gathered round a table in the well of the court shuffled their papers and Lord Ross opened his notebook. It was obvious the 'audience' had a keen sense of the importance of what was to come. Usually for a police officer like myself, sitting in the back of the court, this moment, before a plea of guilty to the charge is entered, should be one of quiet satisfaction. There was no such luxury for me and other officers on the team that morning. We realised quite clearly then that this was the easy part, there was a mammoth and difficult task ahead. I watched every movement. I listened to every word.

Lord Ross indicated his preparedness to start proceedings. The clerk told Black to stand and asked him to confirm his name and address. Those few inaudible muttered agreements from the accused were the only words he spoke during the entire proceedings.

The detectives from English forces involved in the hunt sitting in court may well have been forgiven for thinking the charge Black faced was from another planet. There is a distinct and entirely separate way of doing things in Scots Law. The charge was formed under the Common Law and read thus:

> Robert Black, prisoner in the prison of Edinburgh, you are indicted at the instance of the Right Honourable, the Lord Fraser of Carmylie, Her Majesty's Advocate, and that the charge against you is that you did on July 14, 1990, in . . ., in the district of Ettrick and Lauderdale abduct . . ., aged six years, care of Lothian and Borders Police, at . . . and there did assault her by seizing hold of her, lift her into the front of a motor van, push her under a seat, cover her with a coat and a blanket, order her to be quiet, and convey her against her will in the said motor van to a lay-by on the A . . . road, approximately 1.6 miles north of . . . aforesaid, and in said lay-by place her in the rear of the motor van, take off her shoes and socks, place your hand inside her shorts and pants, place your finger in her private parts, tie her hands behind her back, stick pieces of plaster over her mouth, place a bag over her head, tie said bag around her neck and place her in a sleeping bag and thereafter convey her in said motor vehicle to . . . aforesaid, all to her injury and the danger of her life.

Through counsel, Mr Herbert Kerrigan QC, Black entered a plea of guilty to the charge, and sat down again.

In Scotland the prosecution of crime is done in the name of the most senior law officer in the country, the Lord Advocate. In England cases are described as Regina v so and so, in Scotland the correct form is Her Majesty's Advocate v so and so. The Lord Advocate had, unusually, decided to prosecute this case himself.

Lord Fraser of Carmylie QC rose to outline the facts of the case. It was just 27 days after the crime that he was speaking. Lord Fraser was quietly authoritative as the facts were recited. They in themselves were so horrific they did not require unnecessary eloquence to cause an impression on the court.

Lord Fraser told the judge that a psychiatrist who had examined Black considered him to be a serious danger to children and liable to remain dangerous for an indefinite period. The advocate said the Borders girl was so trussed up she could not cry for help and, more importantly, could not breathe adequately. He said it was medical opinion that if she had been left in the sleeping bag in which she was found she would have been dead within an hour.

There was little Mr Kerrigan could say for the defence. His mitigation was muted. The QC said Black had described the offence as one 'of the moment', he was adamant he did not intend to kill the child. Black, said Mr Kerrigan, had admitted to facing this kind of temptation before but previously had managed to resist it. He had, until now, satisfied his desires on pornography bought abroad. 'He accepts he is a danger and wishes to engage in some sort of programme to get assistance.'

Lord Ross, in his sentencing speech from the bench, said that David Herkes, the alert neighbour, had undoubtedly saved the girl's life and deserved the highest possible public praise. He went on to tell Black that he had subjected the girl to a horrifying experience. 'I am bound to be greatly influenced by the opinion expressed by the psychiatrist . . . the fact that you are a serious danger to children and are likely to remain one for an indefinite time to come. There are no means by which children can be protected other than by detaining you in custody. The sentence is one that makes sure you cannot be released until such time that it is safe to do so.'

Black was sent down for life. As the people in the court began to sit once more, after Lord Ross's departure, Black was hurried out by his police escort. The newsmen rushed off to file their stories. Radio and TV reporters were by this time hard up against their lunchtime deadlines.

A suggestion had been relayed to me that in the shock of the life term he'd just received, Black might be wanting to make a quick 'cough' to other offences. I hurried along the stone-slabbed corridors to the court cells, but I was to be disappointed. It was clear Black was in no mood for talking.

I walked out of the court into Parliament Square and was met by a mob of reporters and cameramen who were demanding to know what was likely to happen next. 'Is he going to be charged with other offences?', 'How many murder charges do you expect to bring?', and so they went on. As I walked to a waiting car I just smiled, unable to help reflecting privately on what the answers may be to those questions.

In all honesty, at that time, I could only have speculated myself. I knew what I hoped, but after only having Black behind bars for a little under four weeks it was far too early to say what I thought we may, or may not, eventually be able to prove.

Since Black had been taken into custody, I had ordered that enormous lengths should be gone into to prevent a picture of him being taken by the press. I knew that if he was to face further charges the proof might well rest on identification. After he was sentenced for the Borders incident the case was no longer active in terms of the Contempt of Court Act. That meant the newspapers could say anything they liked about him and publish pictures if they had them. The last thing I wanted was for some possible future prosecution to founder because Black's face had been staring out of every paper between the time of conviction and further charges being brought.

I thought I had been successful. Each time Black had been outside his head was covered with a blanket. Criminals sentenced at the High Court in Edinburgh are inevitably photographed in the next day's papers, handcuffed to a police officer as they emerge from a side entrance of the building to walk in public the few steps to a waiting prison van. You could hear an audible groan from the newsmen as Black walked from that door, once more, with a blanket over his head.

However my best efforts were foiled. The *Sun* in Glasgow had managed to get a picture of Black from the Edinburgh jail where he had been on remand. An inmate 'trusty' detailed to duties in the reception area of the prison had taken the picture out of Black's jail file and given it to the paper.

I was furious. However, my fury abated rather when a fortuitous phone call was received the next morning by officers at the Black incident room at St Leonard's Police Station. A previously unknown witness from Portobello telephoned to say he recognised the picture in the *Sun*. It was a man he had seen before, on Portobello promenade with a little girl the night Caroline disappeared.

For reasons I have never understood the *Sun* had doctored the picture of Black they used on the front page so it would not be recognised as one from the jail. However, the picture they used inside the paper, to illustrate further background articles about Black, had not been doctored, and was just a straight reproduction of the jail photo, which rather gave their game away. I was later told it was an oversight on behalf of production staff, but I find it hard to believe they could risk their inside man by being so slapdash.

Lawyers acting for Black lodged appeal papers shortly after his sentencing, and an appeal against sentence was scheduled for not long after. I once more went to the Parliament Square court for the appeal hearing, but just minutes before it was due to be heard the appeal was withdrawn before the case could be called. I have never quite understood why the appeal should have been made in the first place only to be abandoned at the last moment. Few, I would have thought, could have argued that a life sentence was too harsh when the recipient was obviously such a danger to children.

CHAPTER NINE

Who is the Stranger?

In the few weeks between Black's arrest and eventual court appearance many newspapers had been using the unusual legal position he was in to their own advantage and running a series of stories about him. He was, at this point, only charged in connection with the incident in the Borders, but it was well known in the media that we were going to be interested in Black for other matters. Various articles appeared about an unnamed man, who was 'going to be quizzed' about a variety of matters.

The stories started off with references to just Susan Maxwell, Caroline Hogg and Sarah Harper. As the days passed the stories grew, and it was being suggested that we were interested in the 'London van driver', as he was usually described to illustrate the otherwise anonymous articles, on behalf of continental police investigating incidents involving children in France and Germany. To say that this speculation was premature is a total understatement. We were just beginning to have a good look at Robert Black. Quite where the trail would take us even we did not know, but of course we had our suspicions.

As the stories began to get out of hand the Crown Office felt it necessary to circulate confidential advice notes to newspaper editors, reminding them of the status of proceedings against Black and indicating that a serious view would be taken of the publication of any material that might jeopardise the case. The last thing we wanted was irresponsible newspaper reporting giving Black's lawyers the chance to say that his right to a fair trial had been so badly prejudiced that future proceedings against him would be unjust.

Just three days short of the eighth anniversary of Susan Maxwell's disappearance, with Black in custody and awaiting a High Court appearance date for the offence in the Borders, I convened a meeting of the six forces involved over the years in order to report back on what we had uncovered so far and where I thought we should be going in the future.

Senior officers from all the forces involved arrived early at the Fettes Avenue Police Headquarters in Edinburgh for talks that lasted for almost the entire day. Naturally they were anxious to hear about Black and the sort of person he was. I filled in all the details to hand so far on his background. A course of action was outlined that would, we hoped, finally ascertain whether we had got our man. The first, easy checks had already revealed by this time that Black did not have a grade one alibi for any of the crucial dates. That is to say he was not in prison or in some sort of secure mental institution. We knew more than that would be needed to end our task. We were going to have to prove where he was, not where he was not. Trying to pinpoint precise movements of any individual even just a month ago is hard enough. Could we discover a way of showing where Robert Black was at three specific times eight, seven and four years earlier?

In absolute terms we still knew very little about him. We had obviously spoken to his workmates and the Scottish couple who owned the house in London where he had lodged for a number of years. Everyone was willing to help but few had any real knowledge of Black. Most had opinions and it is fair to say those opinions were not usually favourable. When we spoke to people who had come across Black, either through work or socially, the first adjective they employed in describing him was 'smelly'. It seemed he rarely washed either himself or his clothes, and was unpleasant to be near.

The Rayson family, who had taken him in, regarded the oddball loner virtually as a son. Edward and Katherine Rayson had probably been motivated by kindness towards one of life's more unfortunates.

Our initial inquiries had shown quite quickly there was little in Black's lifestyle that would give us easy clues to his movements. His hobbies, according to his few friends, were all fairly passive. He appeared to like mostly playing darts and listening to music. Apart, that is, from his more private leisure interests, the ones he did not talk about at work. The mainstream hobbies were not the sort of things that would lead him to travel widely across the countryside. It probably meant that if we were to uncover details of his movements it would be through his work.

We had also found out that Black was quite unusual, inasmuch as he did not appear to have a single living relative, certainly no one we could find. His birth certificate showed him to be the child of Jessie Hunter Black, who had lived in a cottage within the gates of Grangemouth Docks, on the Firth of Forth, just inland from Edinburgh. He was born on 21 April 1947 in nearby Falkirk Royal Infirmary. His mother was unmarried and gave him up for adoption soon afterwards, when he was just six months old. The name of Black's father was not recorded on the birth certificate and his identity has not been revealed by our investigation. We discovered that Jessie Black had emigrated to Australia and died there in 1987, having never made contact with her son since giving him up all those years before.

His early years were spent in the largely industrial Highland town of Kinlochleven. It lies at the head of a long glen that stretches down to the majestic pass of Glencoe, well known to those who travel to the West Highlands of Scotland. There, he was fostered by Mrs Isabel Tulip, now dead, who appeared to have been a Highland stalwart, giving over a considerable portion of her life, and house, to looking after children from less fortunate backgrounds. In those days it was common practice for youngsters, like Black, to be sent from Scotland's urban central belt to rural areas in the hope of putting something back into their lives, to replace the stable family background that was missing.

Even in those days Black was marked out. He was known at the local school as 'smelly Bobby Tulip'. That epithet which would dog him through life had appeared early.

Sometimes it can be more than difficult to trace a person's path through life over a period of many years. Not so Robert Black. He walked life's highway leaving a trail of social work reports and minor convictions. It was not a taxing matter to discover where Black had stayed, and when, during his formative years. He had rarely been out of close contact with authority, particularly council welfare workers, until much later in his life. Certainly, during his minority, his exact whereabouts could be traced through the various social services departments that were entrusted with his care.

Mrs Tulip, whom Black would probably have regarded as his mother, died when he was eleven years old. It seemed she was as close as the young Black was to having a real family. Once more the Falkirk social services department had to find a home for him. They decided to take him out of his Highland environment and move him to a children's home in a small community near Falkirk, in the central belt of Scotland.

It was while he was at this home, in a small community called Redding, that his behavioural problems first began to surface. This anti-social activity culminated in his attacking a young girl, who was also resident in the home, and removing her underpants. The incident was not reported to the police and so no criminal charges came of it, but it resulted in a decision being taken to move him to a home for boys only.

Looking back on this episode, with the help only of old reports and case notes, it was hard to judge the severity of the attack. It was, clearly, bad enough for him to be moved out of the Redding home immediately after.

This was how Black came to be resident in the Edinburgh area. The home that was selected as being most suitable for him was in Musselburgh, originally a fishing village but now merged into Edinburgh's eastern suburbs. This was a most interesting discovery for us.

If you walk towards Edinburgh from Musselburgh, you pass first the city's easternmost suburb, Joppa, and then, continuing along the seafront, is Portobello, just a healthy distance from Musselburgh. The home Black was moved to and Portobello are, at most, only three to four miles apart. In the days when Black was in Musselburgh, the early 1960s, buses ran frequently and directly between the two places. Also, in those days, to walk a distance like this would not be uncommon.

It was clear from the people we were talking to and the social service notes that we uncovered that Black was quite a sporty youth. He enjoyed football and swimming particularly. It has to be said that I believe when he was pursuing his interest in swimming during later life, his main motivation would not be simply to take exercise.

We discovered Black often walked the main road from Musselburgh to Portobello, where there were two swimming pools. One lay at the Musselburgh end of Portobello. It is a fine Victorian building housing the indoor baths. The other pool was an outdoor one that stood in the part of Portobello nearest to Edinburgh. It did not escape our attention that halfway between these two places was Beach Lane, where Caroline Hogg lived. To walk between the two pools you virtually had to pass by her front door.

That outdoor pool is now demolished but the other still thrives right on the seafront, its steps leading down on to the promenade. During the winter months, as the wind whips in off the Firth of Forth, you can see the bathers pulling their coats tight around themselves as they emerge after a swim for the chilly walk round to the carpark and nearby bus stops. It would be a scene well known to Black who, we discovered, swam there frequently.

More sinister still, we discovered that Black appeared to have been the victim of sexual abuse, committed by one particular member of staff at the Musselburgh home. It had taken the form of what can only be described as a complete breach of trust by the man, involving serious offences which would have resulted in a substantial prison sentence for the individual concerned had the matter come to light.

The contents of the files kept on Black during his years in care cannot of course be disclosed here. Suffice to say he did not appear to have a happy childhood. It would be fair to conclude that by the time he left school in Musselburgh at the age of 15, defects in his personality that had shown themselves from an early age would have been exacerbated substantially. This may well have been largely due to his experiences in the home in Musselburgh, at the hands of a cruel abuser.

The argument over whether Black became an abuser himself because of the abuse he suffered at a vulnerable age is as old as chronological speculation over chickens and eggs. There were suggestions that Black had first suffered sexual interference by an adult when he was at Kinlochleven, which he left at the age of eleven. This could not be substantiated and Black himself appeared to deny it during the one full interview he agreed to submit himself to with my detectives.

In my view, one must also forget the current emphasis that society seems to place on the accused and be aware that there may well be many people who have had their own upbringing, in care, made that much more difficult because of their meeting with the young Robert Black.

Through the network of child care agencies that existed at the time, Black gained employment in the West of Scotland on leaving school in Musselburgh. He went to the then thriving shipbuilding town of Greenock, on the Clyde, down river from Glasgow. There, in the shadow of one of the great names in Scottish shipbuilding, Scott Lithgow's, he worked as a butcher's boy. His carers had started him off in his working life with a job and lodgings in a boys' home in the town.

Our picture of his childhood was fairly complete. Abuse both of Black and by Black. We suspected that abuse of him began back in that Highland glen but there was never any firm evidence to back our suspicions. Then, just as had been said in that *Scotland on Sunday* article, the one published the day after his arrest in the Borders, we were discovering that the stories behind the seemingly minor convictions at various courts were the tip of a much more menacing iceberg. His 'form', previous convictions, disclosed at the High Court in August, began with one for lewd and libidinous practices and assaults. The first is a broad charge, unique to Scotland, that covers sexual misdemeanours. The English equivalent of it may be a breach of the peace or minor assault charge. Viewed from the 1990s he seems lucky to have escaped with such a minor conviction for what amounted to a serious offence. He was 17 when, in Greenock, he enticed a seven-year-old girl into a semi-derelict outbuilding and, holding her by the throat to prevent her screaming, inserted a finger into her vagina. He then ran off, leaving the terrified youngster in a state of extreme distress.

This was the first officially recorded example of the digital abuse that would be Black's calling card in the years to come. The incident was dealt with by charging Black with a minor offence and imposing a light penalty. At the town's sheriff court, a halfway house between the English magistrates court and a Crown Court, he was given an admonishment, a warning to be of good behaviour.

From then on a firm and unrelenting pattern in Black's life began to emerge. The social services still had an interest in his welfare and, after his court conviction, they decided it would be best for all concerned to move him away from Greenock, to give him a second chance to start off his adult life on a better footing. He was again helped to find work and lodgings. This time he moved to Grangemouth, the town of his infancy. It was while he was here that Black formed what appears to have been the only normal heterosexual relationship of his life. He seems to have fallen in love with a girl of his own age, an affair which continued for some time, until she eventually rejected him. He may well have felt hurt by that rejection, or his emotions might have been more complicated. In later life he would put great emphasis on the break-up of this relationship. How justified that emphasis was can, of course, only be a matter for speculation.

However, despite the apparently normal nature of the friendship with this girlfriend, his lust for young children was ever present. An elderly couple, with whom he was lodging in Grangemouth, discovered he had been abusing their grand-daughter during her visits to their house. It was a repeat of the offence at Greenock, digital abuse, only this time facilitated not by a hand round the girl's throat, but through a breach of trust. Predictably, there was a massive row with the latest people to take Black in, and find their hospitality betrayed. Again, though, he was lucky. Despite the severity of his actions, Black was not reported to the police. He was allowed to move quietly out of the house and find digs elsewhere in the town.

This gave him the chance to carry on with the job at a local builders' supply company that had been arranged for him by the welfare workers; not for long though. One morning not long after this incident, Black was called before his boss and sacked on the spot, with no real explanation being given. Dismissal may well, we thought, have been brought about because of rumours circulating the town concerning what had been going on at his digs.

So now, at the age of 19, Black decided to head back to the place that had afforded him more happiness than he had known since leaving it. Back to the Highlands, to Kinlochleven, where he still knew a few people and a few people still remembered him, even if it was only as 'smelly Bobby Tulip'.

If he was genuinely looking for a clean start it was not to be. Quite conversely, his return to his roots ended up as though a script had been written for him before arrival. He found work, he found lodgings, and he found a young girl on whom to slake his lust. This time luck ran out and he was reported to the police. Consequently, at the end of March 1967, he was sentenced to a year's borstal training. He left his teenage years and became 20 in the first weeks of the sentence, which he served in a borstal not far from Grangemouth, at Polmont.

The court had heard how he regularly baby-sat for the seven-year-old daughter of the couple with whom he had lodged in Kinlochleven. On various occasions when her mother was out Black had subjected the child to the digital abuse that obviously held a total fascination for him.

My team of detectives looking into his background tracked him constantly, without gaps, until the time of his release from borstal. After that, we assumed, he had decided to make yet another clean break. Like thousands of Scots before him, Black headed for the bright lights of London, to make his fortune in the capital. We would never, of course, discover if his real motive for the move was to make a fresh start in life or to switch to a new environment where he was not known and would have a better chance to be up to his old tricks again.

In London it was more difficult to follow his movements. He seemed to lead a life which would be familiar to many of those who had trodden the streets of London before him. Dingy bedsits, casual jobs here and there, nothing very permanent. Until into the 1970s, when he fell on his feet and met the couple who were to become as close as he ever came to having a real family.

Eddie and Kathy Rayson put a roof over his head and, more than that, took Black into their lives, giving him yet another opportunity to start afresh. But, true to form, Black opted for another course of action. He applied for, and received, various jobs as a lifeguard in a local swimming baths. He was a good swimmer – there was no doubt about that – but as he would admit to us later, attendance at swimming baths was usually in pursuit of his other hobby and he was, in fact, sacked from one of his pool jobs after a young girl complained he had behaved indecently towards her.

The picture we were building up continued in this vein. He was never far from sexual allegations of one sort or another involving young girls and, with the benefit of hindsight, the workmates to whom we were talking were giving us the same, troubled, sort of picture.

Black used to be particularly friendly with one man at the poster delivery company. The pair would often play darts together. After Black's conviction at the High Court in Edinburgh, Ray Aldridge was quoted in newspapers as saying: 'I hope the bastard rots in hell.' It was a sentiment many expressed after crossing Robert Black's path.

Whilst this was all very interesting, it was not taking us a great deal further forward in unravelling the matters with which we were primarily concerned. Just because you are not a very nice person does not mean to say you are a multiple child killer. What we had to find was evidence, real hard evidence that would stand up in a court of law and, if correct, end the agony for the relatives of three murdered children.

I decided we needed to know more about Black the man. The picture we had of him, from those who knew him best, was well painted. There was, however, a need to do something the police had not had an opportunity to do before in this case, that was to speak to Black at length.

Scottish and English police practices vary widely in many respects. One major difference is in the handling of an accused person after arrest. When Black was taken into custody following the abduction of the girl in the Borders he had been caught red-handed and so there was no need for interviews and statements from him. The admissions he made to several officers in the car as he was being driven to the police station in Selkirk were sufficient. If the offence had happened in England, on the other hand, Black would have been extensively questioned before being charged. His statements, post-arrest and under caution, would have been of value to the investigation we were now carrying out. We had none.

It was obvious we had to see him sooner or later. I decided it should be sooner. There was no doubt the best people to carry out the interview were Andrew Watt, the detective superintendent who had been put in charge of the operation to try and track down Black's movements, and his number two, Roger Orr. Andrew, now retired, and Roger were the mainstays of the part of the investigation which began after Black's arrest. His latest convictions are due to the extremely hard and effective work put in by many dedicated professionals, but I must single out Roger and Andrew for special mention.

As the man with overall command of a massive inquiry I could not be expected to be aware of the detail of each and every part of what was going on, and all that was being uncovered. When Andrew Watt retired Roger Orr took over as head of this operation, and the work he carried out in the search for clues to Black's movements was painstaking in the extreme. Years later, when we were giving a talk to command officers at the Bramshill Police College on the whole Black case, there was not a man in the room left unimpressed by the work that had been done in our quest. Even I, who have lived with the case for many years, learned much during the section where Roger made a long presentation.

By the time I felt it was right to question Black he was serving a life sentence in a Scottish jail and subject to all sorts of access restrictions. Basically the police can only see a convicted man, in the normal run of things, if the man wants to see the police. It was pretty clear that Black had no desire for his settling-in at Edinburgh's Saughton Jail to be interrupted by us. So we decided to detain him, under the terms of Scotland's Criminal Justice Act. This piece of legislation, that was fiercely contested by many during its passage through parliament, has been widely praised now that it is frequently used to good effect and has not been turned into the tool for denial of civil liberties some had forecast it would. Under section two, the police have the power to detain a person for up to six hours if they believe he is guilty of, or a witness to, a serious offence. Some believe that time should be extended, but no matter, that is how the Act stands at present. It was decided that Black would be detained under this provision. The move was slightly unusual, but not unheard of, for a man in prison.

Careful consideration was given as to how to structure and play the interview. We were nowhere near enough to building up a complete picture of his movements to ask specific questions about where he was at any particular time and then be able to challenge his answers, as one would in normal situations. The interview, we realised, may well be used as the basis of a future case against him, therefore no mention could be made of the incident in the Borders or his other convictions. That would have the effect of rendering it inadmissible in any future proceedings against him because it would disclose details of previous convictions to the jury. Our interview time was limited strictly to six hours. We would have to find out as much as possible, as quickly as possible.

Even more preparation was put into this interview than most. It would be the first chance for Andrew and Roger to speak at length to the man who had taken up so much of their professional life recently. They, and I, felt as though we were getting to know Black as well as we might know our best friends. There are not many people in one's social circle whose history and background one can recount as well as Andrew and Roger were able to do with Black.

In fact, this is a common feature of police work, especially in the case of murder. I feel as though I knew Susie, Caroline and Sarah. I have firm images of them in my mind and a smile often comes to my face as I think of them. It is a smile brought about because of the loving terms in which these three little girls have so often been described to me by their families. That smile was evidence of an emotion that reinforced my determination to bring what peace I could to these grieving families.

By this stage in the investigation, I also knew Black's history in great depth.

In the run-up to the day we were to carry out the interview advice was taken from a psychologist. Unlike the image portrayed in the TV series *Cracker*, starring Robbie Coltrane, detectives do not work hand in hand with psychologists on a regular basis. It was a most unusual step. We were playing for high stakes and we needed to ensure the odds were stacked as far in our favour as possible.

Thirteen days after his sentencing at the High Court in Edinburgh officers turned up early at Edinburgh prison to take Black away for questioning, under the terms of section two. A senior member of the jail staff was waiting to accompany the two officers and Black to the police station. Black himself had been given no indication of our intentions but he must have been expecting it, sometime, perhaps not quite so soon.

A careful plan had been made between Andrew Watt and Roger Orr. They had only six hours, they must use the precious time to best effect. They were going to concentrate on the abduction of Caroline Hogg. The main reasoning behind this decision was that it was the crime in our patch, as it were, but more importantly, it was the one crime under investigation where we had so many good sightings of the suspect, a suspect who, judging by the artist's impression, looked very much like Robert Black did in 1983.

He was driven the short distance to St Leonard's Police Station on Edinburgh's south side where Andrew Watt had set up his new incident room, the one designed to accommodate officers delving into Black's background and movements. He was quickly ushered into an interview room on the first floor where there is a facility to tape-record suspects being interviewed. Then there followed six hours of intensive questioning by Andrew and Roger, in the presence of the senior member of the jail's staff who had accompanied him.

They knew from the outset that it was going to be a difficult six hours. There could be no doubt about that. Even if Black was co-operative, the two officers needed to question him about his innermost emotions and the feelings which drove him in his two major perversions. Apart from his unnatural attraction towards young girls, Black had a bizarre anal self-fixation which seemed to have been with him most of his life. When his bedsit in London was searched, amongst the material uncovered by officers were five Polaroid photographs Black had taken of himself in a mirror as he practiced his 'hobby'. It seemed his interest lay in discovering how large an object he could use for such self-abuse. He had photographed himself using a telephone handset and various other household items. His trophy, though, seemed to be the leg of the bedsit table which he had specially sandpapered for the purpose.

It was obvious that with just six hours to work in establishing contact, then trust and honesty, it was going to be difficult. We had to try.

At the same time, the prospect of a confession was never far from our minds. It seemed if he was serving a life sentence anyway and if he was guilty of what we suspected him of, confession might well have been a weight off his mind, and one he would be eager to shed.

Hector Clark

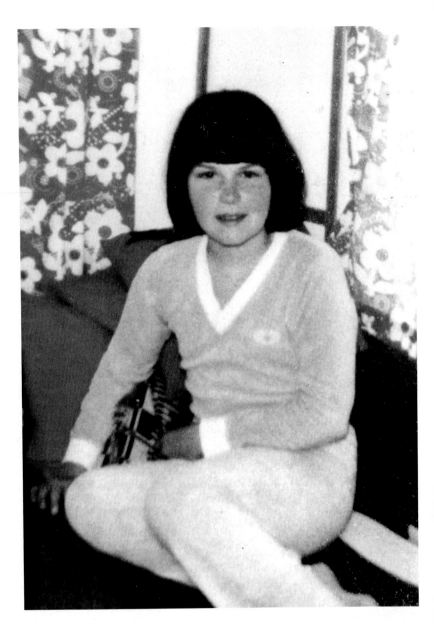

One of the photographs of Susan Maxwell issued to the press after her abduction

Susan's father, Fordyce, out with one of the search parties (©Scotsman Publications)

Black's van was parked in this gateway as Susan walked past. It was probably from this spot that she was snatched

The photograph of Caroline in her school uniform issued to the press after her abduction

Caroline photographed at her friend's birthday party less than four hours before she was abducted

Thousands of people who volunteered to help look for Caroline Hogg cram into Portobello Town Hall for a briefing from police (© Scotsman Publications)

Annette and John Hogg meet the press to appeal for their daughter's return
(© Scotsman Publications)

The author briefs Margaret Thatcher and her husband, Denis, on the
murder hunt during the prime minister's visit to Edinburgh police HQ,
September 1987

The picture of Sarah Harper issued to the press

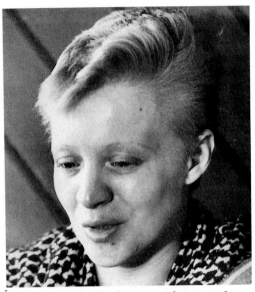

Jackie Harper fights back tears as she meets the press after her daughter's disappearance (© Scotsman Publications)

An aerial photograph of Sarah's street showing (1) her house, (2) the corner shop, and (3) the site of the yard where Black made his deliveries

Left: the artist's impression of the man seen with Caroline Hogg before she was abducted: Right: Robert Black circa 1980

Robert Black on his arrest

CHAPTER TEN

Inside a Killer's Mind

It was shortly after 9 a.m. when Roger Orr and Andrew Watt sat down at a table in the main St Leonard's interview room. Directly across from them Robert Black sat looking down at the table that separated them. He appeared to be quite calm and collected, but there was considerable tension in the room as the two officers set off on their journey of discovery. The tape-recording equipment, the only thing on the table, was set up and ready to go.

The officers went straight into their task. With only six hours there was no time for small talk. Black invited them to call him Robert. Gently prompted by the two detectives, he told them of his early life, his desire to find out more about the father he had never known and the mother who had abandoned him at such an early age. He conceded that, whilst he had these desires, he had not done anything about them, not put idle thoughts into practice.

Black recalled how the death of Mrs Tulip in Kinlochleven had undoubtedly had a profound effect on him. It changed him from being an outgoing and confident child, he said, to one who was much more introverted and shy.

We had already spoken to people who knew him in Kinlochleven and this did not account completely with what they said. Several people had spoken of Black as being fairly overpowering, certainly a confident and loud character. They did not recall a time when he went into his shell, even after his return to the area, after being freed from borstal, following the gap of some years spent in the central belt of Scotland.

Surprisingly, I suppose, Black was quick to volunteer details of his past and his sexual development. He spoke about his time in the home at Redding, near Falkirk. That was the one he had been sent to after the death of Mrs Tulip. He told the detectives he had been sent away from there after he and two other boys had assaulted a young girl. He actually made the incident sound worse than it had been described in the social work reports which had been made available to the investigating team. It might have been possible for him to try and explain away this incident as childish fun, a prank gone too far, but Black admitted that he had lain on top of the girl and conceded he might have tried to have sex with her, but said he thought he would have been too young.

Using classic techniques for this kind of work, the two officers told Black they were not seeking to judge him but just to understand.

It is always difficult in these sort of circumstances to work out if your interviewee is responding simply to please, to make his life, at that moment, easier, or if there is a genuine rapport building up. Sometimes a suspect appears to genuinely welcome the opportunity to be honest, for once to speak the truth because, the suspect realises, the truth can no longer hurt him more than he is already hurt. Whilst Black's admissions came thick and fast, this, in fact, led us to think later that we were dealing with a case of a man wanting to please. If he wanted to make a clean break he could have done so. It was in his short-term interests to go so far, and no further.

One firm childhood memory he had was that of a visit by the singer Max Bygraves to one of the homes he stayed in, but he could not remember any details of the occasion.

Revealing to his questioners details of his childhood sexual experiences, while difficult to talk about no doubt, would not land him in any more trouble than he was in already. It would cost him nothing to co-operate with the officers who had obviously gone to great lengths to learn a great deal about his past. He may have considered co-operation the lesser of two evils.

Black said that from the age of about 16 he had found young children beautiful. He was particularly attracted by the lack of body hair. More than that, he was suggesting he felt a special affinity with children; he was happy in their company. He would have liked to have been a father.

He spoke about the girl in Grangemouth, Pamela Hodgson, who had been his one normal relationship, and claimed to have been devastated when the romance ended at her instigation. The experience, he said, had left him with a lasting fear of rejection and an increase in the shyness he had claimed was engendered by the death of Mrs Tulip.

Black seemed clear that the relationship with Pamela had ended mainly because of the geographic separation which was brought about when he had to leave Grangemouth, almost run out of town, to find work after losing his job at the builders' merchants. He described his relationship with this woman as perfectly normal. The ending of it left him with a fear of rejection, he said. He seemed to have low self-esteem, regarding himself as not particularly good-looking. That in itself may have been indicative of his thinking.

As he became easier in his answers and appeared to be relaxing, so Andrew and Roger decided to steer the interview into more difficult waters. They went back in time from his teenage years, back to the home in Musselburgh. The two men knew full well that Black's experiences in this home had been harsh, to say the least, and were entirely likely to have had a profound effect on his development. We had uncovered clear evidence of Black being abused there; Andrew and Roger wanted to find out his version of it, and discover how much he thought he had been influenced by the experiences.

He spoke almost warmly of some aspects of life in the home at Musselburgh, especially the sporting opportunities it had afforded him. Andrew Watt was a native of Musselburgh and so he was able to talk to Black on his home ground, as it were.

In textbook answers on the subject of abuse in these circumstances, Black said how he had felt trapped when the staff member had begun interfering with him. He did not like what was happening but he had no way of avoiding it. He could not run away, there was nowhere to run. Black told the detectives that the member of staff who had abused him had been previously involved with several other boys at the Red House Home over the years. Black said it was the practice for the current victim of abuse at the hands of this staff member to be forced to recommend a boy to take his place when it became time to leave the institution. That, said Black, was how he had become involved. He said for him there was no enjoyment obtained from the things that happened to him during these years of abuse. There was, however, some advantage in participation; his end of the deal was to receive better reports.

It was about this time that Black, who was, and still is for that matter, keen on football, was given a trial for Enfield Town in an English league. However, his dependency on spectacles ruled out a career in professional football.

Again, as he spoke about his time in Grangemouth, Black was happy to talk about the incident with his landlord and landlady's granddaughter. The incident that had seen him flung out of his lodgings. He described it as exploration, to give him pleasure, not dominance. He claimed, absurdly, that the child also gained pleasure from the experience.

Black was clear his abuse of the girl in Grangemouth – and he admitted there were others as well – was exploratory. He had a fascination. It was a fine example of the self-delusion of the abuser. Here was a man suspected of murdering at least three children, freely admitting abuse of youngsters and claiming his victims would have enjoyed their ordeals.

He went on to talk about how he had fantasies about young

girls and spoke of how he felt more comfortable with little children rather than adults. He volunteered information about self-abuse sessions he had in later life, in the back of his van. He spoke of the objects he carried round in a toilet bag in the van to facilitate these incidents.

As these self-abuse sessions were taking place, Black candidly told the officers, the majority of the time his mind was filled with images of children, young pre-pubescent girls. He said, importantly in our view, that those fantasies centred on indecently assaulting young girls, just in the way the youngster in the Borders had been assaulted by him. There was clearly a potential link to Susan Maxwell and Caroline Hogg as well. Both bodies were too badly decomposed for detailed examination, but Caroline was naked and Susan's underwear had clearly been interfered with. He claimed that the importance of children in his fantasies increased after the ending of his relationship with Pamela Hodgson.

There was more, things that even officers of the experience of the two men listening to this tale could only wonder at. Their long service had brought them into contact with many strange and bizarre stories, many perverts and misfits, but they had heard nothing like this before.

Almost without noticeable embarrassment Black spoke of his fondness for dressing as a child. Children's clothes had been found in the rear of his van after his arrest in the Borders. He said he particularly liked wearing a girl's swimsuit that had been found in the van.

Were it not so tragic, the thought of a six-foot-tall van driver parked overnight in some lay-by, cramming his burly frame into a child's swimming costume and engaging in extreme forms of self-abuse would form the basis of black humour. This was no joke though. All the time Black admitted details of the depravity he had been engaged in, my officers could only wonder what sort of extreme activities he had been involved in but did not wish to talk about. If details of this mind-boggling behaviour were being volunteered, what other activities were being kept hidden, locked up in his mind?

The next part of his interview was extremely distasteful; I recall the barest possible details here because they were to prove to be a vital clue in the case. A key piece of evidence was uncovered through police and scientists working well together.

Black told Andrew and Roger that he kept a toilet bag in the back of the van which contained various implements he used for sexual stimulation by insertion. They were stored in the bag, wrapped up in a sock. He said it was his normal practice when needing to defecate to do so on a piece of newspaper in the rear of his van and then anally insert one of these objects while masturbating. He said he began this form of abuse while a young child living with Mrs Tulip in Kinlochleven and had practised it ever since.

The detectives were not aware of it at the time, but a newspaper found in Black's bedsit would later reveal startling clues.

The two officers showed Black the five Polaroid photographs he had taken of himself in the mirror inserting various objects, including a wine bottle and telephone handset, into his body. He said these had been taken as an experiment. He almost boasted of his achievements with the leg of the table.

The crux of the interview came as Black began talking of his visits to beaches and other areas where children played. He had photographs of many youngsters in his possession. Snaps that could have been taken by any family on seaside holidays. Pictures that could, in other circumstances, be described as totally innocent, were they not in the possession of Robert Black. In his hands no photograph of any child could be described as innocent.

He told how, when he had time, he would visit beaches and beauty spots to watch the children at play. He would, he said, often sit himself down near family groups to observe. He preferred going to beaches. By the seaside there was always the chance he could watch the little ones changing.

The child pornography which Black had collected was kept hidden in a suitcase stored on top of the wardrobe in his bedsit. There were magazines, films and videos. He spoke of the ways in which he used it, and how he had spent several weeks trying to edit together his favourite clips of child pornography from cine films which he had bought in Amsterdam.

The two detectives tried to turn Black's apparent desire to present himself as someone concerned with the welfare of children to their own advantage. At different stages in the interview Black had attempted to give the impression that he would be opposed to the use of children as sexual objects if it caused them any harm. The detectives were happy to go along with this twisted logic for a time. They engineered him round to putting himself in the position of a father, a distraught father, whose child had just had been abducted.

Black agreed his first move would be to turn immediately to the police, to seek their help to get it all sorted out. Then, he agreed, he would want to help such a parent if he could. By this point all the ingredients had been put into the conversation for the abduction of Caroline Hogg to be introduced for the first time. Black must have been expecting it. He'd just been talking of his frequent visits to the seaside to watch children. The subject of child abduction itself. His mind must have been racing as he prepared to talk his way out of the questions that would, he supposed, inevitably follow.

They did not. To put him off his stride, the officers switched tack without giving any signal of the coming change in direction. They started talking instead about his work.

In the weeks since his arrest, Andrew Watt's team had been examining Black's employment records in great detail. He had been in stable work for over 15 years, centring on the delivery of posters for display on roadside billboards. In the mid-seventies Black had begun work for a company which did nothing else. It ran a fleet of vans, the drivers of which dropped off posters for new advertising campaigns at depots dotted across Britain. My officers were discovering how this employment had taken Black all over the country. Everywhere that roadside billboards were displayed Black was likely to have visited, at some time or other. There are not many parts of Britain where this form of advertising is not seen. True to form, he had a favourite delivery area, chosen from perversity rather than anything else. It was the south coast of England, needless to say, because of the opportunities the area afforded for beach watching.

The team had discovered that the posters were delivered to a network of hoarding companies which had depots in or near many large towns and cities. Many of these depots were not permanently manned but had large secure boxes outside to allow posters to be dropped off when no member of staff was around. This had suited Black entirely. It meant he could drive at his own pace on many of the runs. He could stop off for an afternoon here, a stroll on the beach there.

He loved his work, he said. Before entering the poster business Black's employment had often ended in dismissal. He was a poor time-keeper. He sometimes lost jobs because of the allegations about him and children. Van driving was ideal, especially in an industry where he could turn up when he wanted to, within certain wide parameters.

For a loner, a free rein on the highways of Britain is an attractive proposition. It was ideal for Black, and I find the thought of him wandering, loose and unchecked, for all those years, worrying in the extreme. What would those happy families enjoying a day at the seaside have thought if only they had known who the man was that had been sitting next to them, and why it was that he was there? The mothers chatting in the swing park as their children played would have been horrified to learn the truth about the chap leaning on the fence apparently enjoying a breath of summer air but in reality enjoying something else entirely.

In the interview the three discussed the routes he often took, apart from the south coast, the roads he knew best. Like the A444 in Leicestershire. That road was particularly well known to him. The road to Twycross. Eddie and Kathy Rayson's son, John, lived in the Midlands. Black told of how he would often go to visit them and their two young sons. The A444 was the road he would use.

At this point Andrew Watt moved the discussion round directly on to the subject of the abduction of Caroline Hogg. Some four hours of tape had been used up by now. The three men must have all been feeling tired but, no doubt, adrenalin would be flowing. Andrew told Black they had been able to establish that he was definitely in Portobello on the day she disappeared.

Following the arrest of Black, after the summit meeting I had held in Edinburgh, we had been looking at ways of trying to track his movements around the country. The obvious ones in any case are things like bank transactions which, latterly at least, were all computerised and traceable to exact branches at exact times. Before the interview commenced we had enjoyed a major breakthrough in the task, discovered in the offices of the company Black had worked for. Poster Despatch and Storage, PDS as it was known in the trade, had been in the habit of issuing their drivers with what are known as agency cards, for buying petrol. These work just like a normal credit card, with the sales slips being completed and returned by participating filling stations to the card suppliers who, in turn, invoiced PDS. The poster company had cards supplied by three of the major oil companies. We discovered, fortunately for us, that the companies kept hold of some of the receipts. Details of some of the transactions were stored on microfilm or microfiche. We had then embarked on the massive job of trying to tie in receipts to vehicles driven by Black. More of that later. But by the time of the interview at St Leonard's we already had a fair bit of information about his movements.

As the interview neared its climax, one of the detectives showed him a receipt for petrol issued by a garage in Belford, Northumberland, about 25 miles south of the Scottish border at Berwick-upon-Tweed. It was signed by Black on the exact date of Caroline's disappearance, 8 July 1983. Andrew Watt's team had also discovered that Black had delivered posters in Edinburgh that day. They were dropped off at the depot of one of the bigger billboard companies, Mills and Allen. Their Edinburgh depot was in an area of the city called Piershill, less than one and a quarter miles from Caroline Hogg's home and indeed just off the main road leading to Portobello. Through his time in the Red

House Home in Musselburgh this area would be as near to home ground for Black as he would have known anywhere. He must have walked scores of times along the road from Musselburgh to the swimming pools at Portobello, past the street in which Caroline lived.

Now the officers began to turn the heat on Black. He was shown a photograph of himself, taken at about the time of Caroline's abduction, and then shown the artist's impression created by the witnesses to the incident all those years before. His initial reaction told us a lot. He said it looked nothing like him but patently it did. Maybe he had a good reason to lie about the striking likeness?

Black, until this point, had been relatively talkative. He had spoken quite fully and openly about his distressing habits, without embarrassment or shame. He had only once mentioned looking for help with his problems and even then it was after the idea had been raised first by his questioners. So now, with the interview right at the heart of the matter, with it being directly suggested that he knew more than he was saying about Caroline's disappearance, Black suddenly became monosyllabic. He was barely grunting acknowledgment of the words being spoken around him.

Roger and Andrew turned up the pressure and suggested to him outright that he was the man everyone had been looking for. They told him not only did the police think that, but other people who used to know him were forming the same opinion. The detectives told Black, quite rightly, that people who knew him as the poster delivery man were now saying they wished they had told us about Black years ago because even then they had harboured suspicions.

Black was measured in his rebuttals. They were not heated denials, merely stated. The only time he appeared to become upset was when the officers, again stressing they only wanted to understand, not judge, mentioned the word 'murder' in connection with the abduction of Caroline and other youngsters.

He steadfastly refused to be drawn any further. Even when the detectives spoke to him on the presumption that he did visit the promenade at Portobello that day, Black did not waver. He gave only lukewarm approval to the idea of him appearing in a possible identification parade.

The next ploy was to try to reverse his role in the affair, in his own mind. Instead of trying to get him to confess to being a child killer Andrew and Roger began to show him the position in another light. They suggested to him that he, and he alone, held the key to end the suffering of those left behind. The parents and relatives of the three little girls. They of course did not highlight the fact that they suspected Black of causing that suffering in the first place.

They seized on Mrs Tulip, in Kinlochleven, as the closest Black would have had to a mother, and asked him to imagine how she would have felt if it had been her child that had been snatched. Wouldn't he want to end her agony? He had the chance of ending Mrs Hogg's agony. He should take it. People would think better of him. He didn't.

In a final attempt to convince Black that his salvation lay in confession, the two officers turned up the heat further. Emotion flowed in the little interview room as Roger and Andrew outlined various scenarios to Black, giving the opportunity time and time again to edge a little further out into the open. The chance to begin making a confession without fear of the instant revulsion of his audience.

It was becoming clear to the detectives that they were making little headway. Black obviously felt hurt by the publicity that had surrounded his court appearance for the Borders offence and subsequent press revelations of details from his background. He had said as much. It was suggested to him a confession now would prevent further publicity for a time and spare him the embarrassment of his personal habits being laid bare for the world to see during a lengthy trial. The officers were by now making no bones about the fact that they thought Black was Caroline's killer. There was, however, no chink in his armour.

The six hours were up and Black went back to Saughton Prison leaving Andrew and Roger to brief me on the results of their interview.

In evidential terms, they had concluded, the six hours of questioning had not amounted to much. However, it had left them even more certain that Black was the killer, not only of Caroline, but of Susan and Sarah too.

As they sat, as casually as possible, talking to Black and outlining the various options, they had been studying his every movement, analysing each response. In the middle of the afternoon that Thursday in August, as they walked out of the police station, the two officers directing the search into Black's background were more convinced than ever we had our man.

That was, of course, fine for morale purposes, but what we needed to find now was evidence. Evidence that could be put to a jury and leave them in no doubt that Black was the person behind this string of offences that had, over a period of eight years, shocked and horrified the nation.

During the course of several meetings an audit was carried out of the information we had amassed so far, and an assessment taken of what could possibly be uncovered in the coming weeks. The searches of the petrol vouchers were already producing results.

We needed more, and if Black wasn't going to help us we would have to do it the hard way.

CHAPTER ELEVEN

Building the Case

The decision to conduct this major interview with Black so soon after his Edinburgh High Court appearance and sentencing was taken quite deliberately. Our investigation into his past was still at quite an early stage, but we had uncovered enough, we thought, to allow us to speak to him with the authority that would be lent by our apparent knowledge of his life. We thought we could reach through to him. I and others were confident that, by the time we took Black from prison under section two of the Criminal Justice Act, we had enough ammunition in our armoury to demonstrate beyond doubt to him that we were very serious in our endeavours and, more, we were heading in the right direction.

The chance of a confession was always a possibility. If nothing else it was important to give him an opportunity to make a clean breast of it, if that is what he wanted, and save a great deal of time and money into the bargain. Equally we wanted to get a good look into the mind of our number one suspect to see what clues could be found there.

Officers were also, of course, speaking to people who were employed by PDS, the delivery company for which Black worked, and other former employees. He had started his employment with them in 1976 and had worked for the company continuously until 1986. Then he was sacked for bad time-keeping and a poor accident record. It was later to become a significant part of the case against him that his vans were often scratched and dented; he seemingly had a minor accident just about every week.

But unemployment had not lasted long for Black. PDS was taken over shortly after his dismissal, and then quickly afterwards bought out from its new owners by two of the employees. They had reinstated Black. Although his time-keeping and accident records were bad, he had his uses to the company. He would go anywhere at any time. Such was the solitary nature of Black's existence that he would be prepared to hop into his van at short notice, even at weekends and in the evenings, to complete the longest runs the company operated, down to the south-west of England or up to Scotland.

The Scottish run was by far the most taxing. It involved delivery stops throughout the north of England and then in the Border country. The routes would go on to Edinburgh and across to Glasgow before heading south again for more drops in the north-west. The Scottish run also had a plus side. It carried the biggest bonus payment for the drivers. This seemingly trivial fact was, again, to prove crucial.

It would be totally impossible for any van driver, with the best will in the world, to recall details of journeys he made years beforehand. If a man regularly does similar trips he could not be expected to remember the days and dates on which specific journeys were made. The clues were there, however, and Andrew Watt, Roger Orr and other officers were quite simply determined to find them.

The bonus payments for the drivers proved to be a bonus for my detectives. Then there was another case which came into the investigation. This girl had survived, but the method of her attempted abduction was central to Black's eventual conviction. I did not learn of these events until late in the investigation.

Shortly after being appointed to head the linked investigations of the then double murders I had asked the Chief Constables of every police force in Britain to report to me any suspicious incidents involving children that might possibly be linked to these crimes. After Black's arrest I was made aware of an incident in Nottingham that was to have a vital bearing on the investigation and the prosecution of Black.

It was apparent to me and the investigating team that no one piece of evidence was likely to emerge after all this time to help us prove Black's guilt of any one offence. We were always looking towards proving basically that he was a serial killer, that he had acted in the same way on many occasions, usually with deadly consequences. When I was made aware of the attempted abduction of Teresa Ann Thornhill my hopes of being able to do this rose dramatically.

She had been attacked by a man driving a Ford Transit van whose motive was clearly to abduct her. The incident had occurred in 1988 in her home city of Nottingham, but I was not to be made aware of it until over two years later. It had been serious enough but had basically come to nothing. There had been a full investigation but officers in Nottingham had been unable to trace a culprit and the file had been as good as closed for some time.

In the light of the arrest of Robert Black, the Thornhill case took on a new significance for officers in Nottingham, but it became vital for my investigation. It seemed to be a carbon copy of the incident in the Borders, apart from one fact: Teresa Thornhill was 15 years old, but she looked much younger, about eleven.

She had been in a park not far from her home in Nottingham with three friends, one female and two male. They had been sitting chatting one Friday evening in April. Gradually the little group broke up, Teresa and a young male friend being the last to leave the park. They walked together along the street and were passed by a blue-coloured van. The pair then parted. Teresa continued her journey home alone. She noticed a van parked in the street up ahead of her. It could have been the one that had just passed by. The driver had climbed out and was looking under his bonnet.

When she was quite close to the van the man shouted to her. 'Can you fix engines?' he had said, causing considerable alarm to the teenager. She quickened her pace but he leapt forward and grabbed her.

Her assailant picked Teresa right off the ground and started carrying her towards the van. She screamed and struggled for all she was worth but to no avail. He firmly put a hand over her mouth to shut her up. She bit it and then she bit his arm but he kept tight hold of her and kept trying to carry her towards the open driver's door of the vehicle. At this point Teresa, by now absolutely terrified, put up a titanic struggle. She wedged her feet against the side of the van preventing the man from pushing her in the door. In the struggle her attacker's spectacles were knocked flying and fell to the ground.

The teenager's prayers were answered when the boy she had just been with suddenly noticed what was happening and ran to her aid. He pulled his young friend away from the would-be abductor and, hand in hand, they ran off. The man leapt into the van and drove off at speed.

The two youngsters had noticed that there was accident damage to the bonnet of the blue, Transit-like vehicle.

Teresa had been badly shaken, she was bruised and scratched, but worse than that she was shocked to the very core. She was old enough to realise just how lucky she had been. How lucky she was that her friend had passed by and she had not been forced into that van.

The girl had been quite certain about the attacker's glasses falling to the ground. Despite an intensive search they were not found at the place of the attack and police concluded the assailant may have returned to the scene of his crime to recover them.

Perhaps because she was an older girl than the ones that I had been dealing with at the time I was not told about the attempted abduction of Teresa Ann Thornhill until after Black's arrest. Now that I did know about it, we had to try to find out if it was another link in the chain, and it did indeed prove to be a vital part of the case that convicted Black.

Building up the detailed picture of Black's movements and, more importantly, proving it, was not going to be easy. The clues were all to be found in archives of various sorts and by tracing people who had been involved on the edges of Black's legitimate activities. When found, we had to hope that these people might, for some reason or other, be able to recall their movements on certain days long ago, and that way we might shed light on Black's whereabouts and movements.

It was clear that Black only travelled any great distance, in the normal course of events, when he was working. If he was working on the days we were interested in we would have to uncover proof of that from the limited records that were still held by PDS.

We quickly established that there was no direct evidence showing Black was on the Scottish run on 30 July 1982, and 8 July 1983. Clues did begin to emerge though. It was discovered that the PDS drivers had been in dispute with the company during these years. The employers had, in the early Eighties, included Dundee as part of the Scottish run which had, until then, gone no further north than Edinburgh/Glasgow. The drivers were angered at PDS's refusal to increase the bonus that was paid for the trip. In the best possible conditions the extra drop would add at least three hours to the existing journey time, possibly more. The company, though, would pay no extra.

Throughout its recent history, the various owners of PDS had kept details of the work they were carrying out, but nowhere did they record which driver did which run on any particular date. Through this dispute we found a way of getting round that. It was found in the wages book.

Detectives went through the pay records of the drivers in great detail and spent hours interviewing the people who had been responsible for making up the pay packets over the years. We discovered that a Scottish run in 1982 earned the driver a bonus payment of £85.50. Other routes carried smaller bonus payments because the distances were shorter. The Manchester run, for instance, earned the driver only an extra £40. The wages book showed that in the week ending 6 August 1982 Black had been given bonus payments totalling £125.50. That indicated to PDS staff being interviewed all these years later that Black had completed a Scottish run between 29 July and 4 August of that year. Included in that was also a £40.00 payment for a Manchester run.

It was quite elating for the officers involved and myself to discover that such detailed evidence was available all these years later. We decided that a belt and braces approach should be employed to put the matter beyond any doubt that may creep in later, for whatever reason. So next we traced all the other drivers who were working for PDS at the time, examined their wages and found that they had not done the run. It was a double proof. Not only could we show Black had made the trip to Scotland the weekend Susan Maxwell was abducted, we could show that no one else working for the same company at the time had made it. So it had to be Black.

We could show that Black was in Scotland that weekend. We had to go further and narrow down where in Scotland he was, to see if we could prove that he was in Coldstream at 4.15 in the afternoon of Friday 30 July, as Susan Maxwell walked home from her tennis game.

At this point in the inquiry the petrol receipts were going to be useful.

Companies, like PDS, that require their staff to drive vehicles over long distances often obtain petrol credit cards. These allow the employees to draw petrol at filling stations and pay for it on credit. The credit card is run through the sort of switching machine one sees everywhere these days. It records the garage, the amount of fuel drawn and the cost of it, the name of the credit card holder, usually a company name and the signature of the driver. Importantly for us, it often also recorded the registration number of the vehicle that had been fuelled. PDS gave Black, and all its other drivers, cards which were unique to them. The card bore the holder's signature on its reverse to prevent fraud.

We were able to discover that Black filled his van at Stannington Filling Station on the A1 road just north of Newcastle upon Tyne between 1 and 5 p.m. on 30 July 1982. His registration number was on the transaction receipt. It showed he was driving a white-coloured Fiat van ULR 392X. The next debit on his account referred to a transaction north of Edinburgh later that same day. It showed that he had filled up once more, this time at the Bullionfields Service Station in Dundee between 10 and 11 p.m.

So Black was not only on the Scottish run on the day of Susan's abduction but he was just south of the scene of it beforehand, and north afterwards. Could we narrow it down any further? Could we discover his exact route?

Just past the Stannington garage on the A1 north of Newcastle, is the slip road that leads to the beginning of the A697, the 'middle road' to Edinburgh, right through Cornhill on Tweed, over the Tweed Bridge and into Coldstream. He could have gone up the A1, or turned off and gone up the A697.

The day after Susan's abduction there was a petrol stop at the Golden Fleece services just outside Carlisle. The time of refuelling there was narrowed down to between 9 a.m. and 6 p.m., not very helpful. There was, however, enough to be going on with.

Still more was to be found in the records and billing systems of the advertising industry. The stock in trade of PDS were the posters they delivered to billboard companies around the country. Our inquiry discovered that this is no hit and miss industry. The posters ultimately end up on roadside hoardings hired for specific periods of time from the companies which own them. Poster campaigns are precise. If an agency has booked a particular campaign on a particular site then it is in its own interests to ensure the posters go up at a precise time, so they can be sure to pay only for the time the site is occupied with their product. PDS in turn had to deliver the posters precisely, and on time, so they could be pasted up at the allotted moment.

To ensure that our evidence was unassailable, we made a detailed study of the advertising industry and found, to our delight, a method of doubling up the evidence. Most of the agencies that had been dealing with PDS to have their posters distributed had kept records of the transactions. We found we could speak to advertising companies and after sometimes lengthy searches they were able to find invoices and payment slips, delivery notes and order instructions. By cross-referencing them with the rest of the information we were amassing, a belt and braces job was being done.

Our luck ran out in one respect though. Many of the poster pasters were small operations. The depots in various towns were not constantly manned, and systems had been established for dropping off posters in the absence of any staff. At one such place there might have been a container near the front door. In others Black and the other drivers had keys to the depots. Every place on the Scottish run that posters were dropped off had a method of accepting out-of-hours deliveries.

We had reached the stage that we knew Black was on the Scottish run, we knew vaguely when he could have been in the area of an abduction, but we had no way of proving his exact time of calling at any one place along the route in 1982. Was there a way of finding more precisely the time of the fuelling stop at Stannington to give a better idea of when he might have been driving over the Tweed bridge?

Officers went to the garage armed with the credit sales slip from the agency company. It goes without saying that they hadn't a clue from looking at these slips when they had been issued, beyond reading the date on them. This was done at all the places Black stopped for fuel during the times we were very interested in his movements. Sometimes the garage might say that they were only open for certain hours, so his stop had to be during this period, but because opening hours tend to be long in the petrol business it wasn't good enough for me. On other occasions a particular assistant at the filling station could say positively that the slip had been filled in by him or her. They could also, sometimes, say that they had only worked certain set hours. Again it all helped, but was nowhere near enough.

As usual with police work there is an easy way and a hard way. The easy way is through luck, getting a good break early on in an investigation. The hard way is through painstaking and detailed inquiry. We had no alternative but to adopt the second method.

All agency card sales slips are numbered in series. We decided the best way to be more precise in timing Black's transactions was to track down the people who had bought petrol with cards issued by the same company and been given sales slips numbered immediately before and after those signed by Black.

Most people if asked today about their petrol-buying habits of ten years before would laugh. With careful questioning though, amazing results can be achieved. Sometimes the little human dramas of life make odd things stick in people's minds. We had to hope that luck would come into this avenue of inquiry at some stage.

Most of the time we were only able to track down people who, on seeing the receipt they signed, could only confirm that they must have been at the garage in question on the date shown. Other times we were more lucky. Black made scores of garage stops. The timing of each or any one could have been vital to us.

This part of the investigation was often routine, frustrating and frankly tedious. At the same time it was important that nothing was missed. A great deal of time was being devoted to tracking down people who, if they could remember anything at all to help us, were providing important, but dull, evidence. Again like so much police work, detectives were spurred on in this task by the hope that the next person spoken to might be the one who would make a substantial contribution to cracking the case.

Do not let me give you an over-simplified impression of this task. Credit sales slips tracked back to individual companies spread throughout Britain. Ten years later the staff of these companies who bought the petrol very often had moved on to new employment, new areas of Britain, and indeed elsewhere.

Detectives were having to search out people who, when they discovered the nature of our task, were usually only too eager to help, but who would repay our hard work in finding them with mundanities.

However, as officers from Edinburgh spread out across the country with their questions they were being rewarded with more vital clues as we were building up our case, which increasingly looked as though it was going to rely on circumstantial evidence.

The transaction before Black's on 30 July at Stannington in Northumberland was debited to the account of a London agricultural company. This was the afternoon of Susan's abduction. Officers travelled to the firm's headquarters. There the signature was recognised and the employee was traced, but he could not, of course, remember buying petrol there that day. He could say that he was a regular user of the A1 road and, from his habits, he could also say he was likely to have been at the garage between 11 a.m. and 2 p.m.

The transaction after Black's was billed to a systems control company. The man who signed that sales slip had left it years before and emigrated to Australia. We asked the Australian police to interview him, and he turned into a vital witness. This man said he was at the Stannington Garage near enough to 12.45 p.m. His memory was helped by detailed records kept by his former employers which showed he was at a job nearby at a precise time. His arrival time was recorded as part of the billing process for his visit.

So that was how we concluded the timing of Black's visit to that particular petrol outlet to be, probably, between 11 a.m. and 1 p.m. that day. He pulled in at Stannington while heading north. Two roads went to his destination known to us through poster delivery books, Edinburgh, from that spot. One, the A697, led right past the spot south of Coldstream Bridge where Susan vanished.

Another thing we could be sure about was the time and date Black left for Scotland. A human drama had fixed it in the mind of another important witness.

One of the PDS drivers had a son who was appearing at the Old Bailey in London, on a murder charge. On 28 July 1982, Kevin Wilcox was found guilty and sentenced to life imprisonment. The following day Wilcox's father, Derek, reported for work at PDS and was told that he was going to Scotland. He felt unable to make such a long trip with the trauma of the trial and his son's sentence. For his protestations PDS sacked him on the spot. As usual, Black stepped in to cover for the missing driver. He would not have been doing anything in particular that weekend, so the loner was only too happy to head north with the prospect of the bonus payment.

This was the sort of evidence we had been praying for. Derek Wilcox would not forget 29 July 1982 in a hurry.

So Black would have been heading north in his white Fiat van on 30 July. Edinburgh was his destination, but which route did he take?

In the taped interview at St Leonard's police station, Black had said that he did not use roads other than the A1. He went as far as to say he had never travelled north on a road lying west of the Great North Road. During our interviews with other PDS drivers, officers had naturally been asking them if they discussed routes and short-cuts with each other and Black in particular. They had, needless to say. Two of the drivers distinctly remembered Black saying he used the A697. They remembered he had recommended a café along the route.

Why was his denial to us so categoric?

Then we uncovered another factor in route planning at the time. A bypass was being built round the small Northumbrian village of Belford. A steep hill at its north end had long been a hold up and accident blackspot. The PDS drivers said that to avoid the delays here during the construction of the bypass they had always used the A697 route to Coldstream.

A fine example of a hunch that paid off was centred on a photograph we found in the Stamford Hill bedsit where Black lived. It was a landscape snap, a scene typical of many parts of the Scottish Borders. Officers were sent with copies of the picture to drive up and down the roads in the area, particularly the A1 and the A697, to try and locate the exact spot from where it had been taken. We found it. The picture was a scene of hills taken from a road near a little border village called Cranshaws. It wasn't on the A697 road, but it was certainly west of the A1.

Again fortune smiled on us. One detective noticed a field in the foreground of the photograph was rather an odd-looking colour. We spoke to the man who farmed the land. He remembered the reason for the odd appearance of his crop well. One of his staff had made a mess of mixing up a batch of spray and when the chemicals were applied to the barley they had turned the crop a rather unpleasant dark-brown colour. So irate was the farmer that he gave the tractorman in question a written warning over his future conduct. A copy of the warning was carefully stored in the farm files. It was dated 1982, the year Susan disappeared.

Then a re-examination of the statements made by witnesses in the bridge area at the time of Susan's disappearance revealed several references to a white van reversed into a field gate leading off the A697, just past the Border Bridge. If it had been there as Susan was walking home that day she would have walked right past it.

We had known about the van from the first hours after she vanished, but no one had a clear picture of what make it was, let alone anything useful like its registration number. To start looking for a white van somewhere in Britain was a task so enormous as to be not worth starting.

So by now we knew Black was on the Scottish run, he was at Stannington in the afternoon, he lied about not using the road from where Susan was abducted, and we knew he had made poster drops in Edinburgh and Dunfermline by 11 p.m. that night. There was another drop in Dundee, and three more still in Glasgow. We think these were made some time after midnight. Between 9 a.m. and 6 p.m. on 31 July he refuelled at Carlisle and headed south for London down the west side of the country.

From the town of Carlisle there is an obvious route south;

154

straight down the M6 and then on to the M1 all the way to the capital. Black had told his colleagues at PDS that he disliked using the M6 on the section as it makes its tortuous way round Birmingham. Roadworks were common at this spot and there was always the chance you would hit heavy traffic. He told two of the other PDS drivers that he preferred to go off the M6 and take the A50 through part of the Midlands and reach the M1 that way. Susan's body was found in a lay-by in Staffordshire adjacent to the A518 road, just a short distance from its junction with the A50.

We also found a worrying gap in Black's timings on this route south. All the way north we could track him and fit his known stops into a logical sequence. On his way south the timings did not add up. We knew he had drawn petrol prior to 6 p.m. at the Carlisle filling station. The next transaction we could discover was on the following day, 1 August, at the Blue Boar services beside Watford Gap. That could be timed at near enough to 11 p.m. using the same methods as before. What on earth was he doing between 6 p.m. on the day after Susan's disappearance and 11 p.m. the next night?

Thorough checking of all records that we could come across revealed no more poster deliveries. He was untraceable from petrol receipts or any of the other methods we had used to plot his movements for over 24 hours. During that time he would have passed right through the area where Susan's body was found.

Here we had a case beginning to emerge along the classic methods of murder detection. There was motive, quite clearly. Susan Maxwell was a likely target for a paedophile like Black. There was opportunity. He could have been in Coldstream around the time of her abduction, he could have been in the area of the Midlands where her body was found at the time of her disposal.

This already painstaking inquiry certainly gave heart to the officers in the thick of the inquiries, but on its own would have been laughed out of court. We had to carry out a similar excercise for the other two murders and the attempted abduction of Teresa Thornhill.

To establish the simple fact that Black drew petrol at Stannington in Northumberland between 11 a.m. and 1 p.m. on 30 July 1982 had taken more than 50 statements. Those statements were taken by our officers, and those of other forces, throughout the country and as far away as Australia. The process we were now involved in was trying to prove that Black was our man. This was not some sort of short-cut where officers might try to show that the easiest suspect they had was the person that was responsible for three child murders. This was a case of experienced detectives acting on a great deal more than a hunch, which had come at the end of three very long and detailed inquiries.

As Andrew Watt and Roger Orr regularly reported back to me and as the pieces of the jigsaw fell into place, one startling fact became apparent. We had detectives going over every part of Black's background and movements that we possibly could. Hundreds of people were being interviewed, scores of transactions were being examined.

In all this work not one single fact, not one hint nor indication to detract from our suspicions was coming forward. There can have been few exercises like this carried out over the years when each new piece of evidence fitted neatly into place.

This intricate jigsaw continued to be completed as the other abductions and the attempt to snatch Teresa Thornhill came under the same sort of spotlight.

CHAPTER TWELVE

It Must Be Him

Through further inquiries we were sure that a year later, in July 1983, Black was once more off to Scotland. It was more or less the same run he was doing as when Susan was abducted. This time he was driving a white Transit van.

Using the methods that had revealed so much in the Maxwell case, we could be certain he made a drop in Gateshead, just south of the River Tyne from Newcastle, between 5 p.m. on 7 July and 7 p.m. the following day. This was gleaned from the poster receipt book at the depot. It frequently occurred to me that, if Black had been delivering materials which were not so time sensitive, we might have had a much bigger problem tying down his movements.

Then it could be proved he drew petrol at Belford in Northumberland on 8 July between 11 a.m. and 6 p.m. By now the work building the village bypass that had moved a great deal of traffic on to the Coldstream road was finished. Black was back on the A1. The natural route from the Belford filling station to his next delivery would have taken him right through Portobello.

At this point our luck waned for a while. We knew he was heading for Edinburgh. We knew he reached his destination because posters were delivered that weekend at two sites in the Scottish capital, and at another two in Glasgow. However, we were unable to tie down the time he was in Edinburgh.

One possible picture of events was clear to see though. In his six-hour interview Black had told the detectives that he sometimes used to visit Musselburgh, the town of part of his youth. He told the officers he liked to visit seaside places on warm days, in the hope of seeing little girls changing. Friday 8 July was just such a beautiful warm night. Caroline, out to play on a pleasant evening, was about to be abducted.

One of Black's poster drop-off points was at Mills and Allen again, in the Piershill district of Edinburgh. The depot is only one and a quarter miles, on the most direct route, away from Portobello. We knew from his next petrol purchase that all the Scottish drops were made that Friday, because he bought petrol at Carlisle, back in England, between midnight that night and 3 a.m. the following morning, the Saturday. Clearly, to have reached there in time, he had driven north from Belford directly to Edinburgh. It would have been early evening when he arrived in the Scottish capital.

His natural route south would have been again down the west side. We found that he had drawn petrol at Ascot Gate services in Staffordshire between 8 a.m. and noon on 9 July, the day after Caroline went missing. This petrol station is just 15 miles from where her body was deposited on the A444. We could only wonder. Did he leave her then, or did he take her to London first? He ought not to have needed more petrol so quickly. What was he doing with it? Where had he gone?

More importantly, Black made a delivery to a poster depot at Rushdown, in Bedworth, Warwickshire, on 12 July. The depot is just eleven and a half miles from that notorious lay-by. This was the date identified by the entomologist as the first possible one on which Caroline's body could have been left where it was found. If this was the day her body was put by Black in the lay-by, it meant that he had been in possession of the little girl for up to four days. There was no way for us to discover if she was alive or dead, or what he had been doing with her.

There was another reason for Black to have been in that area. The Rayson family, with whom he lived in London, were as close as Black had to a real family. Eddie and Katherine Rayson's son John lived in the Midlands. John and his wife Angeline owned a large, white detached house in a semi-rural area on the edge of a village some eight miles from Burton on Trent. Robert Black was a frequent visitor to 'The Hawthorns', in Acresdale Road, Donisthorpe. John Rayson was in many ways as good as his brother and the driver often called in for a quick visit on his way up and down the country. Sometimes he even stayed overnight.

Try as they might, of course, the Raysons could not remember if they had a guest that weekend. They could remember one vital piece of the jigsaw. Black had told John on several occasions that he had discovered a quick route to the London road from their house, which he also used on trips to the north-west. It was via the M1 to the M5, then on to the A444 past Twycross, on to the A50 road, and the reverse journey on the way back. So here was Black telling a reliable witness that his preferred route through the area was right past the very spot where Caroline's body had been found.

All the time the evidence was piling up. Black had played a canny game during his six-hour interview in Edinburgh but he had said enough to us and his friends and colleagues for substantial holes to be discovered in his story.

Going back to the night of Caroline's abduction, we had the sightings of the scruffy man and the witnesses who saw Caroline with him. We had the artist's impression created with the help of two people who had a good look at the stranger. That artist's impression resembled closely a photograph of Black we found in his own home that was taken that year, 1982. It also was not at all unlike Black when he was arrested years later.

There was more. We had several sightings of a van, a white Ford Transit van. Individually these clues had been meaningless at the time of the initial investigation. Now they were good pointers to the conclusion we were reaching. One of the van sightings was at Bath Street, just beside Caroline's home. The other was at the rear of Fun City. She had left the amusement park that night with the stranger by the West Gate, the gate that led to the carpark.

As this picture was being painted, my team was becoming increasingly confident that a conclusion to a long and tiring hunt was at last in sight. Everything we were uncovering was fitting into the scene. Nothing that we uncovered was out of place. That was the key factor in this part of the investigation. Every single clue that was uncovered pointed to Black, and Black alone. At no time did we ever find something to exclude him from the process.

By now, from our research of his movements, we could say that there was a very good chance Black had been at the scene of both abductions at the time of the crimes. When viewed against what else we knew of our number one suspect that likelihood became more certain. Not certain enough for a court of law. Enough, though, to keep my team fired up as this most difficult operation kept going.

The methods we had used to study Black's movements in 1982 and 1983 were just as sound when we came to look at what he was doing about the time of Sarah Harper's abduction. We knew from PDS that he was by now driving another van, a white Ford Transit, registration number B170 BWC. He seemed to have left London on the morning of 26 March 1986; we knew he withdrew cash from an automatic dispenser in Leicester at 12.50 p.m. that day. By 1986 automatic cash dispensers were commonplace and for the police their great advantage is that the withdrawals are timed exactly.

Checks on delivery notes and receipt books revealed a trail of stops through the Midlands and into the north of England. Hull, York, Brighouse and then Leeds were the drop-offs. One of the Leeds drops was at a company called Myles Spencer, in Morley. It was so close to Sarah's house a man in that depot's yard would have heard her mum shouting for Sarah that night. It was just 200 yards from the point of Sarah's abduction.

We found it difficult to tie down exact timings for Black's visit here. We knew he had filled up in Leeds between 4.15 p.m. and 10 p.m. on 26 March, the day of Sarah's abduction. We knew the delivery was made to Morley between 5 p.m. that day and eight the following morning. It was one of those drops where there was a box to leave the posters if the depot was unmanned, and that is just what happened that night. The posters were not there at knocking-off time one night, but there at opening time the following morning.

We needed to be able to formulate some good estimates of his movements. We consulted the manufacturers of the various vans Black had driven and obtained estimates from them as to fuel consumption rates of the exact models Black was driving at the time. Officers were then supplied with models as close as possible to the actual ones Black drove, and then despatched from PDS's London premises to complete the journeys Black would have made on the three critical dates. This exercise allowed the team to speculate with some scientifically produced background information as to his likely movements.

We concluded from the pattern of stops that it was inconceivable for Black to have dropped the Morley posters off and driven somewhere else before returning to Morley. He must have remained about the town until the time of Sarah's abduction. Because of the time span involved in the refuelling and the poster drop we could not be sure of how long he was there. The overlap between the two was such that he might have filled up, dropped the posters and made an unplanned stop at the little corner shop when he spotted his victim walking past quite by chance. It could equally have been the case that he spent a little more time in Morley looking for a candidate.

We knew, from Black himself, that he usually slept in the van on overnight trips. We knew from other witnesses that sometimes he would park the van actually at the Morley depot to spend the night in its yard.

We discovered that after Leeds his next drop that trip was completed, in Lincoln, between 10 p.m. on the night Sarah was snatched, and 6 p.m. the following night. We also had him drawing petrol between 7 p.m. and 8 a.m. at Newport Pagnall in Buckinghamshire, off the M1 motorway. On this journey he would have passed the A453 road to Nottingham. It was a road he knew well and used often and is only a short distance to the River Soar, into which Sarah had been so callously thrown, possibly alive, that spring day.

As the missing person inquiry into Sarah began in Morley that night witnesses had spoken of a man with a beard who was seen sitting in a white Transit between 7.30 and 7.45, shortly before Sarah's abduction. It was parked right outside the Harpers' house. This driver was never traced despite repeated appeals for him to come forward.

Nor were we able to discover the identity of another man, the one seen in Cross Peel Street, Morley, that night. He was in his mid to late thirties and was wearing steel-rimmed spectacles. They could have been the same man. Our hunch was that they were separate sightings of Black. He had steel-rimmed spectacles in his possession when he was arrested and generally fitted the description of the two men. Morley is the sort of place where the locals recognise the people they pass on the street more often than not.

Again, there was nothing here to positively identify Black as the culprit. Coincidence was no longer an argument available in Black's defence. Here we had him potentially at the scenes of three abductions and subsequent murders. The officers working for me throughout the country were convinced he was the killer. So was I.

It was at this point that the attempted abduction of Teresa Ann Thornhill took on a special significance to the team and our enterprises. The circumstantial evidence uncovered to put Black near to the scene of her brush with death would, in my view, clinch the case. It brought the city of Nottingham into the investigation for a second time and settled things once and for all.

By the time of this attack, 24 April 1988, Black had changed vans again and was now driving a blue Ford Transit, registration

number D748 RAR. Between 7 a.m. and 10 p.m. the day before
that bungled snatch, Black filled up in London. For the next three
days we could trace him to deliveries round the Midlands and the
North-West; Birmingham, Wolverhampton, Stoke, Manchester
and Liverpool. The order of those deliveries was unclear.

Other stops, then on to Mills and Allen in Nottingham. The
drop there was made between 23 and 25 April. No one had been
there to countersign the receipt book between those dates. Our
timings of the journey, after we carried out the exercise using a
similar van, put Black there about 5 p.m. on 24 April. One hour
later a 15-year-old girl was undergoing a horrifying ordeal 500
yards away from the depot, in Gregory Boulevard, Nottingham.

More evidence was found on Black's return trip to that city
just a couple of days later. Through the agency cards we had him
buying petrol at a filling station in the city, very near to the
Gregory Boulevard, on 27 April. Studying the till receipts we
discovered that just three minutes after the transaction of Black's
petrol purchase a 22 pence newspaper sale is recorded. The local
evening paper is sold at that garage. The *Nottingham Evening Post*
was 22 pence and that night it included an article on the
attempted abduction of Teresa. It was a 'crimestoppers' piece, an
article highlighting the fact that a reward was available for
information leading to the arrest of the girl's attacker.

When we went through Black's bedsit after his arrest in the
Borders, we found a part copy of that very newspaper, the 27
April issue. Included with its fading pages was a paper towel and
some empty bags. Like everything else from the flat, they were
examined in great detail by the forensic scientists. The boffins
discovered traces of pubic hair on the bags, and the newsprint
itself gave a positive reaction to tests for semen.

It surely could not have been yet another coincidence that this
newspaper containing the article about Teresa was in Black's bedsit
two years later. I certainly could not believe it so. Remember his
admissions of fantasising and his behaviour whilst doing so.

Eight pairs of spectacles were taken from Black's flat. They
were all shown to Teresa. She said one of the pairs was like the

ones her attacker had been wearing that night. The pair she picked out showed signs of having been repaired. Were they damaged in the fall to the ground during that struggle in the Boulevard?

The front of the bonnet of Black's Transit was found to have had accident damage repaired. We could prove conclusively that on 24 April insurance records showed Black's van had been involved in an accident and had suffered damage to the front, just as Teresa had told us.

There was an additional substantial clue in this case. The attack had taken place beside a bank which had a security video filming outside the premises as well as inside. When we viewed the film, Teresa and her friend could be seen running away from what appeared to be the front end of a van. Only that first portion of the vehicle was seen but it was clearly a dark colour and shaped like a Transit.

I had long been of the opinion that after all the time which had elapsed between these events, there was little chance of one single piece of evidence being discovered to prove our case. However, the picture that was being assembled was better than many had thought possible. We were uncovering a pattern, a clear pattern of deadly activity that suggested a serial killer in the truest sense of the phrase. Black could be seen quite clearly at work in each of these cases. What were the chances of finding another human being who could have been in each of these places on five separate days over a period of eight years? Add to these facts what we had found in Black's van and bedsit. Remember his explanations for these things in his long interview with Andrew Watt and Roger Orr.

Each of the three bodies was found within a 21-mile radius of Ashby de la Zouche, right in the middle of that Midlands triangle where John Rayson lived. Over the years he had moved from Donisthorpe, but his new home in another village not far away at Melbourne, ten miles from Burton on Trent, was in the same general area.

The attack on Teresa Thornhill took place on the edge of the triangle. Black had told various people of the routes through this part of the country that he liked using and they all fitted in with the places where the bodies were disposed of.

After all this powerful evidence a close study was made of the incident he had admitted, involving the six-year-old in the Borders. If that was used as a case study of his method of operation again there was nothing to exclude him from the other incidents. Quite the reverse. The victims were roughly the same ages and appearance, the north-south route, the sexual interference of varying degree, the method of body disposal in the three murders. My conviction that we had the right man left me with an understandable sense of achievement and at the same time an equally comprehensible feeling of disappointment that the excitement of the challenge was almost over.

More importantly was the overriding hope that, once a trial was over, these three families would be able to begin a new chapter in their lives. Each had lost a lovely young girl and the agony of that loss was exacerbated by the years it took to track down the killer. They were three families who had my total sympathy, respect and admiration.

CHAPTER THIRTEEN

Is it Enough?

As our investigation into Black's background and movements progressed, I could only be encouraged as the overall picture continued to build up without a meaningful part of it being out of place. We were conducting detailed inquiries into events nearly a decade old and yet at no time did we uncover one single substantive piece of evidence or information that detracted from our case. Amazingly, everything seemed to fit. Senior officers and I were frankly astonished at the amount, quality and detail of evidence that was becoming available through our efforts.

As each day went by my convictions over Black increased. I was certain that he was a dangerous serial killer who could not help himself. It was equally certain that he was not going to admit his crimes. That course of action was the only one left in his power that, while it could never reverse his dreadful wrong-doings, could certainly have eased their consequences for the parents of three little girls.

It is hard to predict whether a person will confess after arrest. Black was no exception. If he was guilty of what we suspected, he must be a cold, calculating and fundamentally evil person.

Ending a parent's torment at his own expense would not be an appealing prospect. At the same time one can only ask what he hoped to gain. By maintaining his innocence while perfectly aware of his guilt he would, in the long run, make his own life more difficult.

I think he may have been frightened of being sent to Durham Jail. It has a tough reputation in the prison system. Going there on a guilty plea with only limited public release of the detail of his crimes would have been bad enough. Insisting on a long trial that would be painful for him and the parents because of the horrific nature of the evidence that was bound to come out was quite another matter.

He had little to lose. He was doing life anyway; early release was extremely unlikely. Going back into prison, but to a new jail, with a fresh lot of sickening details exposed about his activities would only, I would have thought, made life tougher in the hypocritical criminal pecking order behind bars that leaves child sex offenders at the bottom of the pile.

By the end of 1990 we had a powerful volume of evidence indicating his movements and our information generally put him in the place of each abduction, about the time it was taking place and in the general area of each of the body disposals at an incriminating time. I decided it was time to have another interview session with our suspect. This time, though, the questioning was to take a different tack.

When the Edinburgh interview was carried out our main desire was to gain an understanding of Black, the man. We wanted to discover as much as we could about his obviously troubled mind. He was interviewed under the separate rules of practice in Scotland and so, by the book, could then only be questioned about the offences committed under the Scottish jurisdiction.

The cross-border rules are one both police forces in which I worked found nothing short of a nuisance. The basis of the outdated and confusing mess is the 1707 Act of Union which joined the Scottish and English parliaments but enshrined the differences north of the border to protect Scots sensibilities. All very well. In reality, however, it creates a great many practical and legal problems. For example, if a man from the little fishing town of Eyemouth, just five miles over the border from England, were to fly to China and pick a person off the street at random, who happens to be a UK citizen, and murders him, he could be tried for the crime in Scotland. This is so even though it is an essentially Chinese crime, involving Chinese investigators and Chinese witnesses. If, however, our man in Eyemouth were to go shopping with his wife in Berwick, just south of the Scottish border, and, overcome with emotion, bludgeon her to death in that town's high street, he could not be tried in Scotland.

Our case was very different, however. It is in cases like ours where murders are committed by the same person in both Scotland and England that difficulties arise. These problems are held to be quite unnecessary by some observers. It had to be decided where Black was going to be prosecuted and on that decision rested problems of admissibility of the evidence and what charges could be preferred.

We had a mass of material pointing to Black. We did not have one single shred of evidence implicating him directly and conclusively. There was nothing to forensically connect him to any single offence in the catalogue of cases we had examined. But our case was, in my view, overwhelming when looked at as a whole, a view thankfully shared ultimately by the jury. However, it was clear to me and the team that we were going to have to paint a picture of Black, his movements and tendencies and allow the jury to make up its own mind. Our only almost direct evidence were the eye-witnesses who saw the scruffy man with Caroline Hogg, but that was not a lot to go into court with all those years later. Identification seemed doubtful.

The case, it was obvious, was going to have to show Black was in the general area of each of the abductions when they took place. He could have been in the exact area. He had done it before. This was why the seemingly relatively minor case involving Teresa Thornhill was to be so crucial to us. We had better evidence

169

of Black's direct involvement in that offence than any other. There was her relatively fresh recollection of the man who committed the attack. We had the van caught on the video. We had the damaged glasses recovered from his flat and we had the newspaper containing details of Teresa's ordeal showing up positive to semen tests. All this and Black's self-confessed predilection for pre-pubescent girls.

This would have all been very well if the offences had all taken place in either Scotland or England. We were dealing with a mixture and we could not even be sure where some of the events had taken place. Susan was abducted in England. Caroline was abducted in Scotland. But where, for instance, did they die? At the time of both abductions, Black would have been due to make further deliveries in Scotland. In fact, those deliveries did take place. So should he be charged with murdering these two little girls in Scotland or in England?

For now though, at the end of 1990, the need to resolve these particular matters was still some way off. It was time to speak to Black again. I picked a team of officers to carry out the interview. This time the plan was to ask him direct questions about the offences of which he was suspected. I chose the officers who had the most detailed knowledge of the crimes allegedly committed by Black in their force areas.

The decision was taken to question Black in England, under the English jurisdiction, because the majority of the offences would be English and the Crown Office in Edinburgh had given its blessing to pursue our prosecution in England. Arrangements were made to take Black from Peterhead Jail on Scotland's north-east coast, to Alnwick police station in Northumberland. It was chosen as the first in England with suitable facilities for our purposes. It also housed the court which covered the area in which Susan Maxwell, the first of our victims, had been abducted.

Black seemed to have become quite comfortable in Peterhead Jail and was not keen to leave it. It had the reputation for many years of being the toughest jail in the entire Scottish prison system. All the hardened gangsters and men of violence ended up in Peterhead, making its grey granite walls a most forbidding sight over the lovely little fishing port from which it takes its name. Strangely, perhaps, it was a place where Black had settled in well.

After a series of very violent riots at the jail in the 1980s, one so severe that it needed the SAS to end it, a rethink of its role was carried out. One of the halls in the jail was given over to housing sex offenders and other potential targets of kangaroo court 'jail justice'. This means that offenders whose crimes have caused widespread revulsion to the public can serve their sentence without the ever-present fear of retribution at the hands of other inmates. No doubt for these reasons, Black seemed reluctant to leave the safety and comfort of his prison cell. But he did and it was from here that he was driven the long distance south to Northumberland for questioning by my detectives in a session that would last three days.

This time he was not going to help us at all.

Black, in Edinburgh, had been questioned under the Criminal Justice (Scotland) Act 1981. He was detained and questioned under section two of that Act which allows witnesses and suspects to be held for up to six hours. At the end of this time a suspect might be released or charged. There is no right given to the interviewee to have a solicitor present. Now we were questioning him under the Police and Criminal Evidence Act 1984, with his solicitor in the interview room. The results were somewhat different.

In Edinburgh, Andrew and Roger had been able to build up a relationship of kinds with Black, and make him relatively forthcoming. He had spoken candidly of his fantasies and self-abuse, all very incriminating for a man in his position. Now, in Alnwick, with officers in possession of detailed evidence of his movements and a clear picture of his likely actions, we could get nowhere. With his solicitor present, each and every question, over the three days, was met with the same reply: 'No comment.'

Officers took it in turns, each approaching the interview in their own, and widely differing, styles, but always the answer was the same: 'No comment.' It was, of course, his fundamental right. It was also, as ever in these circumstances, deeply frustrating for me and my team.

It was clear that we were going to have to progress the case towards trial carefully, and in stages. The first stage had already been carried out. It was to make a report on the abduction of Caroline to the Procurator Fiscal, the Scottish way of dealing with crime. He is the local head of the independent Scots prosecution service working to the central body, the Crown Office. Roger and Andrew compiled that report for Duncan Lowe, the Regional Procurator Fiscal for Lothian and Borders at the time. He is a respected lawyer and now the head civil servant in the Crown Office, a position known as the Crown Agent.

Duncan was a man I knew well and had worked with for a good number of years. I knew the report would be expeditiously treated and an early decision made. It was equally clear that the evidence against Black, in the absence of a confession, was rather shaky on the one charge involved: that of abducting and murdering Caroline Hogg. I had little hope of a decision to prosecute from the Crown Office. In isolation, the case did not stand up. The Crown had even instructed me not to attempt to have Black identified by the Portobello witnesses either on an identification parade or by photographs. I wholeheartedly supported that instruction. The passage of time made the prospect of a positive identification unlikely anyway. A negative identification parade would only help Black.

Within six weeks the matter had been fully considered by Crown Counsel and a decision given. Duncan said they would not, at that stage, proceed against Black for reasons of insufficient evidence. However, he said the authorities would withdraw their previous objection to Black being shifted into the English jurisdiction for consideration there. I was further instructed to make a report to the head of the Crown Prosecution Service, the Director of Public Prosecutions on the other matters Black was suspected of.

That was the instruction I had been waiting for. It gave me

and my team a better opportunity to adduce evidence against Black for a whole range of offences rather than just one, and that opportunity would allow a prosecution based on the principles I have already outlined. It was the sort of practical decision one normally gets in Scotland. As perhaps an insurance, I was told to report back to the Procurator Fiscal if the Crown Prosecution Service in England decided not to go ahead, the implication being that a failure to proceed in England may lead them to at least have a go in Scotland.

Detailed arrangements were made to have the case prepared properly for consideration in England. I instructed how it was to be produced, in a standardised way and in a form that could be used in an English court. Senior officers throughout the UK were instructed to compile reports into the offences in their areas. Then other separate reports were drawn up highlighting different aspects of the case we were building.

There was a report which detailed Black's antecedents. His petrol receipts and wages records, an important part of the case for the clues they gave to his movements, were appended to that. There was also a detailed report on the incident in the Borders which was presented as a study and evidence of his admitted modus operandi. We had another report on the relatively small geographic area in which the bodies had been found in England. It was known to us as the Midlands triangle. It was critically important because of the relationship between the places where the three bodies were found and the addresses where Black's friend, John Rayson, lived in that area with his young family. Two addresses where, over the years, Black was a frequent visitor.

When the separate reports were put together they represented a powerful body of evidence pointing to a single conclusion. That was that Black, already convicted of the abduction of one little girl, had also abducted four other girls and killed three of them.

If normal processes had been followed Black would have been charged with offences as the documentation was finalised for submission. There was no need to do that in this case because

173

he was going nowhere for a long time. In addition, the CPS had instructed us not to bring charges but to report the whole circumstances to them.

As these reports were having the finishing touches put to them, new potential problems arose all the time. The Alnwick interview, evidentially useless, was conducted under the specific guideline of what is known throughout the service as PACE, the Police and Criminal Evidence Act 1984. The telling, detailed, comprehensive interview in Edinburgh was conducted under Scottish rules with a different caution administered to the suspect at the start. Would that interview be admissible in an English court?

Then there were the witness statements. The Scottish ones are taken by entirely different methods from those in England. In Scotland, it is normal for two police officers to visit witnesses, interview them, writing down verbatim the answers to questions, and then leave with an unsigned document. In England, the rules of the Criminal Justice Act 1969 require witness statements to be signed and endorsed as a true record and the date and name of the person taking the statement to be recorded. This meant that all the witnesses who had been interviewed under Scottish rules had now to be re-traced and re-interviewed, up to nine years after they were first seen.

I was equally conscious that there were many other legal difficulties that were going to have to be addressed in this case. The problems of jurisdiction are clear, on top of that there were problems of what is called evidence of similar fact and severance of the charges. These are mainly problems for lawyers, but I will come back to them.

We had ended up with a unique situation. Here was a Scottish police force reporting three abductions, three murders and other more minor associated offences, all committed in England, to the English prosecution service for likely disposal in an English court.

The various strands of this exercise came together in what is commonly referred to as a report to the DPP. A short enough phrase. Consider this though; that report was based on nine years' worth of evidence, extracted from interviews of 189,000 people, statement from over 60,000 witnesses and 56,000 separate actions or jobs completed by the police. The number of pages of statements on the computer topped one million; there was the same again in hard copy. It is hard to imagine a bigger inquiry anywhere in this country or, perhaps, even the world.

The weight of evidence was there. It was now, in my view, up to the lawyers. If everything went our way, there was as good a case as it was possible to build up. Some would call it overwhelming.

So, on 21 May 1991, Andrew Watt and Roger Orr delivered the report to the Crown Prosecution Service in London. They drove down to London from Edinburgh with a vast amount of paperwork secured in the boot of their unmarked police car. It was ten months since Black had been arrested in the Borders; the report represented ten months of exhaustive, exhausting and painstaking research by a team of hard-working detectives from both sides of the border.

I realised that it would be some time before a decision could be taken on whether or not to start new proceedings against Black. There were the complicated legal issues to be sorted out. I resolved to be patient and concentrate on everyday matters. As the weeks went by, though, I began to become increasingly concerned at the time it was all taking. It seemed to me that, complicated though some of the issues were, they were not so insurmountable as to warrant such a long and unexplained delay.

One of the newer problems to present itself was disclosure of evidence to the defence. This comes into play only after charges are made. In Black's case, at this stage, there were no charges yet and so disclosure should not have caused a delay.

Months passed by and annoyance on my behalf, and that of many officers in the various teams, began to turn to desperation. We had acted quickly, putting in great efforts to bring these distressing matters to as speedy a conclusion as possible. Now we were encountering what seemed to be an unconscionable delay. My own officers were asking questions. More importantly, the parents of the three dead girls were becoming increasingly concerned as the uncertainty dragged on. For them a trial, and all the new detail of the full horror of their children's suffering, would be an ordeal that would need considerable preparation for. How could they prepare if they were not certain that there ever would be a trial?

Sarah's mother Jackie Harper went public and told a Yorkshire newspaper: 'I want to look forward to the day the trial is over and I can put all this behind me. At the moment it is an open wound.' Former Home Secretary Merlyn Rees, the MP for Sarah's home town, Morley and Leeds South, pledged to raise the issue with the Attorney General. In Edinburgh and Berwick, the parents of Caroline and Susan maintained a dignified public silence; in private they expressed to me exactly the same feelings as Mrs Harper.

I adopted a similar attitude, publicly.

By February 1992, fully nine months after the receipt of the report, there were indications that a decision was near. On 10 March the CPS, with my knowledge, took out summonses against Black at Newcastle Magistrates Court. The allegations had been framed in such a way as to exclude offences which may have been committed in Scotland. The aim, obviously, was to preclude some of the charges being dismissed at a later date because of jurisdictional problems. They were as follows:

1. The abduction of Susan Claire Maxwell in July 1982.
2. Murder of Susan Claire Maxwell.
3. Obstructing the coroner by concealing the body of Susan Claire Maxwell.
4. Unlawful imprisonment of Caroline Hogg in July 1983.
5. Murder of Caroline Hogg.
6. Obstructing the coroner by concealing the body of Caroline Hogg.
7. Abduction of Sarah Jayne Harper in March 1986.
8. Murder of Sarah Jayne Harper.

9. Obstructing the coroner by concealing the body of Sarah Jayne Harper.
10. Attempted abduction of Teresa Ann Thornhill in April 1988.

The summonses concerned offences which had a degree of probability to have happened in England. He was not charged with Caroline Hogg's abduction. That was clearly a totally Scottish matter.

However, because of the forensic and evidential problems there could be little certainty over where the first two girls died. On both occasions Black had Scottish deliveries to make after the abductions. In the case of Susan Maxwell, Black was heading north when he snatched her off the A697 road. He had to go on to Edinburgh, Dundee and Glasgow. If he used the same technique that he was later to employ in the Borders, then Susan would have died fairly quickly. We and the DPP worked on the basis that she died in England. Certainly in the Borders incident, he had said that he planned to take his little victim to Blackpool where he could spend some time with her. It was unlikely that he would have wanted to spend time with a dead child. The same view could have been taken of Susan and Caroline, though I hope that I am wrong.

As a father and a grandfather, it horrifies me to think of first Susan and Caroline and later Sarah, trapped in that smelly van, alone and terrified, at the mercy of a man who clearly had no thought for his victims.

Throughout the long inquiry into Black, I had promised senior members of the Scottish press to keep them informed of the progress of our efforts, particularly undertaking to inform them when summonses were going to be issued or charges preferred. When that time came the promise was broken, not through any fault of mine it must be said. I was aware a decision was imminent. I had been told to expect a call from the DPP's office late in the afternoon or early in the evening. It had not come by the time I had left my office for the day, so I expected a call at home. That evening my meal was a hurried affair. It was virtually certain I would have to return to headquarters in Edinburgh to make the announcement many had been expecting. The national BBC television news programme was on in the background. I was stunned as the newscaster reported a late item: a man was to be charged in connection with the murders of three schoolgirls in the 1980s. Thank goodness I had warned the parents.

Then came the call I was expecting from the DPP's office. I pointed out to my caller that his information was not news to me or anyone else who was watching the television.

A flood of calls came into headquarters. The force information officer, Chief Inspector Bryan Lowrie, phoned round the major news outlets in the area to tell them a news conference was to be held that evening. Just after seven o'clock that night, I faced a battery of cameras and microphones.

At a time I should have felt delight and satisfaction at this important stage in the inquiry my emotion was one of some sadness. I do not like breaking promises. The press throughout this difficult hunt had been good to the police, providing enormous help when we needed it. I was deflated to have let them down. I told them so.

The summonses were received by me on 20 March 1991, and twelve days later I despatched Andrew Watt and Roger Orr to serve them on Black in Peterhead Jail.

At this point, Black said something that, for me, was one of the most incriminating things to come out of his mouth. Like so many instances with criminals of all sorts, it is the slight phrase, the odd sentence spoken off-guard that says more than a hundred replies, well rehearsed beforehand no doubt, in a formal police interview. The two detectives had met Black in one of the jail interview rooms normally used by lawyers meeting their clients. Andrew explained briefly why they were there and handed the papers over to Black. He showed little surprise or emotion. Hardly unusual, he could not have missed the press reports. As Andrew and Roger turned to leave the room Black said: 'Tell Pamela she's not responsible for all this.' The two officers turned back and Andrew asked him to explain what he meant, but once more Black fell silent.

Those eight words, to me, were confirmation, if it was needed, of Black's guilt. He had spoken them for one of two reasons. He either let slip his real feelings in an unguarded moment or he was being clever with us. He may well have spoken of his former girlfriend at this moment as some sort of mitigation. Now he realised the chips were down and he was more than suspected of carrying out these hideous crimes, he may have been planting little thoughts for the future. He may have been trying to let those present think that he was a perfectly normal sort of person driven to these dreadful deeds by the rejection of the woman he loved. Whichever of these, or perhaps other, reasons it was, they were not the words of an innocent man.

The case against Black was first listed for Newcastle Magistrates Court in July 1992. Black was not required to appear. The procedure was a little different from normal because Black was already a convicted prisoner and so bail hearings were unnecessary. The case was adjourned, and then over a period of months to come, adjourned and adjourned again and again.

By this stage, both prosecution and defence had engaged legal teams to work on this complicated and large case. The prosecution was led by a well-known Tyneside QC, John Milford, who had prosecuted a great deal of the major crime in the North-East over the years. His juniors were Toby Hedworth and Roger Cooper.

One of the characters of the Edinburgh Bar, Herbert Kerrigan QC, led for the defence at this stage. Bert Kerrigan is one of the few members of counsel with what is known as dual call, that is to say he has right of audience in the higher Scottish and English courts.

The fact that the case of Regina v Black went into another series of delays is to a large extent understandable. In England, but not Scotland, the Crown is required to enter into advance disclosure of evidence. That is to say they are to reveal to the defence the entire make-up of the prosecution case and hand over

179

all witness statements and exhibits for examination. This has to be done before committal for trial to the Crown Court.

The principle caused us no real problems despite the amount of paper that was involved. The part of the disclosure that delayed us further was that of the material that had been gathered in the investigation but not used by the prosecution as part of its case.

The delays were rather longer than I was prepared to accept as necessary. During ten years of country-wide inquiries, a huge mass of paperwork had been accumulated at incident rooms in six locations, plus the child murder bureau in Bradford, and then there was more. The Staffordshire database for the Susan Maxwell inquiry alone weighed seven and a half tons. All this had to be made available to the defence for examination if they wanted. Ninety per cent of it would never even be looked at but we had to find one central place where this, and a whole lot more material, could be stored safely and computer links to our databases established.

This long established principle was first laid down in the Attorney General's guidelines in 1981 and updated in 1992 after two celebrated cases. Disclosure of evidence had been central to the successful appeal of Judith Ward, who was found to be wrongly jailed for the M62 IRA army bus bombing, and in the infamous Guinness case involving Ernest Saunders and others.

I had office space sought out and ended up commissioning purpose-built office accommodation in the centre of Newcastle near both the committal court and the eventual venue for the trial, Newcastle Crown Court. It took two whole floors of the building to house all the evidence we had. It seemed, to an extent, a bit of a waste of time and money to shift mountains of irrelevant paperwork round the country, but if the prosecution of Black were to fail I was determined it would not be on a technical reason like non-disclosure of information. There was nothing anywhere in that office that we really minded the defence lawyers having a look at. If they wanted it then they got most of it.

IS IT ENOUGH?

There were, and must remain, certain matters that could not be disclosed to the defence team, or anyone else for that matter. Public interest immunity certificates were applied to these matters with the consent of both prosecution and defence. Only a handful of papers were not disclosed.

This latest incident room in the case had to be staffed and officers from the forces involved were seconded to help. The lead was taken by my own Edinburgh team who, with the others, spent many months working with prosecution and defence lawyers helping them find their way round the maze of filing cabinets, computer programmes and card indexes.

By this time, Andrew Watt had moved on to a new job at the Scottish Office, so the onerous job of overseeing this operation fell to Roger Orr.

The accommodation had been arranged at my request; the considerable cost of it was shared between the force from which I am now retired, four other police forces and Northumbria. Their new Chief Constable, John Stevens, was very helpful to our operation at this stage and earned my gratitude. John acquired national prominence when he took over the 'shoot to kill' investigation in Northern Ireland. It was good to see Northumbria in the hands of such a capable Chief Constable following Stanley Bailey's retirement.

By July 1992, after that first call in Newcastle Magistrates Court, my patience with the legal process was wearing very thin. I wrote to the new Director of Public Prosecutions, Barbara Mills QC, to express my deep concern at the apparent lack of progress in the case. She responded immediately and though events moved on, they still were not travelling fast enough for my liking.

Court hearings came and went with the case being adjourned on the nod time and time again. It was not a helpful position for anyone. It certainly was not satisfactory for the parents.

The problems that seemed to be being anticipated by the legal teams were threefold. There was jurisdiction, which I have already mentioned. Then two legal principles; evidence of similar fact and the issue of severance.

On jurisdiction, the prosecution worked on the basis that Caroline and Susan had probably been killed in England. Caroline's unlawful imprisonment would only come into being the second Black's van passed over the Scottish border back into England. The evidence of similar fact is an English legal principle. If a number of offences bear a striking similarity it is permissible to invite the jury to consider that they were all committed by the same person. So if there is evidence to show that he committed one of the offences the jury is permitted to conclude that he committed the others as well. There is actually a leading case involving this principle called R v Mansfield in 1977.

On this principle it followed that it was possible for the Crown to lead evidence to connect Black with each individual occurrence. The idea would be to show he was potentially at each of the crime scenes and the totality of this evidence would be relied on to show he was the killer. The coincidences would be shown to the jury to be so numerous that they could no longer be regarded as such.

The similarities in our case were obvious. In the whole of the United Kingdom there were only three cases of young female children being snatched from public places and transported long distances from north to south and murdered. They were Susan, Caroline and Sarah. This was just like the incident in the Borders – the little girl taken from the street. Black's stated intention had been to take her to Blackpool 'to spend some time with her'. He did not say what he was going to do with her and how he planned to eventually dispose of her. Susan's pants had been removed, Caroline was naked and Sarah had been the victim of a serious sexual assault. All the girls had their shoes removed. The first thing Black had done after the Borders abduction was to take the six-year-old's shoes off and indecently assault her. The similarities were startling.

The third element of the problem lay in the severance of the charges. It is open to the defence to apply to have each and every charge heard separately. If that application had been successful, it might have had a devastating effect on the case.

IS IT ENOUGH?

Putting it simply, the whole prosecution had been structured to show that Black could have done it and was actually caught doing it. The basis of our case lay in the detailed study of Black's movements, activities and whereabouts at the times of the five abductions. In the absence of evidence directly connecting Black to an individual offence we had to go for the serial approach.

Although there were these problems, they were not, in my view, insurmountable. These matters ought not to have taken the time to resolve that they in fact did. Indeed, there is a strong argument to say that they should not have had more than just perfunctory consideration before the commencement of the trial. There seemed to be a reluctance on behalf of the defence team to allow the case to progress as quickly as it might have done.

For the defence to seek to argue before the commencement of the trial, at preliminary hearings, that these matters needed to be resolved was acceptable, but another solution could have been to get a prosecution off the ground earlier. It could have been left to the trial judge to deal with these matters on defence applications in the absence of the jury once the case was underway. But the delays dragged on.

CHAPTER FOURTEEN

Method, Motive and Opportunity

After many months of furious activity on behalf of myself and the rest of the team we suddenly hit a long quiet spell. Most of our work had been done. We had produced the best case we could and I was satisfied our efforts would produce the result we all wanted to see. It was now up to the lawyers to sort out what steps were to be taken and the direction in which it was going to be best to proceed.

During this extended lull in activity the case was never far away from my mind. It would be impossible for me, certain as I was of Black's guilt in these terrible crimes, to begin to put these matters behind me until justice was done. I often found myself reflecting privately, and in conversation with other senior officers, on the many facets to the case and its main characters.

Murder, and murderers, are often regarded by the public in the same general sort of way. It is the most vile of crimes, there is no doubt about that. The murder of a child is always more difficult for the detectives involved for the obvious emotional reasons, not the least of which is the fact that a child murder can certainly never be justified let alone understood. Generally, however, murder is not always the most difficult of crimes to solve. In the vast majority of homicides there is a clear association between the killer and the victim. It may not always be an obvious one but in most cases it is there if you look hard enough.

Motive is the most powerful of the three elements which usually make up a murder. Then comes means and finally opportunity. It is these ingredients which, when sifted, give the detective the opportunity to solve the crime. The murders which are most difficult to solve are those where no link exists between the characters in the drama. A truly random killing can often go unsolved. When there is motive, the chances of a successful outcome to the case are greatly improved.

So when a murder is discovered finding out exactly who had the motive to carry out the crime is often the key to it. It may never be certain in this case if Robert Black meant to kill his little victims. I am convinced he did. But the fact of the matter is that his motive was paedophilia and he was totally reckless as to whether or not his prey lived.

The fact that the three girls were chosen at random demonstrates the theory well. The investigations into the three murders carried out by him were amongst the most extensive ever conducted in this country. Yet the reality of the matter is that at the end of this mammoth effort involving hundreds of officers over eight years we had failed.

Black's downfall came when his motive, his lust for young children, forced him to strike again. Had he not been seen by an alert member of the public he would in all probability still be at large. The truth of it is simply that at the end of those three major inquiries we were no nearer catching him than we had been on day one.

In 39 years in the police service, the majority of them as a detective and 21 above the rank of Chief Inspector, I have had some experience of murder inquiries. Now retired, I am happy to say that, in each and every one of the cases I dealt with, the culprit was identified and, save in one case, dealt with appropriately. One of the cases ended in a not guilty verdict, but I have good reason to blame the jury for this rather than the investigation – not sour grapes, merely a fact of life.

Before I was actually in charge of murder hunts I worked on many as a junior detective. These experiences were all interesting for it is during one's junior years that reputations, experience and credibility are achieved. You listen and learn about the structure and techniques of inquiries and acquire from more experienced officers the knowledge and best practice that any good detective needs.

One of the most horrific investigations I ran was the hunt for the man who quite literally slaughtered a mother and her two young children, and then set fire to the house to try to cover his tracks. This was a classic case in as much as the basic ingredients of murder were all there: motive, means and opportunity. We were able to find the motive quite quickly and so the path ahead to our goal could be plotted appropriately.

The case caused an undoubted sensation in Alnwick, the market town of north Northumberland just a few miles north of my home village, Felton. The killing of Eileen Lynn Gibson and her children, Andrew, who was three and a half, and baby Sally, just six months old, shocked the entire north of England. Mrs Gibson and her husband David lived with the two children in a quiet residential street of Alnwick called Clifton Terrace.

I was head of CID for Northumbria on the January Thursday in 1979 that I was called north from Newcastle to the town where I had spent so much of my youth. The sight that greeted me was devastating. There was still a choking smell of smoke as I walked into the charred house. The fire had never really caught hold but everything inside had been blackened.

The baby's body was in the porch. She had been stabbed. Lynn's body lay in the passageway towards the rear of the house. She had died from multiple stab wounds and her throat was cut. Beneath her chin there was a gaping wound where once her neck had been. Andrew had also been brutally stabbed.

Alnwick is the sort of place where neighbours notice what is going on, not out of interference but kindly concern. That everyone knows everyone else was underlined by the fact that, in common with most people in these parts, Lynn had left her house front and rear doors open.

The milk had been delivered to the front doorstep at eight. An hour earlier David Gibson had kissed goodbye to his wife and left for work. Over the next few hours there had been various sightings of the mother and her children. The little boy waved to a neighbour, another passer-by waved at Lynn as she held the infant in the window. That was the last time they were seen alive.

There was a heavy covering of snow on the ground that day. At lunchtime a neighbour noticed footprints in the fresh fallen flakes leading up to the front door of the Gibsons' house. The prints appeared to be leading right into the house and out again. There was a little red stain on the right heel of each of them. The neighbour recalled smelling smoke but did not do anything about it. A short time later a nine-year-old girl knocked at the front door. Her intention was to ask if she could be allowed to play with Andrew. There was no reply to the girl's knock. The youngster looked through the letter-box.

As she bent down to look her nose was hit by a strong smell of smoke. Even at nine she knew something was wrong and the girl ran off to tell her grandparents, who lived nearby. The elderly couple sped round. They walked into the house through the unlocked front door and were shaken to a standstill by the pathetic sight of the butchered baby just inside the hall.

The fire brigade and police arrived almost simultaneously. The fire seemed to have been started deliberately in the kitchen of the terraced house and had almost burnt itself out.

The people of Alnwick were shocked as news of the tragedy spread around the town. Lynn and David Gibson came from two well-known Alnwick families. Many in the town were related to the couple; the majority of people in Alnwick would either know them personally, or know a member of their immediate families.

I arrived at the scene accompanied by an old friend and colleague, Cecil Hall. He was one of Northumbria's most experienced detectives. We had worked on many murders together before, none as gruesome as this though. Cec and I were founder members of the Northern Regional Crime Squad set up throughout the country, including Tyneside, in 1965 to tackle major crime.

Cecil was what you could call a crafty investigator. He had a wealth of experience that served him well. Even greater, though, was his network of contacts which was one of the most extensive I have ever come across, and which supplied him with a mass of information concerning crimes ranging from the minor to the real headline grabbers. They were unlikely to help in this case, however, and I preferred to rely on Cec's other qualities to help in cracking this one. We went to Clifton Terrace together. The bodies had not been removed by the time we got there and both of us were clearly affected by what we saw.

Lynn Gibson's mother and father, Eileen and Cecil Turnbull, had been shattered, naturally enough. They had lost a daughter and two grandchildren just days after the joy of the festive season. Cecil Hall and I went round to the house to speak to Mr and Mrs Turnbull. We, of course, needed to get as much information from them as possible, as quickly as we could.

I broke the habit of a professional lifetime when I met that couple. I told them we would find who had done this to their family and bring them to book. It was a pledge that I meant from the bottom of my heart and one I was certain I could deliver. These Alnwick people were my people. This was really my town. I grew up amongst them and already I was sure the answer to our search would be found in the town itself. If this was correct it would make our job a lot easier.

In tears, this elderly couple told me they could not think of anyone who would want to harm their daughter and her children. They could think of no reason for what had happened. But harmed they had been, and it was no accident. This mother and her little children had been savagely and deliberately butchered.

The red stains, of course, turned out to be blood. Officers who had been at the scene for some time longer than myself had already gleaned pieces of information that would render this case into the category of those not difficult to solve. The staggering aspect to these particularly savage killings was the motive. Any man who can kill a mother and her infant children must be driven by a strong emotion or wild insanity. In the Alnwick case it was the former and that emotion was fuelled by a desire for revenge.

The investigation was at an embryonic stage and nothing at this point was certain. Sadly for David Gibson, in the absence of clear motive on behalf of anyone else we had to work on the possibility that the person with the greatest motive to kill these three people would be the person closest to them. So David spent the first night of his bereavement in Alnwick police station being questioned with sympathy, but firmness. On the balance of probability, taking into account past experience if nothing else, the husband or father in a case like this must be high up the suspect list. A police officer who knew the families was detailed to look after David during the night. This officer, a woman, lives in Alnwick to this day.

It was soon established that David Gibson was not and could not have been the killer but, sadly, he was unwittingly the motive for the attack.

David worked as a bricklayer for a local building company and he was by all accounts a good one. His labourer was a 33-year-old local man called Terence Emery. They had worked together on many projects and at the time of the killings were on a job at RAF Boulmer, on the Northumberland coast. This is the base for the Sea King search and rescue helicopters that cover the north of England and southern Scotland. Six days before the killings, on the day before Twelfth Night in fact, a workmate saw Emery acting suspiciously in the officers' mess of the station.

The colleague told David who later got a chance to look into Emery's lunchbox, universally known as a 'bait box' in this part of the country. There he found two pieces of frozen meat. It was exactly the same weight, 5 lbs, 3 oz, as a piece of fillet steak missing from the mess freezer.

Subsequently, Emery was challenged by colleagues but he denied all knowledge of the incriminating evidence in his box. An RAF policeman was called; he referred the matter to civilian officers in Alnwick. Emery still denied the theft and was suspended from his work while the matter was investigated. The labourer may well have thought that David Gibson would be a witness at any future trial; he may even have suspected Gibson of 'grassing' on him.

Officers obtained a search warrant and went to Emery's flat in Alnwick. In a wardrobe they found some bars of soap, some scouring powder and some spanners, all of which were identified as having been stolen from the RAF base. Emery confessed to these matters, saying, 'I nicked them from the stores, I think.' He was bailed and, we were told, spent the next few days brooding over his arrest and suspension from work. On 9 January Emery was sacked.

Two days later he took a dreadful revenge on the man his troubled mind had worked out to be the architect of his downfall. It was an outrageous and brutal crime.

Investigation into his background showed Emery to be an unfortunate and unhappy man. His mother left home when he was just three and a half and he never saw her again. When he was six or seven his brother and he were taken into care, and not long after that he developed epilepsy. He was moved around various homes, finally ending up in one at Alnwick. After being released from care in the early 1960s, he went to live in lodgings in Alnwick. His epilepsy continued. He showed no emotion at all when his only brother died tragically early in life. He ran up a couple of minor convictions for dishonesty and assault.

All in all, Emery could only be described as a loner, a misfit who was very deep and insular with a tendency towards violence. It seemed that this was our man, it appeared revenge was his motive. Inquiries revealed that he had been seen in a local shop on the day of the killings wearing clothes that, according to witnesses, may have been bloodstained. Between ten in the morning of the killings and noon we could find no trace of his movements around the town. Before and after that two hours he was well documented, seen by many who knew him well or by sight at least.

We needed more evidence than that though. He was brought to the police station in Alnwick and, like Robert Black was to do in that very building years later, maintained total innocence of the crimes.

As he was examined, officers noticed two small cuts, crescent-shaped, on the back of his left hand. From the post mortem examinations we knew that Lynn had fought hard to protect her children. I remember quite clearly what Emery had to say about those little wounds that might mean so much. 'I did them at home last night on the door. It was tight with the wet and I caught my hand trying to close it.'

To test his alibi forensic experts examined the door. It was not tight at all but opened and closed perfectly normally. What was more, try as they might they could find no trace of blood whatsoever, anywhere on or about that door. In addition, there was nothing about the door that could have caused those distinctively shaped cuts.

We carefully examined all of his possessions and clothes. Emery's Timex watch, which he was wearing when arrested, had a link missing from its metallic strap and there were small spots of blood on the remaining ones. It was of the same group as Emery himself and the two dead children. There was not enough to sub-group the samples, that is to say narrow down the number of people likely to be of that blood type in a random sample.

These days you can be absolutely sure. Then, you could only say which group the blood was from and what percentage of the UK population shared that grouping. It was not possible to totally rely on evidence like this in court. Only when blood was from one of the rare groups was it possible to say what the chances were that it came from one specific person. Even then it was down to chance and not certainty. Now, with DNA techniques, tiny samples of blood and body fluids can give you the powerful evidence needed to convict. DNA profiling is like fingerprints – no two are the same – and if your dabs are there then you must have been there before them.

Emery was quite happy to talk about other matters. He told us he was renovating a house for his current landlady. There were four keys for it, he had two of them and two friends who were to carry out a bit of work on the house had the others. They had not been in it at the time we were talking in that interview room.

Jim Anderson, an excellent, experienced detective who was my deputy as head of CID and a good friend, went round straight away with other officers. The house was in the process of being worked on, just as Emery had said. Dust was everywhere and the entire inside of the house appeared to be covered with a film of builders' stoor, as it's called in these parts. Not quite everything was covered though. There was a pair of wellington boots in the corner, one pushed into the other. They had not been there long, quite obviously, and Jim saw there was blood on the legs.

Next we embarked on a search of the house where the killings had taken place. It was to be a completely thorough exercise, the sort of operation that would turn up hair fragments in the carpets if there were any to be found. It was expected to take days. However, that day, 13 January, was to be a lucky one for us. Two detectives found a small gold object lying in the passageway close to where Lynn's body had been found. It was the missing link from Emery's watch strap.

Blood samples from clothes Emery had taken to the cleaners were found to be incriminating, despite the fact the garments had been through the cleaning process, and that missing link turned out to be rock solid evidence. When the scientists looked at it under the microscope along with the rest of the watch they found a scratch on the body of the timepiece, continuing on to the strap, and the link we found at 3 Clifton Terrace fitted in, scratch and all, perfectly.

The wellingtons revealed blood from Group A with six sub-groups the same as Lynn's. Two hairs of the same colour as hers, and the same size, were embedded in the blood. Her blood was also found on the front door of the house Emery had been working on.

We were there. We even concluded that he had killed the three people with a pair of scissors that were found at the seat of the fire in the kitchen. Despite this overwhelming evidence Emery still maintained his innocence. He did so as well at his trial when it was held before a High Court judge at the Moot Hall in Newcastle. The jury did not believe him any more than I did. He was sentenced to three terms of life imprisonment, one for each of the murder charges, and seven years for arson. The judge recommended to the Home Secretary that Emery should not be considered for release for at least 18 years. The charge of stealing the fillet steak, the one that had begun this whole tragic episode, was allowed to lie on the file with an order it could not be proceeded with without a court order.

The last I heard of him Emery was in jail in Bristol with still a fair time of his sentence to run. David Gibson has not remarried. I take comfort from the fact that he was gracious enough, after that first night in Alnwick police station that must have been so terrible for him, to acknowledge that we had been correct in our actions and he felt no bitterness towards us.

Lynn's dad Cecil died, some say it was from a broken heart; her mum Eileen still stays in a lovely house in the south-west part of the town. I try to call on her when I visit Alnwick, and we have often talked about her daughter and lovely grandchildren over a cup of tea. We have sat looking through family photographs, and though tears are never far away Eileen has a knowing smile as she remembers them and recalls the pleasure they gave her, and she them. We share our thoughts. She is a fine lady.

Those Alnwick killings may have been hard to understand; how could a man be so worked up on such a relatively minor matter to kill three people – two young children and their mother wiped out for five pounds and three ounces of fillet steak? An earlier murder case of mine was in many ways even more chilling. It concerned the murder of a twelve-year-old boy. To call this crime murder is somewhat to underestimate it. What I found myself dealing with, again during the festive season, was a case of cold-blooded execution.

It was the Saturday before Christmas 1980. My son Andrew and I were in the stand at St James' Park in Newcastle watching the Magpies beating some team or other. My bleeper was, as usual, in my pocket, so it was a little surprising for the request to 'ring in' to come over the football ground's public address system. I was told by the duty officer at force headquarters that the body of a twelve-year-old boy had been found. He had apparently been shot. The scene was on some open ground just outside the Northumberland coastal village of Newbiggin by the Sea.

The body had been found by a local couple out for a walk. They were crossing the Spittal Burn, a small stream, by way of a plank bridge. As they walked across it, one of them had noticed a pair of green wellington boots lying by the side of the water. One was on top of the other.

At the time, a major police search was underway for a twelve-year-old boy, Paul Hedley, who'd gone missing a few days before. It had been a difficult case for the local officers. There was no history of Paul running away, but equally no suggestion that some mishap had befallen him.

The discovery of those wellingtons led officers to flood the area to see if there were any further signs. A short time later an underwater search team had found the lad's body in the burn, which was badly swollen by recent heavy rain, about one hundred yards downstream from that plank bridge. It was at this point that I had been called away from the football match.

By the time I arrived at Newbiggin it was dark. Detective Chief Inspector John Hollows was in charge of what had turned into a murder hunt. John, now sadly deceased, was a fine man and a good detective. He quite rightly had left the body in situ in the stream until my arrival. I examined the scene carefully before giving orders for the body to be pulled out of the fast-flowing water.

The fact that young Paul had been shot was obvious. It was equally clear from the gaping wound in his back that the weapon used had been a shotgun. This observation was confirmed by the pathologist as he examined the body by the light of torches that chilly December night. It was more like a Mafia execution than something you would expect to find in a quiet Northumbrian village. Apart from the savage wound below his shoulder the body had been weighed down with pieces of concrete tied to its arms and legs.

Later, at post mortem examination, the pathologist concluded that the shot had entered the boy's body about 40 inches from the ground, and the weapon had been level when fired. The shot had shattered the base of Paul Hedley's spine.

As usual, the first task for the investigators was to try and establish the victim's last movements and then begin to build up a picture of what sort of youngster he was. We had to see if there was anything in his lifestyle that could throw up clues as to who would want to kill him, let alone kill him in such a cold-blooded way.

He lived in a council house on a small estate in the village, with his parents and brother, Anthony. Newbiggin is one of the coastal mining villages in Britain. Those few that exist are found along the shores of Northumberland and Durham. It's quite an attractive place with a pleasant, long beach and had been a frequent destination for the young Hector Clark many years before, on his bike, cycling out for the day from nearby Felton.

Already police had been told that the previous Monday evening Paul had been at home with his family when a friend came to call. It's not his real name, but I'll call him Tom. Tom was older than Paul, 15 to be exact. They left the house together, brother Anthony remained behind. Later, when the youngster didn't show up at the appointed time, his parents began to worry and eventually called the police. Tom, needless to say, was asked what had happened to Paul and he gave officers a story that bore out close examination saying how he'd left Paul, who had then gone to visit an uncle.

There had been mention of Tom's friend, Raymond Scobie, who at 16 was a year older, and had also been questioned in the hours after Paul's disappearance. The search for the missing teenager had been concentrated on the coastal area, because Paul was a keen fisherman. But it had been to no avail; as we were eventually to discover, he was already dead.

Scobie was the legitimate owner of a single-barrelled shotgun. His father had given him a Russian-made Baikal 12-bore weapon, and he had a shotgun certificate for it. Suspiciously, Scobie told us the gun had gone missing and he didn't know where it was.

We decided to question the pair. Scobie was taken into one police station and Tom to another, nearby. The latter immediately admitted the part that he had played in the death of Paul. John Hollows and myself, along with Detective Sergeant Ken Anderson, were visibly shocked as the boy recounted the tale of what had gone on, and why.

He agreed to take the three of us to the spot where the unfortunate Paul Hedley had been shot, and then show us where the murder weapon had been hidden afterwards. We were led to the place where that plank crossed the burn, and Tom told us that was exactly where the killing had been done. He then walked downstream a little and said if we looked under the water at a place he indicated the gun would be found. Divers waded into the stream and, as forecast, came up with a black-coloured gun case containing the Baikal shotgun. The gun was broken open and a spent cartridge was still in its chamber.

Back at the police station, in the presence of his father, Tom recounted the whole shocking tale. He outlined what can only be described as a cold-blooded murder that had been carefully planned, the groundwork for establishing an alibi having been carried out and then the killing executed.

But why?

It turned out that Scobie, rightly or wrongly, believed that Paul Hedley was entering his house illegally and stealing small amounts of cash and airgun pellets. He had decided that the twelve-year-old had to be stopped, and he was going to do it his way.

Tom told how he and Scobie had met the day before on the beach just across from the village. Scobie had told of his plan and recruited Tom as his executioner's assistant. They went up to local allotments for some rope and walked back to the Spittal Burn. There they found some good lumps of concrete and tied the lengths of rope on to some of the bigger pieces in preparation for weighing the body down the next day. Tom told us that, by this point in proceedings, he was very frightened but went along with the plot anyway.

The next task Tom had been allocated was to collect Paul Hedley from his home the following night. Tom went round to the Hedley household and he and Paul walked down towards the burn. They then met up with Scobie, who was carrying the gun. As the three of them strolled along the Spittal Burn, Scobie fired a couple of shots into an oil drum, said Tom. A third was fired at a bird, the fourth at the twelve-year-old suspected of stealing airgun pellets. Paul Hedley fell to the ground just past the little improvised bridge.

The teenagers then dumped the gun, returned to the body and dragged it to a nearby tree where the weights had been concealed the day before. With the heavy lumps of concrete tied on, Paul Hedley's body was pushed into the water. But it wouldn't sink. Tom told us how they desperately grabbed hold of a log and pushed as hard as they could on the body until eventually it went out into the middle of the stream and disappeared from view. Then they quickly caught a bus to a leisure centre in the town of Ashington three miles away to establish an alibi for the time of the killing.

I and the other two detectives in that interview room were quite horrified at what we had just heard. It seemed unbelievable that two teenagers would go to such dastardly lengths merely to punish someone for petty theft.

We travelled to the police office where Scobie was being held, wondering, no doubt, what fanciful tale he would have concocted in the time he was waiting for his turn to be interviewed. But no. Scobie just sat down, again in the presence of his father, and repeated the same horrific story that Tom had just told us.

Scobie did say, by way of mitigation perhaps, that he just meant to fire at Paul, meaning near to him, not actually at him. However, he showed no remorse for what he had done and only little regret. Tom showed some sorrow for his actions.

Both were charged with murder.

By the time the case got to the Crown Court in Newcastle for disposal, the pair had decided to plead not guilty, Scobie on the grounds that he did not mean to hit Paul, Tom on the grounds that he was acting under Scobie's coercion. The jury were happy with Tom's story, and he was duly acquitted of murder. They did not believe Scobie and he was convicted.

The judge ordered Scobie to be detained during Her Majesty's pleasure; because of his age he could not be sentenced to life imprisonment. He was held in various juvenile institutions before reaching the age of 21 when he could go to an adult jail. He was, when I last heard of him, in prison in Lincolnshire.

Tom went on to live a fairly normal life, or at least as normal as it could be with these dreadful events behind him. I do not see why I should add to those traumas that he must still suffer by revealing his whereabouts now.

The Paul Hedley case sticks out as a classic example of gratuitous violence, a killing carefully planned and ruthlessly carried out. I am afraid I am no stranger to man's inhumanity towards his fellow man. An earlier case, in 1971, stands out not as a prime example of classic detection, for it was in fact easy to solve, but as a brutal example of the things that can go wrong in family life *in extremis*.

The scene was an ordinary family home in a quiet street in Whitley Bay, the seaside resort of Tyneside. Its hotels and amusement arcades are well known to people from the nearby city of Newcastle and its suburbs. It has a large commuter population who daily head the six or seven miles down the dual carriageway, universally known as the Coast Road, to their offices and shops in the town.

Robert Small had four children. He was stepfather to 20-year-old Michael and was the natural father of two girls and a boy. He seemed devoted to all of his children and his wife Elsie.

We were later to learn from Robert Small's mother-in-law, Elsie Cahill, that in fact all was not well in their household and had not been so for some time. There was a simmering resentment between Robert Small and his stepson Michael. We learned later too that a next door neighbour, while friendly with Mrs Small, did not get on so well with Robert. There was also something of a general doubt about Mrs Small's friendship with one particular man. Not only were close friends aware of this doubt, it transpired, but so was Small himself. He was becoming increasingly concerned about his wife's socialising habits. Fairly often she would go to 'bottle parties' without him and an increasing amount of her social life was spent outside of her husband's company. It is fair to say, however, that despite our long investigation after it happened, we uncovered no evidence of infidelity on behalf of Mrs Small, nothing to justify her husband's doubts.

But suspicion does not need truth as an ally and these strains and stresses were beginning to wear heavily on Robert Small. Later we were to build up a picture of growing enmity and hatred. That hatred came to a dreadful conclusion on 18 March 1971, shortly after Mrs Small had finished work for the day at the nearby Whitley Bay Ice Rink where she was the catering manager. After leaving her work about three in the afternoon, Elsie Small had popped in for a chat with friends on the way to the family home in Priory Avenue.

Michael Small was aware of the growing friction between his mum and stepfather. There had been a row just a couple of days before. His mum had moved a bed into the little rear room for his stepfather to use. The lad was understandably worried when, on 19 March, he discovered that his mother had not been home the night before. If, as he worried about his mum's whereabouts, his mind entertained fears to her safety, none could have even approached the horror of what had actually happened. No one could imagine the depravity of what was yet to come.

When Michael spoke to his stepfather about his mum's absence the older man seemed totally unconcerned. Small said she'd probably headed south to visit her mother in Stoke on Trent. Michael was so worried he thought he'd go to his grandmother's home to check. As Michael left his own home, his stepfather Robert Small was playing with the two youngest children, Robert junior, who was ten, and eight-year-old Jacqueline. Their big sister Janet, aged 14, was upstairs in her bedroom.

Michael left without saying where he was going and did not return for four days. By the time he did arrive back in Whitley Bay, the lad was becoming very concerned for his mother's safety; she had not been at her mother's.

These feelings of apprehension were immediately confirmed when Michael opened the front door of his home shortly after nine on the morning of 23 March. He found his stepfather lying on the living-room floor. He was breathing in short gasps, frothing at the mouth and unable to speak. Surrounding him on the floor were scraps of notepaper. Michael snatched at them and, as he read the few words he could make out, he realised that something dreadful had happened to his mother. By now in a panic, he ran upstairs and first found his stepsister Jacqueline apparently asleep on a bed. He tried to wake her by shaking her shoulder but found it was cold and hard. She was dead.

His stepbrother was lying on his bed in the next room. Robert junior's face was pressed into his pillow. Michael turned him over and saw that his face was completely blue and the lad's tongue was hanging out. He, too, was quite dead.

Michael told us later that when he next went into Janet's room and and saw she was also lying face down on the pillow he did not have to touch her. He knew instinctively that she would be dead. He ran as fast as he could to the local police station. Officers raced to the house and took Small to hospital.

As a man with a young family then, I was shattered when I arrived at the house along with a detective constable. It was clear that the children had been systematically strangled, by their father in all probability. In the house we found the 'murder weapons' – a belt, two knotted ties and a short length of rope.

A quick search of the house was carried out but there was no sign of Small's wife Elsie. However, as the notes written by Small, and found by his horrified stepson, were read it became clear that she was dead and that her body was hidden somewhere in the house. It fell to me to make the grisly discovery; in the cupboard under the stairs, under a pile of household goods, including a bike, wrapped in a roll of carpet.

The body was unwrapped from the carpet and it was clear that she had been subjected to a terrible attack. Elsie Small died of asphyxiation caused by a vest that had been rammed into her mouth. However, she also had severe head injuries and had been subjected to manual strangulation for good measure. She was meant to die.

Our prime – and indeed only – suspect was not in a fit condition to be interviewed. He had taken a massive overdose of various drugs and for a time the doctors thought it was in the lap of the gods if he would live much longer. He was transferred to a Newcastle hospital when it was thought that his kidneys had failed. In the end, though, he started responding to treatment and about ten days after the killings the doctors said he was well enough to understand and respond to questioning.

It transpired that Small wanted to speak to the police and, in his hospital bed, he recounted what can only be described as a litany of horror. In front of myself, another officer and medical staff, Small told how he had confronted his wife in their home when he found she had apparently started packing a suitcase with a view to leaving him. Small told us that his wife had said she wanted out of the house and she was going to press for a divorce as quickly as possible. The argument developed apace and this father of four picked up a piece of pipe that was lying in the kitchen, went back upstairs to where his wife was and struck her over the head with it. At this point Small said Elsie had shouted words to the effect of 'I won't do it again', which he took to be an admission of wrong-doing on behalf of his wife and those few words turned his dreadful rage into a frenzy.

He told us that blood was pouring from Elsie's head and he decided that he had to keep up the attack. In all his anger and rage he worked out that if he stopped, Elsie would only go to the police, with all the consequences which would follow from that course of action.

So in the midst of this building dedicated to the science of relieving human suffering, Small calmly told us how he just kept hitting his defenceless wife. I recall to this day that he used a good old Tyneside word to give force to his description. 'I kept braying her, braying her, and braying her,' he said.

In the middle of this attack Robert junior had come in from school, but even his arrival back at the family home was not sufficient to make Small stop. He pushed Elsie into the back bedroom upstairs, the one she had just arranged to facilitate their separation, let Robert junior into the house, told him to stay downstairs and then went back upstairs to continue the attack on his wife. His rage-fuelled strength had not been enough to kill the poor woman that he had once loved and now hated with such a passion. In desperation, with their son downstairs, he grabbed a vest that was lying on the floor nearby and stuffed it into Elsie's mouth, to shut her up for good.

That night he played the perfect dad, never mentioning his wife's absence, and went about domestic life as normal.

After the children were breakfasted and off to school the next morning, he went back upstairs, pulled his wife's body out from under the bed where it had been stored overnight, wrapped it in some old carpet and hid it in the cupboard under the stairs. It was at this point that Small suggested to Michael that his mother had gone off to Stoke.

Over the next couple of days Small carried on with his act never letting, for one moment, anyone who came across him think something was wrong. He told me that all the time he was acting out this charade he was considering whether or not to hand himself into the police. He eventually decided not to, a decision that would cost three more lives. On the Monday he kept the children off school and at home. He had decided to kill them as well.

From what he told me, lying in his hospital bed, Small was obviously considering whether or not to kill the children right up to the moment the carnage started. When he put his horrific plan into action all three youngsters were upstairs in the house playing. He walked to the living-room door and called up for young Robert to 'come down for a minute'. When the boy walked into the room Small strangled him with a tie. Next he shouted Janet down, saying her brother had taken a fit. She walked in and met the same fate, strangled with the same tie.

Small recounted this story to us slowly, deliberately and quite calmly. He then told us what he considered to be the most difficult part of what he had done. After killing the two older children he walked upstairs and talked to little Jacqueline in her bedroom. He led her downstairs, sat her on his knee and put the tie around her neck.

A shiver went right through me as Small recalled how the little girl had looked at him as he tightened the tie and said: 'Oh no, daddy.' His eight-year-old daughter became his fourth victim.

Quite how a man can first of all kill his own wife and then spend days reflecting on whether or not he should kill his own children as well defies understanding. However, that is exactly what Small did. His tortured reasoning seemed perfectly logical to him. After murdering his wife he had decided to kill himself. Initially he was going to put his head in the gas oven but had concluded that this might cause an explosion injuring his friends next door. So that plan was scrapped. Then, he thought, if he was arrested for his wife's murder, his children would suffer, being brought up without a father and mother. So on the basis of this logic, which to a rational person seems more like a rather sick joke, Small decided the only thing he could do, for the sake of his children's welfare, was to murder them.

He proved to be more skilful at murder than suicide and lived to face the consequences of his terrible actions. He was charged three weeks after the killings. He cut a pathetic figure. Damage to his kidneys was so severe he had to be supported by two detectives as he shambled into court. The deaths had, of course, shocked the whole community. There could be no sympathy for Small.

Despite the enormity of his crimes I felt, in a strange way, sorry for him. He was near enough the same age as myself and was the sort of bloke who, if we had met in different circumstances, I could have seen myself becoming friendly with.

In the summer of 1971 Small, then aged 42, appeared at Newcastle Crown Court and admitted the murder of his wife. He pleaded guilty, on the grounds of diminished responsibility, to the manslaughter of his three children.

Robert Thornton Small served only twelve years in jail before being released on licence in 1983. He went straight back to Whitley Bay and finished the job he had started all those years before with the piece of lead pipe. He went down to the beach and drowned himself by walking out into the sea, his mind clearly still fundamentally disturbed by the guilt. It was just three weeks into his freedom.

The sad case of Robert Small must be consigned to the file of life's experiences that can really only be described as inexplicable. Quite why a man should do what he did is more a matter for speculation amongst psychiatrists rather than policemen. However, in what became known as the 'poison and the passion' murder you did not need psychiatric training to deduce the motive for Paul Vickers to kill his wife. It was lust. A jury decided that he, quite simply, risked an eminent career for the love of one woman and chose to get rid of another he had rather inconveniently married, by doing her in, over a period of years, in one of the most cold and deliberate murders I have ever come across.

For many months Dr Vickers lived with the knowledge that the woman he shared his life with was dying, at his own hand. He was playing God alright. He had decided Margaret was no longer needed and the easiest thing to do was to use his vast medical knowledge to kill her in what was very nearly the perfect murder.

205

Paul Richard Jarvis Vickers had made up for his slow start in the medical profession and achieved eminence as a consultant orthopaedic surgeon at the Queen Elizabeth Hospital in Gateshead, on Tyneside. His reputation as a doctor had spread throughout the north-east of England and he had a long waiting list of patients eager to benefit from his skilled hands.

Another reputation had spread more discreetly amongst a few friends and colleagues. Outwardly he was head of the perfect family. Paul and Margaret Vickers lived in the middle-class suburb of Gosforth with their son John, 16 at the time of his mother's death, who went to a public school in London. Their large semi-detached home in leafy Moor Crescent contained all the trappings of Vickers' successful career as a surgeon, although few people had the chance to see them.

Margaret Vickers was shy, painfully shy, to the point almost of needing help with her problem. It had blighted her career as a teacher before marriage and after the wedding it meant she was not often seen socialising with her husband. There were just a few friends and hardly any relatives. Callers to the door of the family home found the welcome from her frosty in the extreme. A woman doing some secretarial work for Vickers called round one day to drop off papers and was spoken to on the doorstep. On another occasion, after Margaret had just come out of hospital, an acquaintance popped round with a bunch of flowers. The front door was only opened far enough to admit the bouquet; the author of the little act of kindness was not so lucky and remained outside.

Mrs Vickers was also permanently physically disabled which made walking difficult. She eventually died in June 1979. She had succumbed, so it seemed, to her many illnesses.

In the months leading up to her death Margaret Vickers had become even more withdrawn, and her appearance had become unwashed and dishevelled. She seemed distant and was obviously suffering clinical depression. In 1978 she had been diagnosed as suffering from schizophrenia. She was admitted to a general hospital for tests and doctors found that she had virtually no active bone marrow in her body and was therefore suffering from chronic anaemia.

Her husband had appeared shocked when he was told about the latest developments in his wife's difficult condition. During the course of a conference shortly afterwards, at the General Medical Council in London, a concerned Dr Vickers approached fellow professionals for advice on his wife's many problems. He spoke in particular to a Professor of Psychiatry from Manchester University. He asked him if the drug his wife had been prescribed, Stellazine, could have been having a detrimental effect on her. Could it have been causing her blood disorders? Ever the concerned husband, Vickers would often speak at length to other doctors as he, apparently, tried to find the cause of his wife's ever worsening state.

She was eventually admitted to hospital, for the first time, on 9 June 1979 and died in the early hours of the morning a couple of days later. Vickers was in the hospital when she passed away, though not at her bedside. There was a post mortem examination carried out, which was perfectly normal, concluding that Margaret Vickers had died of aplastic anaemia. It had been suspected that she may have been suffering from cancer but no signs of malignancy were found in her body.

Paul Vickers buried his wife in an unmarked grave in Gosforth, and that was the end of a sad and rather unhappy marriage. It was not to be the end of the story.

The doubts entertained about Vickers by those who knew him best were centred on his relationships with women. In particular there was one, Pamela Collinson, a woman some people thought of as quite vivacious but in reality I found her rather plain and ordinary. After his wife's death this relationship became more public, and the pair had apparently decided to marry. A wedding was arranged for a London registrar's office but then cancelled at the last minute. It seemed that the cancellation was not of her doing and Collinson went to the police in London. She was a spurned woman out for revenge.

It may have been that she was trying to pressurise Vickers into going ahead with the marriage after all. She had, at one time, claimed to be expecting his child. Whatever, it appears Vickers had decided against going ahead with the wedding, a decision that would cost him dearly.

Nearly a year to the day after Margaret Vickers' death, Pamela Collinson alleged in a London police station that Vickers had been obtaining drugs by deception. She did not tell Detective Chief Inspector Robert Green what she believed the surgeon had been doing with them. She no doubt delighted in telling Vickers shortly afterwards that she had been to the police to make the claims.

He would have been expecting a visit from police officers and was not to be disappointed. After he was interviewed, and released, at Gateshead police station, officers began to suspect what the doctor might have been doing with the drugs. Detective Superintendent Joe Bulch was called in to investigate and I was the supervising officer.

Joe was a great operator. He excelled in those cases that had the 'long slog' label attached to them and had some great victories behind him as a result of his painstaking and thoughtful approach. For those of us who worked with him, one of Joe's greatest qualities was his sense of humour and infectious smile that helped to keep morale high when the results were not coming as quickly as officers might have hoped.

It was a delicate case. Not only was Vickers one of the North's better-known surgeons but he was also politically active and ambitious. He hoped to become a Conservative Member of the European Parliament. Admissions from him and his former lover came easily though.

She admitted obtaining drugs fraudulently on prescriptions sent to her in London by Vickers. She told us that she believed he wanted supplies of the anti-cancer drug, CCNU, to carry out unauthorised trials. He couldn't get the drugs on Tyneside. She said that she had recognised the names of her family and friends on the prescriptions. It was just possible she herself had completed that part of the forms.

METHOD, MOTIVE AND OPPORTUNITY

The doctor was equally forthcoming. In a statement he sat down and wrote in his own hand, Vickers admitted sending prescriptions to Collinson and getting the drug back by return. He said he believed his wife's real medical problem was a brain tumour and he admitted giving her eight of the CCNU capsules to try to counteract it. In the presence of his solicitor, Vickers said he'd broken a cardinal rule of medicine and treated his wife himself. In all he said there were about 20 prescriptions involved, each for four capsules. Then, in a twist to the tale, Vickers suggested that Collinson was trying to blackmail him. He was released without charge and Joe Bulch and our team set to work.

We had to examine the background of all the parties in the case and see what that turned up. It appeared to Joe that politics had brought Paul Vickers and Pamela Collinson together. They had met through their Conservative Party interests and an affair had begun.

In her London flat, Collinson had kept a thick wad of handwritten letters from her lover, which, although undated, were clearly written at a time when Margaret Vickers was still alive. He once reflected in one of these letters: 'What are we going to do with Margaret?' In others there were complaints about the problems divorcing his increasingly difficult wife would bring.

Next, Joe turned to medical experts for opinions on the ability of the drug CCNU to cause the condition that Margaret eventually died of. The perceived wisdom was that it could. A single dose of CCNU to a susceptible person would have been enough to cause the anaemia, the chances of inducing enough to kill a person would increase with a more frequent dosage.

The most stunning, and suspect, part of Vickers' story was that he had decided to treat his wife on a whim. No one had diagnosed a brain tumour; there was no concrete evidence that she was in fact suffering a brain tumour. Vickers had simply decided that she was and started, by his own account, administering this powerful drug.

A leading Tyneside cancer expert told Joe that it was beyond belief that any member of the medical profession could embark on such a course. Other medical experts examined the other drugs which had been properly prescribed to Mrs Vickers and concluded that none of them could have contributed to the condition from which she eventually died.

So from their own mouths the pair stood condemned on the illegal use of drugs: he for administering them, she for knowingly obtaining them. Even if you believed her protestations that she did not know they were destined for Margaret Vickers, Pamela Collinson was still involved in fraudulently obtaining these drugs.

Everything in the case pointed Joe and the rest of us to the conclusion that Vickers had murdered his wife: not a killing in a moment of rage, but a long-drawn-out painful death that this man, trained to heal, had brought about and lived with, at close quarters, for two years. She had simply been a burden to him and his political ambitions. He had needed a bright and out-going wife to take to functions and play the role of the successful politician's partner. Poor pathetic Margaret, handicapped, painfully shy to the point of agoraphobia, was never going to meet that bill.

Then there was the other woman. The woman who he loved and, if he married her, would be just what a man in his position needed. Until, that is to say, love turned sour.

Both stood trial at Teeside Crown Court. Vickers was found guilty of murder, Collinson acquitted. On 20 November 1981 Mr Justice Boreham sentenced the surgeon to life in prison and recommended that he serve at least 17 years. In passing sentence the judge felt moved to comment on what he had heard the preceding days. His words are worth recalling here: 'To judges it is a familiar thing to have to witness what may be called man's inhumanity to man. But when a medical practitioner whose vocation is clearly to alleviate pain and suffering deliberately kills then this, even for a judge, is a new field. And when, as here, the victim is your wife and the killing is achieved not in a moment of passion but by a process that was cruel, deliberate and fatal then, in my judgment, inhumanity has plunged to the very depths.'

As the court's eyes were on the judge I watched Vickers to see if emotion would finally reach him as he met his fate. It did not.

The General Medical Council struck him off, needless to say, for 'the most shameful abuse of his professional privileges and skills'. He appealed against his conviction shortly afterwards and was turned down. Further appeals to the Home Secretary in 1988 and 1990 were also refused. Again in 1992 the Home Secretary turned down a request to reopen the case to have late material included. A further appeal was turned down in 1994.

John Vickers was 29 then. Joe Bulch, now retired, was sadly widowed, but is now remarried with a new young family. Paul Vickers remains in jail; of Pamela Collinson I know not, and care not.

The sentence imposed on Paul Vickers was appropriate. In truth, in all my years in the service I have never been one to complain about the sentences handed down by courts. To sit in judgment on one's fellow man is an important responsibility and one which I am certain everyone involved discharges with honesty, common-sense and, where appropriate, sympathy.

There are rare occasions, though, when there is a sentence imposed which the public generally believe too lenient or, less frequently, too harsh. There are more rare cases when an extreme decision causes outrage in society, though no doubt the judge thought he was doing the right thing at the time. It is for that reason I hardly ever complain. There was, however, one case that did give me cause for concern – a brutal fratricide, brother killing brother, that earned a violent man just three years in jail. I found very little to justify such leniency.

Ian and Ronnie Brown – those are not their real names – were pioneers of inner-city drug culture dependency. They were living in self-made squalor in Edinburgh in the late Sixties and early Seventies, abusing just about anything they could get their hands on, particularly heroin and cocaine. For the Brown brothers there was no halt to their spiral of descent through society. They ended up broke, jobless, on the dole and dependent totally on their 'fixes'. Edinburgh became notorious for its heroin addiction and related AIDS problems in the Eighties, but the seeds of the epidemic of both that hit certain parts of the city were sown long before that. Ian and Ronnie were amongst the trailblazers.

The epidemic was recognised and tackled robustly by the police in Edinburgh. The description, 'drugs capital of Europe', was regularly attached to the city where I now live. It was a totally unjustified label and one that has now been firmly cast aside. Drug abuse is down, the number of drug-related deaths has declined and the availability of hard drugs on the streets is greatly reduced to the point of scarcity. Housebreakings carried out by addicts turned into petty thieves to feed their habits have greatly reduced. The incidence of AIDS is under reasonable control.

Edinburgh's multi-agency approach to the dangers posed to the whole of society by drugs is largely to thank for that situation. The police made a substantial contribution to this much healthier picture of Edinburgh today but have been reluctant to claim the credit they deserve.

The Browns were both in their mid-twenties when first Ronnie then his brother moved to Newcastle to find work, or drugs, or some change to their pretty miserable existences. Ronnie had rented a bedsitter in Jesmond, a suburb of Newcastle with many fine houses now largely turned into flats for students and others who could not afford large rents. The brothers Brown shared the house in Jesmond with the occupants of seven other flats.

The long and the short of their story is that one night in September 1972, in the early hours of the morning in fact, they fell out. The subject of their fall-out was the last syringe full of barbiturate. Neighbouring tenants heard three thuds and screams but did nothing. Incredibly, one man leaving early for work was ushered into the Browns' bedsit by Ian and saw the dead body on the floor. There was a considerable amount of blood about the place but he did nothing.

Eventually, Ian phoned an ambulance. The crew realised the

man was dead and called the police. Ronnie had died from three stab wounds to the back and neck.

I was called to the scene. It was not a pretty sight – so typical of households devastated by drug abuse, needles lying around, dust and filth everywhere. Unwashed dishes lay not only in the sink but generally scattered about. Ronnie's body lay pathetically on the floor; a sharp industrial metal scraper lying nearby on the floor was badly bloodstained.

Things took their natural course and Ian freely admitted killing his brother with the scraper. They had both injected themselves with barbiturates the previous evening before crashing out. The trouble had started through the night. Ian woke up and saw Ronnie taking another fix with a syringe and when Ronnie refused to share this last drop of their cravings an argument started. It ended with a violent attack culminating in three stab wounds in Ronnie's back with the scraper.

A good Detective Inspector, John Lawton, who was later to become my deputy in Northumbria CID, needed only a couple of days to tie up the loose ends of the sad case of the brother who died for a fix.

Ian eventually went for trial charged with murder, but on the first day his plea of guilty to manslaughter on the grounds of his drug-induced diminished responsibility was accepted by the Crown. He was sent down for five years and came out after just three. He's now back in Edinburgh, hopefully doing better all these years later than when drugs almost destroyed his own life as well. Three years does seem a small price to pay for such a killing, even if the victim was your brother.

For sheer, unrelenting, gratuitous violence, though, the killing of Jean Makepeace, in her 25th year, and her son Lee, only three, takes a lot of beating. Certainly I have seen little worse than what happened to them.

They were half of the Makepeace family. The rest were husband Tom, who was in his late twenties, and the couple's other son, Paul, about one year old. They lived in a terrace of half a dozen houses on a new estate in the village of Ellington in

213

Northumberland. It's a nice enough spot, close to the sea, close to several larger towns and, in those days in 1981, close to jobs in the local pits. Not so now, I'm afraid.

Tom worked at Ashington Pit, and they were friendly enough with their neighbours, socialising with some of them. Jean had a sister, Anne, who lived in the same street of the Highthorne Estate, with her husband Alan Ogilvy, who was 29, and their two young children.

It was a typical northern community where everyone knew everyone. In fact, it had been Jean who introduced Anne to her husband-to-be some nine years before the events which I am describing.

The tranquillity of this little village estate was shattered about midnight on 21 April 1981. An emergency call sent ambulances and the police racing to Jean Makepeace's house. They found her dead on a bed upstairs; her son was lying nearby whimpering quietly. Both had horrific injuries and Lee died shortly afterwards in hospital. Paul was unhurt.

I was called out from home and, on reaching Ellington, was met by Detective Chief Inspector Fred Stephenson, the officer who would later be in charge of the search for Susan Maxwell in the days immediately after her abduction.

The close-knit nature of the community in which we set to work allowed myself and the other detectives to quickly build up a picture of the Makepeace family and gather clues as to what had happened that terrible night.

The first people we spoke to were the Makepeaces' next door neighbours, Susan and Brian Hill. They told us the Makepeace family were quiet, normal folk, working hard to better themselves. Their young children meant, as with so many other parents, that there was time only for limited socialising and most of the couple's lives revolved around the home, together. Jean and her sister Anne were close, they obviously trusted each other. They held back-door keys for each other's homes.

Mr and Mrs Hill told us how they had heard Jean screaming just before midnight. It had been quite clear. She was screaming

'Stop it Alan, stop it.' They had also heard at least one of the children shouting out as well. Mrs Hill estimated the cries from Jean had gone on for about five minutes, then Lee's voice could be heard, crying out, along with Paul's, then there was just the sound of Paul.

Susan Hill had knocked frantically on her neighbour's front window, but there was no reply, although she did think she could hear someone moving about inside. Mrs Hill went back to her own house and she and Brian tried to work out what to do for the best. As they spoke, they heard a key turn in the back door of the Makepeace home.

Susan ran outside once more, and as she looked through the window into the Makepeaces' kitchen she saw a pair of brown-coated arms putting a toy tractor immediately behind the back door. She thought then that she recognised Jean's brother-in-law, Alan Ogilvy. Seconds later Mr and Mrs Hill heard the front door open, they ran through their own home and saw Ogilvy, quite clearly this time, walking out of the house. His clothes were in some disarray. His shirt tails were hanging outside his trousers. They watched as he walked up the street and went into his own house.

Susan Hill was frightened. She went round to next door once more, but could get no reply to her shouts. The front door was open and she went in. On finding no one downstairs she walked up and discovered Jean lying on the bed with Lee close by. Jean was already obviously dead. She was just 25. Lee died not long afterwards in hospital. Susan Hill's screams brought her husband running to join her. Together they found Paul in the next room, unharmed but extremely frightened.

Brian Hill ran back to his own house to phone for help. He was returning once more to No. 22 in order to rescue Paul from the carnage when he met Ogilvy walking out of his house. He had obviously changed his clothes. Ogilvy, oblivious of the fact that he had been seen minutes earlier, started asking Brian what was going on. He then claimed he had seen two youths causing a disturbance outside his sister-in-law's house. Now extremely nervous, Brian Hill carried Paul to the safety of his own home where his wife comforted the terrified tot.

Police began to arrive on the scene and Ogilvy walked up to one of the first officers there and told him that he, too, had been assaulted. He then said that he had bruised his hand in the struggle but explained scratches on his face as the result of a game of football earlier that evening. Then he retracted that statement.

The officer, PC John Dodds, realised something was far from right and continued to engage Ogilvy in conversation to make sure he did not leave the scene. At one point, in front of the officer, Ogilvy fastened up a shirt button that had been undone, confirming the garment may well have been put on in something of a rush.

By now the street was buzzing. There were the lights of the emergency vehicles flashing away through the night air. Half the village had turned out to see what was going on. Forensic scientists were arriving along with the pathologist and officers from the identification branch to photograph and minutely examine the scene. Turning into the street, right in the middle of this, came Thomas Makepeace, walking home after his shift at the pit.

A senior officer broke the news to him. His restraint was remarkable. His life had just been shattered in the cold reality of the early morning.

Officers were careful not to let Ogilvy out of their sight. He started becoming restless and appeared to want to go into the house where we thought he'd just committed a double murder. He was arrested and taken quickly away to Morpeth police station a few miles away.

The house was examined in great detail. The rear kitchenette door was found to be locked and no key available. Behind it there was the toy tractor and a kitchen chair. Both, in my view, had been placed there to give the impression that whoever had done this dreadful deed had not entered the house by the back door, thereby switching suspicion from himself. Ogilvy had a key to that door.

There was a note Jean had left for Thomas, lying on the table. It read: 'Can't find back door key.' More interestingly, examination of the pad on which the note was written showed another message had been penned that night. It's indentation on the next page showed up under oblique lighting. It had said: 'Alan, will you see if you can find spare back door key because I can't find mine, and push it through the door – Jean.'

We discovered that Alan Ogilvy had finished work in the middle of the afternoon and, after a game of five-a-side football, had gone to a local hotel where he and others had drunk about six or seven pints of lager each. Then he went home.

Officers found a Prestige-make carving knife in the bathroom upstairs. It had been washed. Ogilvy's house was full of evidence as well. There was blood on his jeans, blood on his watch and blood on his brown bomber jacket. Were these the brown-coated arms Susan Hill saw? Of course they were.

A post mortem was carried out on the two bodies and by morning the pathologist, Dr Ranasinghe, was able to give me the horrific result. Jean had been stabbed no fewer than 62 times. Lee had fared worse. He had been subjected to 76 stab wounds, most of them in his neck area. Other evidence showed the weapon used was certainly that Prestige carving knife. The tip of its blade was bent over and left a distinct wound on both bodies.

As far as Jean's body was concerned there was another unusual and unsavoury aspect to the case. I do not intend to discuss it here, it adds nothing to the evidence nor did it enhance the outcome of the events, other than to show exactly how twisted the mind of Ogilvy was. For the avoidance of doubt, I can say the feature says more about the nature and behaviour of Ogilvy than anyone else in the case.

Fred Stephenson and I interviewed him through the night at Morpeth. Despite overwhelming evidence he stuck to his story about being assaulted by two mystery youths. He admitted he knew the back-door key was missing, he knew Thomas was on nights. His own wife was out. Then suddenly he said that he did not remember being in the house downstairs, but he seemed to say that he remembered being in the bedroom. 'What about the bedroom?' we asked.

He said he could remember lashing about with the knife in the bedroom. He claimed to be unable to remember anything else. It turned into a hard interview to conduct in some respects, because all the time he was making incriminating admissions without actually confessing to the murder of two members of his family. Then he blurted out: 'God, I didn't rape her, did I?'

It seemed that the suspect was providing the motive for a murder he refused to admit to. Then he broke down as he seemed to partially recall what had happened. 'Not the bairn. I didn't get the bairn, did I? He's not dead is he? I must be mad.'

Motive and defence in quick succession.

He went on to dictate a statement. Just one page long. He admitted having a struggle with Jean, lashing out with the knife, but that was it. He said: 'I don't know why I done it.' Draw your own conclusions as to why Ogilvy went to that house that night. You will not be far wrong.

At his trial, the jury believed his plea of diminished responsibility and found him not guilty of murder but guilty of manslaughter. It was not an unjustified decision; his admission was reluctant, his recall partial, but it was difficult to believe that anyone could inflict 138 stab wounds on his sister-in-law and her lovely young son and know exactly what he was doing. He got life.

Ogilvy is still behind bars, in a jail near Gloucester I think.

I am not complaining – CID work was my own choice – but the undoubted drawback of this side of the police is the fact that work comes without warning, 24 hours a day, exactly as happened in the case I have just described. The more senior one's position in the CID, the more likely the call-out in the middle of the night, the more likely one is to be rushing away from social engagements or whatever to answer the pressing call of the bleeper.

So it was, right in the middle of the festive season in 1975. I was fast asleep in bed at home in the early hours of New Year's

Eve when the telephone rang. Within 45 minutes there I was standing on a cold, dark piece of waste ground in the middle of Newcastle upon Tyne: my companions that morning were about 20 other police officers, a doctor and a dead body.

The body had been found by a man walking home from a late-night party at a friend's house. He'd walked up a back lane for a pee out of sight of the passing traffic. The open patch of ground was just off Westgate Road, one of the main routes in and out of Newcastle. The road climbs up a long, steep hill from the city centre taking traffic towards the Tyne Valley and rural south Northumberland. The body was that of a youngish man. He was lying face upwards, and it was obvious that he'd been beaten to death with a half-brick and a piece of a kitchen sink, both of which were still lying nearby.

The waste ground was off a small street called Cross Villa Place. At the junction of this side street and Westgate Road was a small alcove in the wall. There was very heavy bloodstaining in it. This was obviously where the attack had taken place. Not far away was a cardboard box; in it the broken base of a fluorescent light fitting. It too was heavily bloodstained. By the light of our powerful torches, it was possible to see that there were marks along the ground indicating that the body had been dragged from the alcove to the waste ground and probably finished off there. On the road between these two points, I saw a gent's wrist-watch lying on the ground. It was a Sekonda make, with a metal strap on it. There was blood on the case.

As the murder scene was being examined for more clues, I telephoned the then head of Northumbria CID, Detective Chief Superintendent Alan Bailey, at his home, and a major inquiry was put in place. On this job I was Alan's deputy. Six months later he was to retire and I would succeed him in the post.

We were able to identify the body from fingerprints. It was that of Kevin Austin Cannon, who lived just 800 yards from the murder scene. His parents told us that Kevin worked as a kitchen porter in the Swallow Hotel in the centre of Newcastle. He had been on late shift the day before from 3 p.m. to 11 p.m. They had not realised their son had failed to return home. Kevin used to walk the distance from the hotel to his home every working day, using the fastest route past Cross Villa Place. He had obviously been attacked on his way home.

Kevin was just 20 years old. The youngest of five children, his mother described him as quiet and sensitive. He suffered learning difficulties and had led a sheltered life at home.

The pathologist, Dr Ranasinghe, reported that death was caused by haemorrhage associated with multiple fractures to the face and head. Dr Ranasinghe and I worked on quite a few cases together. He was a shrewd and likeable Sri Lankan who was consistently able to use his great skill to throw up many pointers to investigators over the years.

That night the murder was front page news in the Newcastle *Evening Chronicle* and was featured prominently on the local television news programmes. The publicity brought forward a number of people who had passed Cross Villa Place the night Kevin died and had seen some sort of assault taking place.

Extra detectives were drafted in to the murder team. This put quite a strain on the city divisions because already another difficult inquiry was underway in the murder of an old lady in nearby Westerhope.

We were making house to house inquiries, looking into Kevin's background, checking hospital casualty departments, speaking to people with assault convictions in the area whose modus operandi matched the circumstances we were investigating. We also had the clue of the watch. Kevin's parents were certain it did not belong to him. The chance was that it must belong to his killer.

Sekonda were heavily advertised popular watches at the time. They were made in the old USSR and imported into Britain by a London company, Global Watches Ltd. They had sold nearly a million of this make of watch. The model we had found, an alarm type known as an 803, was one of about 3,300 sold to various shops in Britain and a further 1,100 sold to a mail order company. It was hopeless to try and tackle whose watch it might have been from the retail outlets and so we turned to the guarantees issued with the watches. Buyers were asked to fill in a form and return their guarantee card to Global. Of 900,000 Sekonda watches sold about 400,000 cards had been returned. Unfortunately there was no way of discovering which model of watch any particular card referred to. Consequently we had to look at them all.

None of the shops selling the watches kept records of whom they had been sold to. We hoped the mail order outlet, Freemans, could tell us who had bought Sekonda watches from them. Two teams of detectives were established to look at each of these matters, one to examine who bought watches from Freemans, the other to plough through the guarantee cards. We had to hope that the owner of the watch which had been found was the sort of person to bother to fill in the card.

Global's records showed that of the 400,000 cards they had, 15,000 were from people who lived in the Tyne and Wear area. Like so much of police work, this avenue was always going to be a long, hard slog. What we had to do was try and make it as easy as possible.

From the outset the odds were against us. More people had not bothered to return their guarantees than had, so on the balance of probability our watch owner would not have returned it. But there was always a chance. So we narrowed down the inquiry as far as possible, in the geographic sense. We started from the scene of the murder and worked outwards in a carefully structured inquiry.

Of the 15,000 Sekonda watches known to be owned by people in Tyne and Wear and who had filled in the guarantee card, 448 were resident in the police division in which Kevin had died. Each one of those people was traced and interviewed. Most importantly, we established if the people to whom we were speaking were still in possession of their watches. We battled on, extending this line of inquiry further and further afield.

In the meantime, we had hoped that Freemans could just press a button or two on their computer and give us a print-out of all the people who had bought a Sekonda watch model 803 from them. Needless to say our hopes were soon dashed. All the company could in fact do was to give us a list of their 6,000 agents in Tyne and Wear, and then leave it to us to go round them all asking if, firstly, one of their customers had bought a Sekonda 803 watch and, if they had, could they remember who it was.

There were 453 Freemans catalogue agents in the west of Newcastle police division alone. Each was seen, each of these inquiries drew a blank. So then we widened it out to the east of Newcastle. There 311 agents were seen and 17 days after the murder we struck gold.

Policewoman June Stafford was to be the heroine of the investigation. No doubt beginning to tire a little of the routine nature of these inquiries, June knocked on yet another door in the east end of the city and started asking the same old questions. It was the 764th time officers in the teams had made such a visit. Then came the replies that we had been looking for. June played an absolutely poker-faced blinder and did not betray the excitement she felt at what she was hearing. Mrs Barbara Craigie told June that she had bought a Sekonda 803 for her husband's Christmas present. Kevin Craigie, her husband, said he had lost it in the city centre days after Christmas. June affected not to be overly concerned, left the house and called into the incident room. How she managed to contain herself amazed me. If it had been me, I would have been hard pushed to hide my excitement.

Nineteen-year-old Kevin William Craigie was brought in to the West End police station for questioning. I interviewed him along with Detective Inspector John Bowyer, who later, incidentally, went on to take charge of searches of the Kielder Forest area of Northumberland for bodies and property from the ill-fated Pan Am Flight 103.

Craigie at first gave the same explanation of the loss of the watch as he had given to June. He said he was in town with his friend James Greenhill. Then Craigie changed his story slightly. He changed the date on which he said the watch was lost. First he had said it was lost on 12 January, many days after the killing.

Then he said it had in fact been lost on the actual night of the killing. He was detained.

Greenhill, who was 21, told us the same story. He too was detained.

John and I came to the conclusion that their stories had been rehearsed. They matched each other's well, a bit too well. We managed to break the story down through further inquiries and as Greenhill was interviewed through the night he suddenly 'coughed'. He admitted the murder and made a voluntary statement which amounted to a full confession. He and Craigie had killed Kevin.

Next Detective Chief Inspector Peter Docherty and Detective Inspector Tom Heron interviewed Craigie. I can think of no two men more suited to the task. Craigie, too, admitted the crime. He was shown the watch we found and identified it as his own. He made a full voluntary statement as well.

It is interesting to note that Craigie had not returned his watch guarantee card. It was lying completed in his house ready for posting but had not been sent. There was another twist to this part of the inquiry. Greenhill too had bought a Sekonda watch. He had returned the guarantee card.

Herein lies the sort of pitfall police work often encounters. If we had seen Greenhill first he would have produced his watch and, to an extent, there was a good chance that would have been the end of the matter as far as he was concerned. Similarly, Craigie might have escaped detection if we had not followed up the Freemans angle and just relied on the guarantee cards. That's the nature of police work. A great deal is down to chance.

The forensic scientists took away clothes from both men's houses and there were bloodstains to connect the pair to the killing. Horrifyingly, it became clear poor Kevin died because these brutes had run out of beer money. They had spent the whole of the day and evening in various pubs drinking heavily. Then the cash ran out. They set out up Westgate Road with the specific intention of finding someone to rob. Kevin overtook them as he walked home from work that night. Craigie said they decided to 'roll him'. The young man was nudged over the wall into the alcove and the attackers both started laying into him. Craigie said he hit Kevin with 'the tin thing', presumably the light fitting found in the cardboard box. He went on: 'We went through his pockets but there was just a couple of pence. There may have been some two-bob bits.'

These were taken and the drinking went on. The pair went to a nearby nightclub and tidied themselves up in the lavatory. Craigie realised his watch was missing, and so they went back to the scene of the robbery. Kevin was still breathing when his attackers came back. They could not find the watch. The pair decided to drag their victim on to the waste ground out of the way. The watch must have been lodged somewhere in Kevin's clothing and fell out as he was moved.

Greenhill used the half-brick, Craigie the shiny white one, as he called it – the piece of kitchen sink – to finish Kevin off. They were both responsible for his death and they knew it. Later that night they calmly, or stupidly, mentioned the loss of the watch to a passing police patrolman, who did not note the vague report from two drunken young men.

They had also stolen a small bunch of keys from Kevin. As they walked away the keys were thrown on to the roof of a car sales showroom. The next morning the bunch was found. One of the keys fitted the front door of Kevin's house, the other the box containing his treasured record collection.

The motive for this murder – greed for a couple of quid to buy yet another drink. The robbery was conducted with such gratuitous violence that an entirely innocent young man suffered an untimely and painful death. Both men pleaded guilty to murder at Newcastle Crown Court on 26 May 1976 and were sentenced to life imprisonment. Craigie, who was married with a young son, was released on licence in July 1991. Greenhill, a single man, came out two months later. I know their current whereabouts but will not reveal them here. They have paid their debt to society and deserve the chance to try and rebuild their lives. How many would share that view?

Such is murder and its consequences. Murderers are occasionally regarded as glamorous and interesting people. Craigie and Greenhill proved, if proof was needed, a counter for that belief. Each of them lost 15 years of their lives for the sake of a drink. Their victim lost his life altogether and Kevin's family, like those of all murder victims, had an irreparable and painful hole put into their lives.

Amidst all these memories of wasted lives, both of victim and killer, my concerns about the delays in proceeding with the prosecution of Robert Black continued. After what seemed like an eternity, again in the absence of the accused, the abduction and murder charges were finally raised at Newcastle Magistrates Court.

Anyway, after considerable delay, again in the absence of the accused, Black was committed for trial at Newcastle upon Tyne Crown Court. The date was 7 July 1993, twelve months after the first court hearing in the Magistrates Court and just seven days short of three years after Black's arrest in the Borders.

If Black had decided to appear at any or all of these hearings, he would have been transferred from Peterhead Jail to Durham Prison. It, like Peterhead, has a reputation for toughness. I had a feeling part of Black's reluctance to attend court was his desire to stay away from Durham in the safety of the isolation wing of Peterhead where he was cut off from other inmates who might have felt the need to do him harm. Indeed, when the case eventually reached the Crown Court for the first pre-trial review, on 12 November 1993, Black again remained hundreds of miles away in his cell.

The first hearing was just a couple of hours put aside in the morning to sort out one or two legal matters. The venue was the new and very impressive Crown Court complex on the Quayside in Newcastle, right on the Tyne.

The judge by, perhaps, a quirk of fate was not only a Scot, but a grand one at that. In England, Mr Justice Macpherson of Cluny and Blairgowrie may be a judge of the High Court of Justice, Queen's Bench Division. Once more back over the border in his native Scotland, Sir Alan Macpherson takes on a different persona. He is Cluny Macpherson, 27th Chief of the Clan Macpherson and direct descendant of the reluctant Jacobite, Cluny Macpherson. The spelling changed over the years. He is one of the old school of judges, apart from his immaculate Scots pedigree of Wellington, Oxford, Scots Guards, and Commanding Officer of the 21st SAS Regiment (TA). He presided over the hearing in a businesslike and impressive manner, setting the style of things to come. He even managed a slight dig at Mr Kerrigan's experience at the Scottish Bar. The QC had suggested to the judge that they may like to sort out the severance issues and evidence of similar fact in a further pre-trial review. On being told by Mr Kerrigan that the argument may take ten days, the judge said he felt sure two days would be more than adequate, wryly observing: 'We work on English days in this court, Mr Kerrigan, not Scots ones.'

As my team and I sat in the rear row of the court it went through my mind, for the first time, that at last we were getting somewhere. The hard labours of the previous twelve years were beginning to show fruit.

CHAPTER FIFTEEN

The Trial

From that first pre-trial hearing in November 1993, the case really began to pick up speed and after years of seeming inactivity the wheels of justice started turning at a rate more to my liking.

There were more hearings to sort out the complicated problems that had for so long delayed the case coming to court. Sitting in the Royal Courts of Justice in The Strand, Mr Justice Macpherson dealt with the disclosure of evidence and information other than that used in the prosecution case. There was an application for the CATCHEM report to be withheld from the defence. I could see little point in this request. There was nothing in CATCHEM of a controversial nature, but be that as it may, the application was made, and granted.

Then, after Christmas, it was off to Chelmsford Crown Court and the first appearance of the man who had been retained to lead Black's defence. Mr Alan Rawley QC asked the judge to rule on two key issues in the case, which were crucial to the way the prosecution of Black would have to go.

In reality, if the judge had decided against us on either of these matters I believe the case would have foundered and Black would not have been brought to justice. Firstly, Mr Rawley submitted that the charges should be separated out and heard individually, which would have been disastrous. We had little direct evidence on any one of the charges. The Crown Office in Scotland had already decided there was insufficient evidence to prosecute Black on the Hogg case alone, and the CPS was certain it was all or none. Then our intention of leading evidence of similar fact was challenged. The Crown case was to centre on leading evidence on the three abductions and murders, detail Teresa Thornhill's ordeal, and then introduce what had happened to that little Borders girl.

The judge said it was clearly a case where evidence of similar fact was admissible. He said the murders bore the same signature, a clear indication that he at least considered them to be the work of one man. He decided that details of the Borders incident could be disclosed to the jury and that all the allegations would be heard together. Things were going well.

When I watched the speed at which this judge dealt with these matters, and the skill he exhibited in responding to counsel's arguments, it was hard to understand what had delayed the CPS for such a long time.

Other key parts of the defence case, he said, could be left for rulings when the trial was underway. It was the desire of John Milford and the prosecution team to lead evidence of Black's propensity to commit offences against children. They wanted the jury to see the pornographic pictures Black had collected in a scrapbook in his home depicting young girls in obscene poses with various objects, and for them to hear the telling matters he spoke about in the taped interview in Edinburgh.

By the time the trial date was reached Black's defence team had been completely changed. First his silk, Mr Rawley, found a case he was appearing in at Manchester badly overrunning and he asked for the case of R v Black to be adjourned. Quite rightly the judge refused the request. Rawley was replaced by Ronald Thwaites QC, a colourful character from the Old Bailey beat. By the time Mr Thwaites entered the case the defence, under

Mr Rawley, had made a number of admissions to the Crown, concerning Black's movements on key dates. They had virtually conceded that he was near all of the abduction scenes at the relevant times, leaving it for the prosecution only to have to show that he was in fact rather nearer than had been admitted. The effect of these admissions was to greatly reduce the number of witnesses that would have to be called and so cut down the length of the trial.

Mr Thwaites' first action was to withdraw all the admissions and revert to the more standard defence tactic of admitting nothing. When I heard this my heart sank. Not because we had anything to hide, but merely at the prospect of weeks of extremely tedious evidence stretching out in front of me, and more importantly, the jury. If we were going to have to prove every single petrol purchase, every single poster delivery, it would take months.

Black's new silk took over the brief with only three weeks or so to go to the opening of the case. Shortly after this change in the driving seat the navigator decided to withdraw. After an involvement stretching back four years Mr Kerrigan resigned from the brief. It was, seemingly, because he felt having been party to the previous strategy decisions on the handling of the case his position became untenable once those decisions had been changed. Whatever, with three weeks to go Black found himself with new senior and junior counsel.

In an unusual step Mr Justice Macpherson invited the press to meet him at the court on 12 April 1994, the day before the trial started. He wanted to ensure that the reporting of the case did not become a problem to either himself, the administration of justice or the press themselves. I was aware, of course, of the large media interest in the case. In the weeks running up to my retirement as Lothian and Borders Deputy Chief Constable on 2 April, I had seen many journalists to give them limited assistance, as is usual, in the preparation of background material for use once the trial was over. The force's first civilian press officer, Dan Hewitt, sat through one briefing I gave on the structure of the case to a large gathering of the writing press, and then numerous TV and radio interviews. The local commercial and BBC television and radio stations in the areas where the victims were from, and national television reporters were all given more or less the same interview on the understanding it could only be used after conviction, so I knew media interest was high. I was, however, surprised to discover over 50 news organisations were represented at that briefing with the judge, who was sitting in 'civvies' in the clerk's chair in his court. He had assembled round him the court clerk, the police officer in charge of security and others to answer questions from the news gatherers. It was the first time in my experience that such a step had ever been taken by a judge and the journalists were clearly surprised at his friendly and helpful approach, and obviously appreciative.

Because of the anticipated interest from the media the court authorities had decided to hold the trial not in Newcastle's new and impressive Quayside court complex, but in the Moot Hall, the original court building right beside the keep of the now demolished castle that gave the city its name. For me to be sitting once more in the rear seats of the Moot Hall's number 1 court was truly coming home. From these rather uncomfortable benches I had watched the conclusion of many of my cases being played out. The courtroom is most impressive, oak panelled with a high judge's bench and rather terrifying dock right in the centre. It has waist-high woodwork topped with a row of ornamental, but sharp, spikes.

On the first day of the trial, and indeed every subsequent one, Black arrived in an unescorted police minibus at half past nine. His head was covered with a blanket as he was led into a side door in the court with at least 12 television crews straining at the railings trying to get a shot of him. Identification may have been an issue in the case and we were determined to ensure there could be no risk to the trial by someone publishing a picture before it was permissible to do so.

A jury had been selected, but not sworn in, earlier in the week, and warned that the case could last for three months. The judge wanted them to have a 'cooling off' period, a couple of days to consider if they could make such a commitment.

Before they came into the court to confirm their availability and be sworn in, pleas were to be taken from Black. Just days before the start of the trial the defence had asked us for one of his suits, to allow him to look smart for the jury. The entire contents of his bedsit had been taken first to Edinburgh and then on to Newcastle to be stored in the office I had rented. We had no wish to be obstructive, but four years in an exhibit bag does little for tailoring and the suit requested was rather beyond wearing.

So when the press and public got their first sight of Black since his Edinburgh court appearance he was wearing clothes which must, I supposed, have been borrowed. He wore a light grey suit that was too tight across the shoulders, and just about everywhere else for that matter. He was now completely bald on top with only a fringe of short heavily greyed hair round the sides and back of his head. He had a short beard and moustache. As he walked up the stairs from the cells below the court that lead directly into the dock Black carried a blue covered legal notebook, which he appeared never to use throughout the trial, although he had it with him every day in court. As he emerged into the courtroom for the first time the accused did not look round him at the benches to both sides and the rear packed with over 50 reporters. He sat down beside a prison officer in the dock and adopted the position he would be in for the majority of the days ahead, slightly turned to the left towards where Mr Milford sat just a matter of two feet in front. His legs were usually stretched out, he seemed relaxed.

The court clerk ordered him to stand and then read through the ten charges he faced asking, at the end of each one, 'Are you guilty or not guilty?'. With just slight hesitation on a couple of occasions he replied 'not guilty' to each one. There was still quite a noticeable Scots accent in his voice.

He was charged with kidnapping and murdering Susan Maxwell and Sarah Harper. He was also charged with preventing their lawful burial. The charges in the Caroline Hogg case were the same apart from substituting unlawful imprisonment for the kidnap charge of the other two. This was because the kidnap of Caroline was solely a Scottish offence and therefore beyond the jurisdiction of the English court. Her unlawful imprisonment, for the purpose of the charge, would begin as soon as Black's van crossed the Scottish border back into England. The last charge concerned the kidnap of Teresa Thornhill.

Mr Thwaites then made two applications to the judge concerning the books of photographs the prosecution had prepared to assist the jury. He wanted some of the pictures of Black in years gone by removed. They included a passport snap, which in common with most such photographs, was not flattering. 'They make my client look like a mental defective,' said the QC in support of his argument. It was a description many would have agreed with, I thought.

Then the judge made a number of rulings concerning the reporting of the case. At the request of the defence he ordered that no photographs of Black be published because identification was still an issue. He made an order protecting the identity of Black's little victim in the Borders, and then another of the cross-border problems arose. When he jailed Black for life in 1990 the judge, Lord Ross, ordered that the name of the village from where she was abducted, Stow, should not be published. Then at this hearing Mr Justice Macpherson explicitly said he had no objection to revealing the name of the village, which the press duly did. He ordered, sternly, that 'Mr Black's current address must not be given.' He did not want the jury to know that he was already serving a jail sentence.

The jury was brought into the court and asked by the judge if they had any valid reason for not hearing the case. None attempted to be excused and so they were sworn in, one by one, without objection from the defence. There were six men and six women, only two of whom looked to be over 30-35 and two more looked to be under 20. Interestingly, one of them had the same name as a notorious murderer who was hanged for his crimes. Throughout the coming days he was the one who, it seemed to me, was the most attentive. He spent most of the trial leaning forward listening intently and watching everything.

Mr Justice Macpherson, it was obvious, is the sort of judge that likes to look after the jury very well. He sat for the first day, as is traditional, with the High Sheriff of Northumberland, Barbara Lyndon Skeggs, and her chaplain. He introduced them to the jury, and throughout the rest of the trial went to great lengths to ensure their comfort and understanding. I did not see him enter the court one time without thanking the jurors for standing as he did so. At each turn of the case he would look over at them to see from their faces if any was having difficulty following evidence, or finding the right pages in the volumes of exhibits and productions they had been given at the outset.

The first afternoon and following morning were given over to Mr Milford's opening speech. He spoke for over five hours outlining the case against Black and the circumstances of each of the charges against him.

As the prosecution detailed the matters they hoped to prove in the coming days the jury looked on attentively. In my experience juries are strange creatures. They seem to take on a life of their own and over the course of a long trial you can see distinct patterns in their behaviour emerging. During this opening speech they looked to be apprehensive at times, no doubt worried about what horrors lay ahead of them. Mr Milford explained the case just as we had investigated it. The prosecution was split into five separate parts. Maxwell, Hogg, and Harper, on to Thornhill, and then revealing the details of what had happened in Stow to give the jury their plan to work from, as it were.

At the start of the second day, before the continuation of the opening speech, counsel for the defence, Mr Thwaites, asked the judge, in the absence of the jury, if he may be allowed to make an opening speech directly after the Crown case was outlined. He argued in such a complicated case as this it would be useful to the jury to be warned in advance of the matters of contention they need look out for, where the defence was likely to contest. The judge reflected for some minutes before ruling out such an opening. He had allowed one only once before, he said, in the case he tried of the police officers accused of perjury over the Guildford Four. He said he had been roundly criticised for his decision in that case, but that was not a matter that concerned him.

So after lunch on the second day of the trial the witnesses began giving their evidence.

As the trial proceeded the defence agreed more and more of the evidence without contest. It is fair to say most of it could not be contested, and the judge made it plain whilst he put no time limits on justice he did not expect the court's time to be wasted. Sometimes he interjected if he felt the Crown was proving a point that was not being doubted by the other side, or becoming repetitive.

It was clear from the witnesses speaking about what they saw in and around Coldstream on the day of Susan's abduction that the horror of the kidnap and subsequent murder had left a deep impression on their minds. Even witnesses who had been quite young at the time remembered vividly the matters they were asked about and gave their evidence in a most convincing fashion.

The jury got a clear picture. There was a white van seen in several places about the bridge over the River Tweed. Importantly, it was a white Transit-like van with curtains at the rear window. The jury had been told Black slept in his van and hung material over the back windows. There was little Mr Thwaites could do. He could only sow seeds of doubt here and there rather than mount a full-scale attack on any witness or thread of evidence. He managed to elucidate the fact that it was a busy day, there were lots of other vehicles about, not just the white van. Minor matters like that were brought out.

Then, with the evidence of Caroline's abduction for which Black was not charged because of the jurisdiction problems, things went equally well. The children who had seen the smelly stranger on the promenade at Portobello gave their stories convincingly.

Although eleven years had gone by, they too were clear in their recollection. One of the witnesses, who was only in his early twenties when giving evidence, even remarked to one of the detectives outside the court as he left that he was certain the man in the dock was the man he had seen with Caroline that day.

None of the people called for the Crown were asked to identify the accused in court. Dock identifications are suspect tactics at the best of times, but after more than a decade it could have been a dangerous process for the Crown.

Thankfully the statements of the dead girl's parents were all agreed by the defence which saved them the ordeal of going into the witness box.

Jackie Harper and her mother were the only relatives of the murder victims to attend the hearing. It must be a difficult decision to make, whether or not to go. It would inevitably be a dreadful experience, but some people may well want to see the man who has brought them such misery and hear all the evidence so they can be certain in their own mind that the right man has been caught. Anyway, the arguments against attendance are equally powerful and Mr and Mrs Maxwell and Mr and Mrs Hogg stayed away. One newspaper, reporting Mrs Harper's presence, said she was escorted by a representative of a tabloid newspaper. It was in fact a detective from West Yorkshire who had been detailed to look after her.

The Crown case proceeded apace, making much better headway than had been anticipated. Much of the evidence was simply given to the jury from statements read by junior counsel; certainly nearly all of the evidence surrounding poster deliveries, and the trips detectives had made in similar vans to Black's to gain an impression of the journeys he made was unchallenged. Very little of the fuel purchase evidence was challenged either, which saved a lot of time, and for the jury, excruciating boredom.

The defence had little choice but to accept another key plank of the case, the likelihood of disposal of Sarah's body being in the Trent at a path used by fishermen close to junction of the M1 Motorway which formed the third apex of the Midlands Triangle.

So the prosecution case proceeded without a hitch through the kidnap and murder of Sarah, and then on to the kidnap of Teresa Thornhill. Interestingly Black had been charged with her actual kidnapping, not an attempt to. In his opening speech Mr Milford said that he was sure kidnap itself was the correct charge because, although she had only been carried from one side of the road to the other, she was clearly an unwilling participant.

By the time the end of the Thornhill evidence had been reached I was confident the jury had been given the chance to have a very clear impression of the strength of the case against Black. Apart from the (in my view) considerable weight of evidence putting him at the scenes of four similar offences and proof beyond any doubt of his sole participation in a fifth, it was, in the words of the Crown, 'coincidence beyond all doubt'.

Until this point in the trial Black had seemed fairly unmoved by what he was hearing. He stared intently at the witnesses. As Teresa gave her evidence, Black did not appear to take his eyes off her once. She for her part did not look at him at all, not even a stolen glance. Nor did she look at counsel, one on either side of the dock, as they asked their questions of her, obviously fearful of seeing Black even out of the corner of her eye.

However, on the day the Midlands Triangle evidence was being led, and his former landlord and landlady took the witness box for the Crown, he appeared to be hit quite hard. Then their son, Raymond Rayson, told how he found a suitcase full of child pornography and little girls' swimwear in the lodger's London bedsit. The other son John told of Black's frequent visits to his Midlands home, and the jury even saw a video taken at the Rayson twins' fourth birthday party; Black could clearly be seen in the background with a camera taking shots of the youngsters at play. The jury heard that on one of the days Black visited Donnisthorpe he and John Rayson had gone for a drink to a pub at Twycross. Another friend of the family was certain that Black was at John Rayson's house when she visited on the weekend of 18 July 1983. The day Caroline's body was found – at Twycross.

This day his composure deserted him. First he fidgeted, then he looked down at his feet, then finally his head went down, almost touching his knees at one point. The Raysons were as close as he had been to having a family, and for him to hear them giving evidence for the Crown was obviously a shock, though it should not have been.

This occurred on about the eleventh day of the trial. By then I had lost count of the number of times I had been asked if it was true Black was about to change his plea to guilty. Rumours were constantly sweeping the court, a by-product of a lot of reporters hanging round with not a great deal to do. However, by the end of proceedings this day I too thought a change of heart on behalf of the accused was a possibility. Counsel went to the cells to see him and stayed for some time, but in the event no change was made and the trial continued.

Throughout these days of evidence the defence made a number of applications to the judge, in the absence of the jury, with mixed results. Primarily Mr Justice Macpherson ruled the transcript of the Edinburgh interview with Black could not be admitted in evidence to the jury. He held that the interview, dealing largely as it did with Black's account of his self abuse, was not relevant in this case. He went on to say that there was no criticism of the way the interview had been conducted. I felt he added this last bit for police consumption lest it be thought Andrew and Roger had in some way been at fault in their interview technique. Similarly he ruled they could not hear what Black had said to Andrew and Roger in Peterhead when served with the summons, 'Tell Pamela all this has nothing to do with her.' A reference, of course, to the one girlfriend he claimed to have had a relationship with.

Importantly he did allow the jury to hear what Black said in the car taking him to Selkirk police station, but they also were told that some of these comments were denied by Black when he appeared in front of a sheriff some days later. He also allowed the various implements found in Black's van on arrest, and his collection of child pornography to be shown to the jury, but at least two of the women jurors handed that quickly past with no more than a fleeting glance at the sickening scrapbooks.

Various police officers were called to tie up loose odds and ends. Under cross examination Roger, Peter Robinson and Peter Herward were asked about various vehicles that had featured at one time or another in the investigation but never eliminated. Peter Herward was cross examined over the case of the man reported to the Crown Prosecution Service all those years before, the one who had sold a fire extinguisher to the Maxwells, and been convicted of sex crimes against his own children. The fact that the CPS had not proceeded for reasons of insufficient evidence rather dented any good the defence might have hoped to bring from this episode. So just before lunch on Friday 29 April, the thirteenth day of the trial, the last prosecution witness was called. It had been some years since I had given evidence in a court of law.

I simply indicated that in 39 years of police work, I had no knowledge or recollection of any unsolved cases of female child murder involving the transportation of the victim's body over long distances between the points of abduction and disposal southwards. As I left the witness stand Mr Justice Macpherson asked if I knew of any criminal investigation that had been larger or more thorough. I told him I knew of none bigger but was not the right person to comment on the thoroughness of what we had done.

The jury were then sent home for the May Day bank holiday weekend and told not to return until the following Wednesday. The defence was being given a little extra time to prepare their case.

At this point, with the jury members on their way home, Mr Thwaites made an application to the bench to dismiss the charges, the prosecution having failed to establish there was a case to answer, he argued. Sometimes these submissions can be lengthy. Mr Justice Macpherson quickly ruled that he thought the weight of the prosecution case could only be properly decided by the jury.

Amazingly the main legal stumbling block to the case had not risen its head once. There that been no discussion whatsoever of the jurisdiction of an English court to deal with murders which may have been committed in Scotland. I drove home to Edinburgh that Friday afternoon wondering what defence could be put forward apart from: 'Yes I was there, but no I did not kill those girls.'

So the morning came that Mr Thwaites unveiled his armoury for the defence. There had been much speculation as to exactly what he had up his sleeve. One fairly obvious tactic would be to reveal his client in his full horror, pick holes in the Crown case and then make a powerful plea to the jury in his closing speech.

This is exactly what he set out to do. It had been a secret until this point, carefully guarded from the jury, that Black was doing life. Rather than, as is usual, trying to put the best gloss on his client, counsel for the defence outlined a pretty black and disgusting picture to the jury. He told them he had been jailed for life by the High Court in Edinburgh, he told them of Black's lifelong interest in young girls. He said child molesters deserve no public sympathy. However, in a neat turn of phrase he urged the jury not to allow the Crown to make a molester into a murderer. He said the greatest secret of the whole trial was that the prosecution had not a single shred of evidence against Robert Black.

I reflected quietly to myself as he claimed the police had seized on Black's arrest for Stow and gone on to dissect every detail of his life. He painted a picture of detectives broken by the long and unyielding case desperate to clean it up once and for all and to make Black a 'murderer for all seasons'.

In a sense he was right. We had dissected Black's life, we had gone to extraordinary lengths to delve into his background and movements on the days in question. What Mr Thwaites did not, of course, say is that our motivation was not that of broken detectives desperately looking to pin three child murders on a stooge. The truth was that what Black had done at Stow was just how we would have imagined his three previous victims had been snatched. He was the classic suspect. His method of operation, his description, and his opportunity made him a prime suspect. As I have said already as soon as we started investigating deeper we turned up not one single major fact that would diminish his candidature for that role. That simple truth would not be at all helpful to the defence case.

In the event Mr Thwaites went on to call the witnesses who, he would later say in his closing speech, were the people who could shed light on the real killer or killers of the three little girls. He produced people like Mark Ball, who recalled his story of seeing a girl with a tennis racket struggling to free herself from the driver of a maroon Triumph 2000. He produced other witnesses who had seen a variety of other vehicles and potential suspects at the scenes of the various abductions. In reality he was unable to bring forward a single witness to cast real doubt on the prosecution case, merely a succession of red herrings.

So in the fifth week of the trial Mr Justice Macpherson came to his court in Newcastle's historic Moot Hall, on Monday 16 May 1994 to sum up the evidence to the jury. The judge is a man of remarkable bearing. He comes over as a warm and friendly individual, and throughout the trial went to great lengths to ensure the jury were as comfortable as the circumstances permitted. Yet, when the need arose, he just switched to being the sort of firm and authoritative figure one would expect on the High Court bench.

He took the whole of the morning and most of the afternoon to go through the evidence and point out the areas where the jury might like, if they felt it right to do so, to pay particular attention to various aspects. About three o'clock on that Monday afternoon he sent the jury home saying the next morning he would ask them to begin their deliberations. And on Tuesday morning, after ten minutes of legal direction, he did just that.

The media attention in the court had come and gone during the trial. Now every seat was taken as the six men and six women filed out of their uncomfortable jury box and down the corridor into their room. The waiting began.

THE TRIAL

Nervous energy abounds on occasions like this. People stood round the Moot Hall in groups, chatting, speculating, just killing time. No one likes to go far from the court at moments like this in case the jury comes back more quickly than imagined. Then there is the certainty that they will not.

At the end of the first day's deliberations the judge called the jury back to the court and sent them to a hotel for the night after first establishing that they were not hopelessly divided.

The next day they were sent out again, and given a new direction, that they could return a majority verdict if ten or more jurors could agree on any of the charges. At three the jury were called back to see if they were confident of reaching a verdict that afternoon, or anticipated needing more time, and another night in a hotel. The foreman of the jury spoke a few words that gave me considerable confidence things were going in the right direction. One always has the fear in a long and complicated case like this that the jury may become badly split and never reach a verdict. A re-trial may be a possibility in such circumstances, but not a certainty. However, the jury foreman said quietly to the judge: 'It's the amount of evidence,' indicating they were being bogged down by the detail. That simple phrase raised my spirits because it became clear what the problem was. Not division, but comprehension. An entirely understandable problem. They were being asked to take in a huge amount of information and then deal with matters far beyond the experience of the ordinary folk who make up juries.

On day three the jury again retired at 10 a.m., and everyone was settling down to another long day's waiting. It was not to be, however. Shortly after 11.15 a buzz went round the court precincts as the jury bailiff hurried into the courtroom and alerted the clerk the jury was ready. People came scurrying from all over and piled into every available seat. Sarah's mother Jackie Harper had been at the court during many days of the trial. Liz and Fordyce Maxwell, and Annette Hogg came for the summing up and verdicts. They had seats reserved for them in the public gallery. I and some of the other detectives involved in the case over the years sat down below them to the rear of the dock. The jury filed back into their seats. I watched intently as they did so. Not one of them looked at the man in the dock. That, to me, was a sure sign of their verdict. Guilty.

The judge took his seat and issued a warning to the packed court. He asked that the verdicts be heard in silence. The clerk rose, the jury foreman rose. He asked if they had reached verdicts on all ten charges faced by the accused. They had.

On the first charge, the kidnap of Susan Claire Maxwell, was their verdict guilty or not guilty. When guilty was the reply an audible gasp, most probably of relief, went round the court. Guilty, guilty, guilty, and on went the replies to each of the charges. Black sat in the dock looking, it seemed, at the foreman, but showing not one sign of emotion.

The judge told him to stand. 'Robert Black,' he said, 'you have said not one word in this court, neither you nor the public would expect me to say many now.'

Mr Justice Macpherson went on to tell Black that he was an extremely dangerous man. The judge sentenced him to life imprisonment on each of the charges saying he expected him to spend the rest of his days in prison. He added that he would publicly recommend he should serve at least 35 years on each of the three murder convictions. Before adding that minimum recommendation the judge paused to ask the defence QC if there was anything he wanted to say. 'Absolutely nothing,' was Mr Thwaites' reply.

As Black was led down to the cells he turned in the dock and looked up at the detectives, and retired officers, sitting behind him and said: 'Well done, boys.' Another indication of his foul character. He had just been convicted of terrible crimes against innocent young girls. He must have known their families were in court, behind him, and true to form he embarked on the most inappropriate course of action and made a lighthearted quip. I did not expect remorse, for one moment, nor shame. But certainly not that.

As the press ran out to file their stories I sat for a few seconds, overcome with emotion at the end of a long and hard road. Outside a scrum of cameras and reporters met me at the court gates. I found it difficult to reply to their questions as the mixed emotions of all that had gone before welled up inside, the most powerful of these the sorrow of the sheer misery this man had caused to the families of three beautiful little girls.

From this bunch of reporters and in subsequent interviews that afternoon, the inevitable two questions kept recurring. First should we have got him sooner? Second how many more murders is he suspected of?

The answer to the first was, and is, clear in my mind. Everything humanly possible was done to bring Black to book as quickly as possible. Yes, he had two previous convictions for sexual assaults on children, but the last one of them was recorded nearly twenty years before Susan Maxwell disappeared, and was for a domestic situation in the Highlands of Scotland involving a breach of trust, Black's assault on the little girl as he babysat in Kinlochleven. Using the parameters for the inquiry I had set at the outset we had totally eliminated 4,000 MO suspects. That is to say people living in and around the areas involved in the investigation with previous convictions which would lead them to be considered as a potential suspect. If those inquiries were widened sufficiently to bring Black into the frame, by virtue of his two previous crimes, the list of people to be totally eliminated would have grown to many tens of thousands. An impossible task. The simple fact was that all the people who had suspicions about Black, or reason to suspect him, failed to tell us.

As for the second question. My answer today is the same as it was on the last day of the trial. It is for the British police service to decide what action to take over future inquiries into Black's activities. I am retired and it would be wrong to attempt to tie the hands of others. Of one thing, though, I am certain. It is inconceivable that this vile and depraved man has not attacked other children, and may have even murdered them.

CHAPTER SIXTEEN

Conclusion

Robert Black is now, thankfully, in jail for a great many years. It is my firm conviction that such is the magnitude of his crimes he should never be allowed out. Capital punishment is not available. If it was, Black would have been a prime candidate.

It may well have been that he did not mean to kill his little victims. It is actually probably the case. However, having had one 'accident', Black went on to repeat his crime several more times knowing death was the likely and indeed only conclusion.

He does, though, have one powerful matter left at his disposal. Such is the depth of his depravity, such is his lust for young girls, I believe quite firmly in my own mind that this man has been responsible for other abductions, other murders. My fondest wish for him would be to develop a conscience and bring some peace of mind to the relatives of missing children who have died at his hands.

For years I was a witness to the suffering of three families as the unsolved murders of three little girls continued to prey heavily on their minds. Knowledge of the truth brings with it a large helping of peace as those left behind are finally allowed to close a painful chapter of their lives. The memory will always live on but the pain will begin to heal. This Black has in his gift. It would not, in the circumstances, be difficult for him to ask to see Roger Orr or another officer and confess. It may well be good for his soul, too.

On the face of it, there seems little consistency in the conclusions of the cases I have been discussing in this book, I have never been a critic of the way judges dispose of serious criminal matters. I have always taken the view that you win some and you lose some. In the case of a police officer 'losing' in the course of his work, the real loss is suffered by society. If a judge gets it wrong the officer may be entitled to feel disappointed but it is society as a whole that is losing out on the protection competent sentencing brings with it.

After involvement in countless criminal cases which I have watched closely as they go through the judicial system, I am convinced that every judge I have come across has disposed of cases in an honest and genuine fashion. As I write these words, I can imagine many disagreeing with that contention but for me it remains a firm fact.

Whether or not the judge has been right in what he honestly believed is a different matter. How can it be that one judge makes a minimum recommendation for the life sentence imposed on an eminent doctor for killing his already ill wife and yet a man who kills his wife and three children in circumstances of almost similar premeditation can be out walking the streets again within twelve years?

The Alnwick misplaced revenge killer Emery may well come before the parole board within the next few years, despite the current climate of demands for stiffer sentencing. Yet the teenager who murdered at Newbiggin will probably have to wait for a long time before he sees the outside of the prison walls, despite his relatively tender years at the time of his killing.

Perhaps more than some people with a little experience of life and death, I feel I have an understanding of the crime and the pressures that drive people to commit it. Whether these pressures be real or imagined, understandable or totally beyond comprehension, I have seen the results, witnessed the devastation of those left behind and grieving, and had an inside track on the mind of a number of killers.

Some cases I have dealt with over the years have left me baffled as to motive but I feel my close contact with the killers has left me with a valuable view on the current debate, a view that is not often expressed even by those more qualified than myself.

I start from a simple and obvious contention. The main purpose of punishment must be as a deterrent. In this country there is only one sentence for murder, that of life imprisonment. Murder is increasing. Therefore it is clear that life imprisonment is not deterring some would-be killers. The question of course has to be, 'Would capital punishment be a more effective deterrent?' and that is a more difficult subject. One needs to understand the recent development of the legal position and sentencing policy in this country to be able to begin to reach conclusions.

For the first half of this century hanging was seen as a powerful deterrent to murder and it was the most frequently imposed sentence. Indeed, early on it was slavishly applied with reprieves being the exception rather than the rule. Up to 1957 it was automatic for an accused person to be sentenced to death when convicted of murder. It was then up to the Home Secretary, or Secretary of State in Scotland, to decide if the ultimate penalty should be commuted to one of life imprisonment. Through the middle 1950s there was a determined and growing campaign to abolish the death penalty. The abolitionists made some impact and a compromise position was reached after much debate and argument. That culminated in Parliament passing the Homicide Act of 1957 which restricted the availability of the death sentence to only certain categories of murder. They were, briefly:

a) Murder in the furtherance of theft.
b) Murder by shooting or explosion.
c) Murder committed in preventing or avoiding lawful arrest.
d) Murder of a police officer doing his duty.

e) Murder of a prison officer on duty by a prisoner.
f) A second conviction for murder arising from a separate incident.

The Homicide Act of 1957 effectively created two categories of murder: capital offences and non-capital ones. Conviction on a charge of capital murder carried a mandatory death penalty. However the chance of a reprieve was still there. All other murders, like domestic killings, knifings and so on, attracted a mandatory life sentence since the capital element was missing.

If the law in place immediately after the 1957 Act was applied to the cases I have been describing then only Scobie, Greenhill and Craigie would have qualified, if that is the right word, for the death penalty, but Scobie, the Newbiggin executioner, would have escaped the gallows because of his youth.

Over the years, before and following the Homicide Act, pressure continued to grow for complete abolition. There has been a number of well-publicised cases where public clamour for reprieve was ignored, not least those of Ruth Ellis, the last woman to hang in Britain, and Derek Bentley, who died for a murder committed by his younger accomplice. The death penalty also hung over juries, making it more difficult to secure a conviction. Seemingly jurors would rather, in the main, set a guilty man free than an innocent one to death. It was unacceptable for murder cases to be decided on the possible punishment rather than the facts of the case laid before the jury. The common feeling was that justice was not being served by the death penalty for this very reason. So after lengthy campaigns in the House of Commons and in the country, hanging was effectively taken out of the judges' armoury when the 1965 Murder (Abolition of Death Penalty) Act was passed.

Thereafter there would only be one possible sentence for all convictions for murder. It was a great victory for the abolitionists and a victory that brought dire warnings with it from supporters of the death penalty. They said the murder rate would rocket which, of course, it did. I cannot now be sure where I stood on the issue at the time, although one thing was certain: the only deterrent left against murder was the thought of life imprisonment. No one can argue that that deterrent was effective in the cases I have been describing. It clearly was not.

As Robert Black sat in his van, or in the midst of some summer scene amongst children at play, would he have hesitated for one second in his evil intentions if he thought capture would bring with it the prospect of the gallows?

Would Robert Small's tortured mind have been capable of working out the consequences when, in his fury, he took a piece of lead piping to the wife he suspected of cheating on him? Would the deterrent of the rope have been sufficient to cut through his blind rage and save the life of Elsie?

Would the innocent Kevin Cannon have been allowed to pass by on his way home unhindered by two youths who butchered him for the price of another pint?

One can only speculate at the answers to these questions. With society increasingly concerned at the seemingly daily acts of violence perpetrated on its most vulnerable members, it is worthwhile speculation.

The other purposes of punishment is reform. To encourage offenders not to repeat their crimes. Society has to take a view on whether a particular offender is likely to commit further crimes. This power is vested in the judge. Just as Lord Ross had concluded at the original High Court appearance that Robert Black would be a persistent danger to children, and jailed him for life, so other judges have taken somewhat different views of serious crime based on their opinion that the person standing in front of them is a one-off criminal and should be treated as such. The Scottish judge, the late Lord Dunpark, caused a sensation a few years ago by admonishing a Royal Marine Commando who had shot dead his wife and infant child in cold blood for no apparent reason. The man had been convicted of the crime of culpable homicide, the Scots Law equivalent of manslaughter, and the full range of penalties was available to his lordship, from the lowest, admonition, to the highest, life imprisonment. Lord Dunpark chose the former.

Now, I do not quibble with either of these sentences. I quote them here merely to illustrate how punishment can be made to fit the crime. For Black, with no remorse and his basically flawed personality, there can be no release from prison. The marine, Graham Sherman, in the judge's view, snapped for a variety of reasons all brought about by the various pressures upon him. Lord Dunpark was quite entitled to take the view, as he did, that the combination was a one-off and the marine would not offend again. So far neither has he. I feel sure that if he had put a foot wrong the newspapers would have highlighted the fact.

Even someone of my years of experience finds it no easier to understand now, at the end of my career, the cruelty that man is prepared to inflict on his fellows, than when I began 39 years ago. A young boy shot, executed, on suspicion of stealing a few pounds. Two families destroyed for no rational explanation whatsoever. An eminent surgeon murdering his wife to save the inconvenience and embarrassment of a divorce. Brother killing brother for a fix.

The increase in homicide has been relentless in this country. When I first joined the police in 1955 those convicted of murder were automatically sentenced to death. However the case was eventually disposed of, the imposition of the death penalty had a dramatic effect on everyone concerned. To my mind, this is the one facet of the death penalty that is sometimes forgotten by people today. It is one of the more powerful parts of the penalty in a deterrent sense, and a main plank of the arguments put forward by those wanting to retain it.

Execution had a whole aura surrounding it that was unique. As a murder trial neared an end the publicity surrounding it increased as the indivisible question was indirectly posed: will they hang? Each case was followed minutely from the verdict being announced, through sentencing, reporting of the representations by whoever to ask for commutation of sentence. The power of the last-minute reprieve. Until even the very last executions in Britain, the posting of the notice on the jail gates brought with it a small crowd who stood outside when the appointed hour arrived.

CONCLUSION

All these rituals when taken together granted murder the status it should have: the most heinous of crimes requiring the most stringent of punishment.

One may be forgiven for thinking nowadays that certain sections of the media find murder and murderers really rather attractive. I believe that has contributed to a downgrading of the crime in the public mind. Too often we have seen people embarking on murder as a method of achieving, in their mind, fame – to the rest of society, notoriety. Perhaps that quest would not be embarked upon quite so readily if the would-be killer realised that his deeds would end in his own death.

Take my word for it, there is no glamour in picking over the life of a murdered person and looking to those shattered people left behind for help. There is no remedy for the illness suffered by those survivors. I have yet to recognise glamour in the shattered, dead body of a human being torn apart by violence, so often undeserved, so frequently unnecessary.

It is not that I complain of my role. It is after all what the police are for and why I joined the police service. We do, however, need to consider how the murder rate can be reduced to protect those who are too often its victims – the frail, the old, the young and the weak.

Not long after joining the force I was involved on the fringes of an investigation that resulted in a man being hanged. Even though my rather junior role in the matter left me far out of the real action in the case, I was near enough to feel a real sense of shock the morning the man went to the gallows, despite the dastardly nature of his crime. This one event probably coloured my view of the subject. My opinion was that in general capital punishment was simply too much and hanging, as a method of execution, was quite barbaric.

Of late I have begun to take a different stance.

In the middle of this century the popular view of capital punishment was that it acted as a deterrent but one that should be reserved for the murder of police officers, prison officers and others who die in the line of duty protecting public safety. Under the Homicide Act of 1957, the one that paved the way for abolition, the idea was that the murder of public servants in the execution of their duty, and limited other categories, would attract the rope. 'Ordinary' murder would not.

In fact, in the years between the passing of this Act and the eventual abolition of the death penalty, a curious situation arose. The incidence of capital murder increased and non-capital murder, for which the culprit would not have faced the gallows, decreased. One would think if death was a deterrent to murder it would be the capital crimes that would decrease. Non-capital murder, crimes of passion, street fights that go too far, people pushed to the limit of their endurance and snapping, jealous spouses, are all the categories where thought probably does not go into the crime in great quantities. How can you deter when a crime is carried out through blind rage, or abject misery? It seemed that the murders that could be deterred with the threat of hanging would be those very ones that in fact increased. The prospect of the rope, I would have thought, might make the armed robber think twice before carrying a gun on his exploits. Seemingly it did not.

For me, though, the driving force that has caused a change in mind over the years is simple. Why should the killer of an innocent child or a frail pensioner escape more lightly than the killer of a person that entered into a particular job knowing the risks? A policeman on the streets with training, support and expertise is doing a job for which he is well paid. That is not to underestimate the killing of a police officer, but why should his life be more highly thought of by society than an innocent child, or a defenceless old person, which, arguably, was the position imposed by the 1957 Act.

In my time as a senior detective, no one has been hanged for a crime investigated by myself. I can only speculate on what effect such a conclusion to one of my cases might have had, and what effect it may have had on me. I suspect I am rather glad to have been spared the experience.

I do recall, however, being acutely worried at the time of

abolition. It seemed entirely likely that there would be a sharp increase in the homicide rate. That there was an absence of the ultimate deterrent for the more vile, senseless and brutal murders did worry me.

My view now is that there has to be a way of dividing murder into two categories so appropriate penalties can be imposed. Murder, whilst capable of precise definition, is in fact a broad crime covering a multitude of widely differing acts and courses of action.

Premeditation to me seems the best yardstick of the crime. Paul Vickers was guilty of a murder carefully planned and ruthlessly executed. He lived for many months sure in the knowledge of what he was doing and why. The law says that a drunken man who kills in a street fight that goes one step too far is guilty of the same offence. That cannot be so.

There is no more certain support to this theory than to look at murderers themselves. Many lifers in jail today are there through pathetic inadequacies or drink. The sort of people in the wrong place at the wrong time. These are not the people who should die for their crimes, distressing though the results of their actions are. It is the smaller number of individuals who carefully enter into murder, having planned their actions and weighed up their possible consequences, that concern me. These are the people who, if deterrence ever works, are capable of being stopped before they go too far.

Such a period of preparation, even if it is a matter of only minutes, is time to reflect on the consequences. To then press ahead with the killing is to be criminal in the extreme. These people have opportunity or time to reflect on their actions and withdraw before it is too late. When they decide not to take that course of action they deserve what they get.

The Saturday night drunk in a fight in the road does not weigh up the potential effect of each blow he rains down on his unfortunate victim. He does not continually assess the condition of his sparring partner carefully calculating how much further he can go without causing irreparable harm. No more does the husband, or wife, driven by blind rage, deserve to be judged as one who is the master of their actions and the consequences of them. Yes, they should pay a heavy penalty but, no, it should not be the ultimate one.

Now that, after all these years, I have come round to this conclusion any nagging doubt that may still exist could be overcome by a change in the method of execution. Reprieves would still be available and in the curerent climate would probably be the norm rather than the exception. That would ensure the ultimate penalty would apply only to the most extreme cases of premeditated murder, the sort of offence that shocks and horrifies the nation, the sort of outrageous activity that Robert Black got up to.

Hanging, to me, seems utterly barbaric – technically improved but in concept little changed from the middle ages. A more modern method of execution would have to be found – possibly lethal injection – before I could favour a return to the days that capital punishment was available to judges. That day is unlikely to arrive but I am entitled to suggest it.

So how would this doctrine of premeditation apply to the cases I have been discussing? It is a rule that would work well and without doubt.

Robert Black not only carefully planned his abductions but carried them out three times, at least, after the death of Susan Maxwell. He deserved to die.

Terence Emery should have no more mercy shown to him than he himself showed to Lynn and her children that snowy day in Alnwick, when he went to their house with a clear plan in his mind.

Robert Small's first killing, that of his wife, was carried out in the heat of argument and would not have sent him to the gallows. The killing of the children was deemed manslaughter, so he would escape with his life, although fate intervened anyway.

Paul Vickers lived with his plan for months. Notwithstanding his special position in society as a healer, he slowly and deliberately poisoned his wife for his own ends and, therefore, he too deserved the ultimate penalty.

CONCLUSION

Scobie virtually boasted about the preparation he had put into the killing of Paul Hedley. He would have qualified for capital punishment but his age would have saved him.

Greenhill and Craigie would have survived despite the brutality of their attack on Kevin Cannon; premeditation was not a factor in their crime. Neither was it in the case of Brian Ogilvy.

I neither require nor expect all to share my opinions. But as a man with 39 years' police service behind me, over half at a rank of superintendent or above, I am entitled to hold a view. I have seen many things I would have preferred to have been spared from. I have met, and indeed pitted wits with, a good many killers. Worse still, I have seen the devastation left in the wake of these murders. The relatives for whom the grieving will never end. The bitterness, the lack of comprehension on the faces of those left behind as they continually ask: 'Why?'

In Scotland crime generally is decreasing but the ultimate crime, murder, is on the increase. In England and Wales all crime is still going up. Something has to be done to reduce the carnage. To my mind, the reintroduction of the death penalty for extreme, premeditated and carefully executed murders may be an answer or, at least, a partial solution. Something has to be done to reduce the toll of wanton murder, for one thing can be certain: we will never stop it entirely. In its wake the devastation of families continues.

Now Liz and Fordyce Maxwell have left Cramond Hill Farm and relocated their family to Berwick upon Tweed, 15 miles away in my native Northumberland. Fordyce is the agricultural expert on *The Scotsman*, Liz a journalist with the local paper. They support each other magnificently and, drawing on their combined strengths, they have come to terms with their terrible loss. Susie's name is in no way a forbidden word in their stone-built home. Each time I call in my greeting and welcome is warm. They are, quite simply, a lovely family.

John and Annette Hogg have moved away from Portobello but still live in the east of Edinburgh. It is extremely fair to say that Annette has had the most difficulty in coping with the aftermath of Caroline's murder. I do not blame her for that and I recognise the very loving and sincere way in which John protects her as much as he can. I do what I can on my occasional visits and provoke the odd smile. I see a lovely family, now broken, but determined to lead as normal a life as possible.

I am less well acquainted with Jackie Harper, though of course I have spoken to her a lot. My former colleagues in West Yorkshire maintain a more frequent contact. She too has moved. Her loss was no less tragic than the others. She had her children, one born since the murder, to bring comfort, but grief will continue to come with her memories.

Teresa Thornhill was the lucky one. She still lives, unaffected, in Nottingham.

The little Borders girl has moved home and her brush with death has left no lasting effect. In the days after the incident her older sister was troubled more than she.

These two surviving victims and their families, along with the Maxwells, Hoggs and Harpers are people to be admired. They all have my sympathy, respect, support, and good wishes.

The evil of man has had some effect on us all.

As for me, I now live in contented retirement in a lovely village on the western outskirts of Edinburgh and there with my memories, both good and bad, I will remain.

DRAMATIS PERSONAE

BAILEY, Sir Stanley, CBE QPM DL, Chief Constable of Northumbria Police (now retired)

BODEN, Derek, Detective Superintendent, Staffordshire Police (now retired)

BYFORD, Sir Lawrence, CBE QPM, HM Chief Inspector of Constabulary (England and Wales) (now retired)

CHAMBERS, Frederick, OBE QPM, Deputy Chief Constable of Northumbria Police (now retired)

CUNNINGHAM, Brian, Detective Chief Superintendent, Lothian and Borders Police (now retired)

GOODSON, Alan, OBE, QPM LLB, Chief Constable of Leicestershire Police (now deceased)

JOHNSON, Brian, CBE, QPM, DL, now Chief Constable of Lancashire Police

KELLY, Charles, CBE QPM LLB, Chief Constable of Staffordshire Police

McLACHLAN, Charles, CBE QPM LLB, Chief Constable of Nottingham Constabulary, later HM Inspector of Constabulary (now deceased)

ORANGE, Leslie, LLB, Detective Chief Inspector, Northumbria Police, later Chief Superintendent (now retired)

ORR, Roger, Chief Inspector, Lothian and Borders Police

PRINGLE, Stanley, OBE QPM, Deputy Chief Constable, Lothian and Borders Police (retired)

SAMPSON, Sir Colin, CBE QPM, Chief Constable, West Yorkshire Police, later HM Chief Inspector of Constabulary (Scotland) (now retired)

SUTHERLAND, Sir William, QPM, Chief Constable, Lothian and Borders Police

WATT, Andrew, Detective Superintendent, later Chief Superintendent, Lothian and Borders Police (now retired)

David Johnston is Head of News at Radio Forth in Edinburgh and covered the developing murder hunt from the day of Susan Maxwell's abduction in 1982. He is also the author of *Lockerbie: The Real Story*, the first book published on the 1988 disaster. He is married and lives outside Edinburgh with his wife and two daughters.